James Stephen Jeans

Conciliation and Arbitration in Labour Disputes

A Historical Sketch and Brief Statement of the Present Position of the Question at

Home and Abroad

James Stephen Jeans

Conciliation and Arbitration in Labour Disputes
A Historical Sketch and Brief Statement of the Present Position of the Question at Home and Abroad

ISBN/EAN: 9783337417833

Printed in Europe, USA, Canada, Australia, Japan

Cover: Foto ©Suzi / pixelio.de

More available books at **www.hansebooks.com**

CONCILIATION AND ARBITRATION

LABOUR DISPUTES

*A HISTORICAL SKETCH AND BRIEF STATEMENT OF THE
PRESENT POSITION OF THE QUESTION
AT HOME AND ABROAD*

BY

J. STEPHEN JEANS, M.R.I., F.S.S.

AUTHOR OF "ENGLAND'S SUPREMACY," ETC., AND LATE SECRETARY OF THE IRON AND
STEEL INSTITUTE

LONDON
CROSBY LOCKWOOD AND SON
7 STATIONERS' HALL COURT, LUDGATE HILL
1894

INSCRIBED

TO MY VALUED FRIENDS

WILLIAM JACKS, M.P.

President of the British Iron Trade Association

AND

WILLIAM SPROSTON CAINE, M.P.

Past-President of the British Iron Trade Association

IN TOKEN OF

MY HIGH APPRECIATION OF THEIR CHARACTERS AND LABOURS

INTRODUCTION AND OUTLINE.

THE "condition-of-England question" at the present moment, and for a considerable time past, has been dependent upon the solution of the problem of reconciling capital and labour. In consequence of the difficulties that appear to stand in the way of such a reconciliation, an infinite amount of mischief has been done to all the industrial interests of this country, and the outlook for the future has been clouded with trouble, uncertainty, and gloom. It is not only that employers have lost vast sums of money in resisting claims made by their workmen, and in supporting their own, but the public confidence in all industrial undertakings has been greatly shaken, until the value of such investments, as such, has been seriously deteriorated, and capitalists who were formerly eager to embark upon manufacturing enterprise have ceased to have confidence in it,—to such an extent, indeed, that it is shunned by many as if it were a certain plague.

So long as this condition of things exists, English commerce and industry must remain in a parlous and undesirable state. The backbone of our commercial supremacy, of our great command of shipping business, of our success as a colonising people, of our superior wealth and all the advantages that it confers, is our manufacturing industry. If that industry is menaced by the unrest and turbulence of labour, by the exactions and unreasonableness of capital, by industrial war on a gigantic scale,—such as that which formed so painful and disastrous a feature of the history of labour in 1893,—capital will be withdrawn from it, new developments will be checked and frustrated, our ever-watchful rivals and competitors will gain a march upon our own manufacturers in the markets of the world, and our circumstances will be environed with even greater perils than Hudibras predicates for "the man that meddles with cold iron." We repeat again, therefore, that the question of the hour is the solution of this great problem. The crucial question of questions is, not the incidence of taxation, not the operation of foreign tariffs, not the exhaustion of our coal supply, not the stringency of money, not the merits or demerits of bimetallism, but the avoidance of serious disputes between capital and industry. Solve this problem effectually, and we guarantee the continuance of English commercial supremacy, we give new life to home industries, we provide new outlets for capital, we secure protection to employers, and we relieve the working men and women of England from the thraldom and dominion of what must to them be the greatest curse of modern times.

It would be going much too far to affirm that the solution has already been found. Again and again it has been believed by sanguine admirers of economic systems or phases of systems that they had finally reached a panacea for the greatest of industrial evils,—at one time in conciliation, applied in a particular way; at another time, in courts of arbitration; at a third time, in the establishment of sliding-scales; at a fourth time, in co-operation; at a fifth time, in profit-sharing. But, unfortunately, every one of these systems has at one time or another broken down; and the bitter and disastrous experience of the year 1893 proves, to the reluctant acquiescence of any candid mind, that we are nearly as far from a solution as we ever were —if we are not still farther.

Many strikes have no doubt occurred in consequence of the ignorance of the workmen, or of their leaders and advisers, as to the actual conditions of the business in which they were engaged. There is often a wide difference between the prices as published in the newspapers or trade circulars, and the realised prices received by employers. This is especially so in the case of coal. The realised price of coal is affected by the proportions free for sale, and sold under contracts of longer or shorter duration. It often happens, moreover, that the employers, in busy times, find it necessary to check sales; and while not refusing orders, they put up a prohibitive price when they see that they have already as many orders as they can execute. These quotations are mistaken by the workmen for realised prices. Of course, all this liability to mislead would be got rid of, if, for the purposes of a sliding-scale or some other amicable mode of settlement, the employers and employed agreed upon the ascertainment of the actual realised selling prices from period to period; but the employers are not to be blamed if they do not attempt such an ascertainment, unless they have guarantees that it will be accepted as a basis of settlement.

Labour disputes are more or less liable to occur in every industry, according as the rate of wages paid is more or less liable to sudden and frequent fluctuations. Thus, in the textile industries, where the wages are usually fairly steady, and where oscillations of any account are comparatively infrequent, the occurrence of a general strike is rare. In the mining industry, on the other hand, the variations of wages are more common than in almost any other, and hence labour disputes are specially frequent.

Some interesting evidence on this point was submitted to

the Royal Commission on Labour (Group A). Mr A. K. M'Cosh, vice-chairman of the Lanarkshire Coal Masters' Association, stated that for a long period wages had been subject to great fluctuations in the Scotch collieries, varying from 6d. to 1s. per day, and that he remembered one time when they were twice reduced by 2s. a day within a single month! It was natural, after this, that Mr M'Cosh should add, that "if the variations were less violent, there would be less friction between employers and employed, and it was to ensure this result that the employers desired the adoption of a sliding-scale." *

The facts just stated make it sufficiently clear that one of the greatest securities that could be provided against suspensions of labour would be the steadying of price, and that any system that could be devised with this end in view would be almost certain to effect immense advantage. It is, however, difficult to see how such a system is to be provided. The so-called law of supply and demand does not provide for a steady demand at all times alike. But even if this were not the case, artificial means are constantly being employed to raise or depress prices,—such, for example, as "cornering" the market, syndicating or monopolising the products of industry, and restricting the output. Of late years the oscillations of price from these causes appear to have been more violent and more frequent than formerly, and it is to be feared that this will continue unless commercial gambling can be got rid of.

Comparatively little attention has been given in the following pages to the French system of *Conseils des Prud'hommes*, established in France under the Napoleonic code, and afterwards extended to Prussia, Belgium, and other Continental countries. This system is well suited to the settlement of

---

* Group A, *cf.* 13633-7.

matters of detail—to small grievances and minor disputes—but it is not quite adapted to the more serious causes of difference which result in a general suspension of industry over a large area of operations, and are liable to affect prejudicially many allied and collateral interests. At the same time, the evidence submitted before the Royal Commission on Labour appeared to show that there was a real *raison d'être* for a tribunal that would adequately meet these minor troubles; and it is quite possible that the system of councils of experts, under such legal sanctions as exist on the Continent, would be more effective in this direction than the present system of joint-committees, or, as often happens, no system at all.

Anything in the shape of compulsion is, however, so repugnant to the spirit and to the traditions of the English people, that it might be found difficult to adopt a system that would depend essentially on legal sanctions. It is clear that this is the view of the most experienced among both employers and employed as to the principles on which conciliation and arbitration should be based. No one seriously recommends that the acceptance of either system should be forced upon industry, or that legal penalties should follow upon the non-acceptance of an award. While this spirit prevails, we must always more or less remain between the Scylla of non-acceptance of conciliation and the Charybdis of non-fulfilment of awards that have no proper legal sanction. The moral force of a voluntary sanction is, however, always the strongest with men of honour, and we may hope that this will ultimately enable us to dispense with legal requisitions. In not a few cases, indeed, the workmen have shown that they were fully alive to the moral obligation which devolved upon them, first, to accept a reference, and next to carry out the decision of the referee, and the leaders of the workmen have again and again threatened to give up their positions, if any attempt at repudiation of an award was

b

made by their constituents. In order to minimise the risk of rejecting an award, it is obviously desirable that it should be so framed as to operate with as little harshness as possible, and especially that it should not be either retrospective or applied to a long period of time. Workmen would be likely to submit to an adverse award for a period of three months, when they would rebel against an award that committed them for six months or a longer period.

Until workmen have learned patience and self-control more generally and largely than at present, there will always be a liability, on the part of certain of the more hot-headed and impulsive among their number, to quarrel with any terms that may be suggested or adopted with a view to the settlement of their rate of wages, hours of work, or other general conditions of labour. The remarks that were recently made on the selection and attitude of Lord Shand, by one of the miners' representatives in the Midland Counties is a notable case in point. Such remarks are greatly to be deplored, even when they have a semblance of truth, but when their accuracy is at least questionable, they should be severely reprobated; and it is satisfactory to be able to add that on the special occasion in question the workmen did, as a body, repudiate the remarks that are the subject of animadversion.

The collapse of many of the earlier boards of conciliation and arbitration may be held to prove either that the system was not fully understood, or that it was not acceptable to either of the interests concerned. Generally the causes of collapse have been either the refusal of one side or the other to accept decisions, or the withdrawal of a certain number of dissatisfied members. In the case of the Wear Shipbuilding trade a conciliation board was founded as early as 1850, but as the early decisions were adverse to the men they declined to go on with it, and it collapsed after two years.

It is hardly necessary that I should add that in the preparation of the following chapters I have derived very important assistance from the Reports of the Royal Commission on Labour. Many previous reports have been published on the systems of conciliation and arbitration, including that which was written some fifteen years ago by my friend Mr J. D. Wicks, of Pittsburgh, under instructions from the Governor of Pennsylvania, and that which Mr Carroll D. Wright, of the Bureau of Labour at Washington, prepared in his capacity of Chief Commissioner of that Department. But I have been guided mainly by the more recent Reports of the Royal Commission on Labour at home, and have made free use of the information which they contain on the various circumstances under which the application of one or other of the systems dealt with has been attempted in foreign countries.

While the *rationale* and the essential phases of the system of conciliation and arbitration are necessarily varying from day to day, so that it is difficult to keep fully abreast of their kaleidoscopic movement, it is believed that this little work will be found to fairly well record and reflect the course of the system up-to-date. It includes, at any rate, the essential features of the recommendations of the Royal Commission on Labour on this branch of their inquiry, for which I have to acknowledge my obligations to the *Times;* and it reproduces in an Appendix the full text of Mr Mundella's Bill of March 1894, designed to make better provision for the settlement of labour disputes. These two documents represent the latest and (in some respects) the most important deliverances on the subject.

So far as my own record goes, I may be permitted to say that I am not quite new to the methods which in the following pages I have endeavoured to reduce to something like a practical system. It is now more than twenty years since I had occasion to study and to write upon the application of arbitration both in the North of England and in the West of Scotland. At a later date I had practical experience as an arbitrator in one of the most important industries in the North, having been associated in that position with such men as Mr David Dale, Mr Thomas Burt, M.P., and Mr John Burnett, of the Board of Trade. I was also favoured with intercourse on the same subject with such notable pioneers of the system as Mr Mundella and Sir Rupert Kettle, from whom I received much encouragement and assistance in my earlier writings; while I have had the marked advantage of more or less continuous intercourse, during the last twenty years, with men who have acquired such marked distinction, and who have deserved so well of their countrymen in this sphere of labour, as Mr David Dale and Mr William Whitwell. I mention these facts, not in order to exalt my own function as the humble compiler of the following pages, but in order to provide some little guarantee that I do not come quite unprepared by previous knowledge and experience to the task which I have undertaken.

CONTENTS.

SECTION I—GREAT BRITAIN.

CHAPTER	PAGE
I. The Progress of Industry	1
II. The Problem of To-day	13
III. Attempts at Solution of the Problem	19
IV. Industrial Conciliation	25
V. Industrial Arbitration	31
VI. Matters Proper for Arbitration	43
VII. Industrial Sliding-Scales	50
VIII. The Coal-Mining Industry as it Was	55
IX. Sliding-Scales in the Coal Industry	62
X. The Coal Industry of South Wales	69
XI. Sliding-Scales in the Pig-Iron Industry	77
XII. Arbitration and Sliding-Scales in the Staffordshire Coal and Iron Industries	81
XIII. Arbitration and Sliding-Scales in the Finished Iron Industry of the North of England	87
XIV. Conciliation and Arbitration in other Industries	102
XV. The Attitude of Employers	109
XVI. The Attitude of Workmen	115
XVII. Pending Proposals and Legislation	123

SECTION II.—FOREIGN COUNTRIES.

CHAPTER		PAGE
XVIII.	Labour Disputes and their Settlement in the United States	131
XIX.	Labour Disputes and their Settlement in Germany	142
XX.	Labour Disputes in France	154
XXI.	Labour Disputes in other Countries	159

APPENDICES.

I.	Sliding-Scale adopted in the Coal Trade of South Wales	173
II.	The "Act for the Amicable Adjustment of Grievances and Disputes that may arise between Employers and Employed," &c., in New York State	174
III.	French Law providing for Conciliation and Arbitration in cases of Collective Disputes between Employers and Employed	180
IV.	Rules of the Board of Conciliation and Arbitration in the Staffordshire Potteries	184
V.	Mr W. J. Parry's Scheme for the Establishment of a System of Boards of Arbitration	188
VI.	Mr Mundella's Conciliation (Trade Disputes) Bill	190

INDEX . . 192

CONCILIATION AND ARBITRATION.

SECTION I.—GREAT BRITAIN.

CHAPTER I.

THE PROGRESS OF INDUSTRY.

THE great charter of the working classes in modern times was the Act 5 Geo. IV. c. 96 (1824), which gave power to do many things that the law had previously disallowed. Under this Act they were at liberty to cease working, to take steps to diminish the quantity of their work, and to do many other things that were visited by condign penalties at an earlier period.

From this date, therefore, the working classes entered on a new epoch. Their new-found liberty, apt to degenerate into license, was kept in check by the penal provisions enacted to prevent the use of force and violence. Trade unionism measured its strength with capital, not stealthily and with many secret devices, but in the broad light of day, and with openly-avowed purpose. It is not altogether a marvel that the newly-acquired freedom of labour was now and again employed indiscreetly and to little purpose. It required a long process of education and experience to teach the true mission of labour combinations. Many a bitter struggle, many a hard name, many scenes of strife and sorrow had to be endured before this lesson was fully taught. Over and over again it was found that the unions created by the men were akin to Frankenstein's monster—a power and an influence which was more easily originated than subdued.

A recent writer has defined the duties of trades unions to be—(1) to oppose all reductions of wages ; (2) to cause a rise of wages whenever practicable ; and (3) to convert non-unionists into unionists, either by persuasive or by coercive means.* As applied to the "new trade unionism," this is probably a very imperfect definition. The functions of this organisation reach far beyond the settlement of wages, or the making of converts to their cause. A line of cleavage between the new and the old has been opened up, of which the true import has not yet had time to develop. We can only hope that new powers and a new programme may be made to consist with wise and rational conduct.

In its ordinary relation to capital, the first object of labour, whether represented by the individual or by the community, is usually that of securing the highest practicable rate of wages. But we are still as much as ever at variance on the question of how that desideratum can best be secured. Abstract political economy, with all its glib and plausible theories, has really done very little towards a solution of the difficulty. Adam Smith justly remarks, that "the property which every man has in his own labour, as it is the original foundation of all other property, so it is the most sacred and inviolable." But beyond this threshold of the subject even Adam Smith cannot take us without leaving us "in wandering mazes lost." Theories as to the laws of supply and demand, as to the differences due to constancy and inconstancy of employment, as to the hardship, disagreeableness, and dangers of work, and their effects on wages, as to the difficulty and expense of learning some trades in comparison with others—these and cognate matters, though all more or less relevant, are yet extremely inconclusive, and leave untouched the essential principle that aims, under all circumstances, at the equitable and just distribution between capital and labour of the earnings which both are necessary to produce.

Nor do we see that John Stuart Mill helps the case when

---

* Ward on *Workmen and Wages.*

he avers that "wages depend mainly upon the demand and supply of labour, or, as it is often expressed, on the proportion between population and capital. . . . Wages not only depend upon the relative amount of capital and population, but cannot, under the rule of competition, be affected by anything else. Wages (meaning, of course, the general rate) cannot rise but by an increase of the aggregate funds employed in hiring labourers, or a diminution in the number of the competitors for hire; nor fall, except either by a diminution of the funds devoted to paying labour, or by an increase in the number of labourers to be paid." *

This formula, although obviously just in the abstract, is yet, in the concrete, liable to be indefinitely varied. Whence, otherwise, the suspensions of industry, the struggles between capital and labour, the frequent disputations and unceasing restlessness that mark our industrial annals? The workmen in some trades will tell us that "the number of labourers to be paid" ought not to have any effect on their wages; that neither ought "the diminution of the funds devoted to paying labour" to have any such influence; that custom, and not competition, should determine their earnings; or that their wages should be varied according to the selling price of the commodity they are employed to produce. Others, again, will go a step further, and insist that neither custom nor competition should be allowed to interfere, but that the profits of the capitalist, and these alone, should be made the basis for the regulation of the labourer's hire.

There is not, and probably in the nature of things there cannot be, any mathematical precision, or even approximate uniformity, in adjusting a quantity so indefinite and so liable to fluctuation as the earnings of labour. The amount the capitalist can afford to pay, the elastic factor spoken of as the law of supply and demand, the selling price of the commodity in respect of which labour is remunerated, the extent of competition and unemployed labour, the wages paid in cognate and collateral industries, are each and all considerations that will

---

* *Principles of Political Economy*, chap. xi.

exercise more or less weight, if they do not become absolute determinants of the problem. Hence we come to face the vital and absorbing inquiry, How are these various considerations to be most completely and satisfactorily effectuated?

There are still those with whom the law of supply and demand are synonymous terms for strike and lock-out, and who do not, even in this age of reason, scruple to avow their belief in these remedies as the only really ultimate solvents of industrial differences. It is a humiliating reflection that our civilisation should be so much of a failure, and our intelligence so greatly at a discount, as to allow the slightest credence or toleration to such a belief. But we may rejoice that the spirit which upheld the Combination Laws, and dominated with tyrannous sway over the rights and privileges of labour, has now given place to a purer, a healthier, and a more reasonable conception of the reciprocal duties of employers and employed. It would be well if we could add that the larger amount of justice now done to labour had resulted in more friendly relations, and more cordial sympathy and more hearty co-operation, between those interests.

The evils of strike and lock-out being conceded, and the urgent need of their prevention being a foregone conclusion, it becomes imperative that some other mode of settling industrial differences should be established in their place.

Hitherto we have only heard of two other remedies with any pretensions to practicability. The first of these is co-operation and profit-sharing; the second is arbitration and conciliation, either conjunct or separate.

Co-operative production has many obvious merits, but it is equally beset by seemingly insurmountable weaknesses. Those who think that in the actual organisation of productive industry there is a disproportionate assignment of profits to capital, ought, under a system of co-operation, to have their minds set at rest. It is the immediate purpose of industrial partnerships to hold the balance evenly between capital and labour; and Lord Brassey was at one time sanguine enough to believe that "when co-operative production has been introduced into all branches of industry successfully, and on a sufficiently extensive scale, we shall then have the universal gauge or measure of workmen's rightful claims." * On the face of it, there could be no better, simpler, or more equitable expedient for adjusting wages than that of providing that every person employed shall have a pecuniary interest in the success of the business; that interest being, as far as possible, in proportion to the services rendered, while the capital employed is remunerated by a reasonable rate of interest.

On these or analogous principles co-operative production has been undertaken at various times by Messrs Fox, Head, & Company, of the Newport Rolling Mills, near Middlesbrough; Messrs Briggs, of the Whitwood Collieries; the Ouseburn Engine Works Company, at Newcastle; the Paisley Manufacturing Society; the Lurgan Damask Manufacturing Society; the Hebden Bridge Manufacturing Society; the North of England Industrial Iron and Coal Company; the Eccles Quilt Manufacturing Society; the Northumberland Miners' Association; the South Yorkshire Miners' Association; the Printing Society of Manchester; and by numerous other more or less extensive industrial concerns. Nor has the movement been limited to our own country. It has been adopted on the other side of the Atlantic by such religious sects as the Shakers, Mormons, Economists, and Perfectionists. The Working Men's Manufacturing Company, with a capital of £25,000, was established in 1872 at Emmaus, and various co-operative foundries have been originated in New York and Massachusetts. In France, the same principle has been adopted by Monsieur Godin, of Guise : and in Germany, Belgium, and some other European countries, experiments have now and again been made in the same direction.

With all these examples before us, it cannot be said that co-operative production has not had a fair trial. It has, indeed, been tried in every important industry that can be named, and for a period sufficiently long to test its stability and practical

---

* *Contemporary Review*, July 1874.

merits. The result has been disappointing, although not, of course, equally so in every instance. The friends and promoters of the system can still confidently claim that it has been redeemed from utter failure by not a few notably successful examples. But its weaknesses and defects have, nevertheless, been so conspicuous under the most crucial tests as to induce the conclusion that in no form which it has heretofore assumed can co-operative production be absolutely relied upon as a safe and sure panacea for the manifold evils that beset our industrial affairs.

Co-operative production has hitherto taken one of two forms. Either the workmen have been admitted, by the principle known as industrial partnership, to a share in the profits of the business, without any investment of capital, and, therefore, without the risk of loss to which capital is always liable, or they have found the whole of the capital themselves, and thus become responsible for the supply of all the essential conditions that production demands. In the former case, it has been found by such firms as Fox, Head, & Company, and the Messrs Briggs, that the workmen remained loyal to the principles on which industrial partnership was founded only so long as they continued to receive a direct gain. Both had found it to be a necessary condition of the system they adopted, that neither employer nor employed should be attached to any association, or subject to any outside interference whatsoever. So soon as a third party was allowed to step in, and prescribe what was the duty of the employer on the one hand, or the rights and requirements of the employed on the other, there came an end to that freedom of contract and faith in one another that alone made it possible for the employer to admit the employed, not only to a knowledge of the results of his business, but to a participation in whatever profits accrued therefrom.

Those, therefore, who became associated with industrial partnership rendered themselves by the very act aliens to trade unionism, and the two systems continued for years to wage an almost unceasing warfare. The unionists seldom lost an opportunity of trying to persuade the men who had thus strayed from their fold that "Codlin's the friend, not Short"; and that by adhesion to the main body of their order, they would reap greater gain than could otherwise accrue. Such blandishments failed of their intended effect while the workmen found industrial partnership promoting their pecuniary advantage. In a few years the Messrs Briggs paid to the men at their Whitwood and Methley Collieries bonuses amounting in the aggregate to over £30,000. In August of 1873 they distributed among 1,754 workmen upwards of £14,250, as their share of the profits realised during the previous year. All this was paid in addition to the ordinary rate of wages current in the district. Messrs Fox, Head, & Company, at their Newport Rolling Mills, where a much smaller number of men was employed, paid in a few years between £6,000 and £7,000 by way of bonus; and at the works of the North of England Industrial Iron and Coal Company, the workmen under the same system were the richer by a similarly large amount.

But in the nature of things it could hardly be that trades so liable to fluctuation should continue year after year to pay a large bonus in addition to the ordinary rate of wages; and although it was no part of the industrial partnership system that the men should share in the losses of the business as well as in the profits, it was yet impossible that, when trade became depressed, the continued loyalty and adhesion of the men could be purchased by the premium which prosperity made possible. Apparently untrained to the wisdom and expediency of sacrificing an immediate benefit for the sake of ultimate advantage, the men forsook their allegiance, and industrial partnership was abandoned both by Messrs Fox, Head, & Company, and by the Messrs Briggs, the former finding that their workmen refused to allow any reciprocity of advantage, and the latter declaring that their men had returned to the union, under the instructions of whose executive they acted in all matters arising between themselves and their employers.

Not less dismal and disheartening has been the failure of co-operative production in cases where the working men have found the capital as well as supplied the labour. The story of the Shirland Collieries acquired by the South Yorkshire Miners' Association is as sorrowful a record of trouble and failure as the annals of industry can supply. Scarcely less disastrous has been the career of the colliery which was taken up by the Northumberland Miners' Association in the vicinity of Chesterfield. The Ouseburn Engine Works at Newcastle is another notable addition to the long catalogue of failures, due either to the lack of commercial foresight and competency, to the inefficiency of the management, to the want of cohesion and agreement among the members of the co-operative concern, or to the absence of reserves adequate to tiding over a season of adversity. Although the Ouseburn Works were the property of the men themselves, this did not prevent a number of them from striking for higher wages, thus proving the difficulty of conducting, on a democratic system, an undertaking embracing many classes of workmen, with varied and unequal qualifications.

Such and so significant have been the results attending the adoption of co-operative production. No elaborate analysis of the facts is needed to prove that, whether due to any inherent weakness in the system itself, to the inadequate and incomplete character of the experiments, to the want of confidence and competency on the part of the working classes, or to the general but vague and shadowy explanation that the times are not yet fully ripe for its acceptance, co-operation has not succeeded in proving its claims to reconcile the conflicting interests of capital and labour, and the unequal distribution of the profits of production must be righted in some other way.

Concurrently with the failure of co-operative production, and its consequent abandonment by those who have given it the most prolonged and patient trial, the expedient of arbitration, which aims at reaching a similar result by a different way, has been growing in public favour, and proving itself an "easy, artless, unencumbered plan" for the equitable and satisfactory settlement of industrial differences. Of this system, the modes and forms are almost as numerous and complicated as of co-operation. One trade has adopted what is known as Mr

Mundella's plan of a "long jaw," which implies and involves the settlement of a dispute by simple conciliation, or, in other words, by a friendly meeting of employers and employed, at which the parties chaffer and haggle and bargain and argue, until an eventual compromise is effected. Another trade prefers the more formal and obligatory system of a regular court, armed not only with the power of making an award, but also with authority to enforce it. Others again prefer a course equally distant from the informality of the one system and the strictly judicial procedure of the other. No accordance of experience or opinion has yet made known whether any particular system is better than another, or which is absolutely the best. We are only feeling our way to this consummation of patient and careful experiments.

It is the purpose of these pages to focus and crystallise the experience of the past and the obvious requirements of the present in respect of this new mode of dealing with industrial differences. Professor Tyndall has affirmed, in his public lectures, that the destiny of this nation is not in the hands of its statesmen, but in those of its coalowners. In another and still more important sense, it might be argued that our national destinies will henceforth be controlled by our trades unions. Subject to wise and temperate governance, these may be made a great power for good. With the advent of arbitration they entered upon a new career of usefulness. Without their aid, arbitration, in its fullest and most effectual modes, would scarcely be practicable. It is the function of the union first to accept or reject arbitration, according to the views entertained of the circumstances under which it is proposed; but, having accepted it, to pledge all the workmen concerned in the issue to loyalty and good faith, thus ensuring to the employer a measure of security and confidence in the execution of his contracts that might not otherwise accrue. In the fulfilment of this mission, trade unionism may redeem itself from the failures and disgraces of the past, and become as conspicuous for the distribution of benefits and blessings as heretofore it has been for such plague-spots as rattening and Luddism.

Certain employers of the old school have been slow to recognise the altered condition of things. Accustomed under *l'ancien régime* to have their own way with their workmen, or to regard them perhaps as machines, to be driven as fast and as long as their energies will allow, without any exercise of their own will, they view with uneasy and dissatisfied feelings the tendencies of the times towards social equality. Absolute equality there can never be in a society composed of men unequally endowed in knowledge, in skill, in aptitude, and in mental and physical force; but the equality which authorises and enables two men to meet at the same table, the one to sell his labour and the other to buy it, is as nearly as possible absolute for this particular purpose; and while " the good old rule, the simple plan," of casting freedom of contract to the winds, and measuring the value of a man's labour by his dire necessities, and the despondency which the superior power of capital can inspire, are still traceable in certain quarters, we should like to infer from recent events that their reciprocal duties, as well as their mutual rights, are being better understood and more conscientiously fulfilled alike by employers and employed. The hostility of class to class is being broken down. The fear which formerly prevented working men from asserting their rights lest they should lose their employment has given place to an assurance of security and protection induced by the ægis of unionism and the more reasonable and rational conduct of employers.

But while conciliation has done more than any other system devised in recent times for the prevention of conflicts between capital and labour, it is still only on its trial, and is even now, from day to day, enduring strains under which it sometimes threatens to give way. Hitherto arbitration has been in danger because men refused to make the experiment which its application involved. Industrial leaders have not been eager to learn the lesson inculcated by Bacon when he says, that "the risk attending want of success is not to be compared with that of neglecting the attempt—the former being attended with the loss of a little human labour; the latter, with that of an immense benefit."* But pressure, solicitation, coercion, and other influences have recently brought the system into the fierce glare of public criticism. It has been put upon its trial under the most crucial circumstances that could well be imagined. For it will not be denied that the industry of this country has never experienced vicissitudes so perplexing, so abnormal, so beset with distracting doubts and difficulties and fears, as those that have marked the epoch during which conciliation has been on its trial. During that interval we have seen the culmination of both prosperity and adversity. Wages have been advanced, " not by steps, but by strides ; not by strides, but by leaps and bounds." The tide turned, and the working classes found their fall almost as rapid as their rise, and quite as unexpected, until they were plunged in the very trough of the wave while yet they believed themselves bounding on its crest. Capital has been called upon to endure similarly varied experiences. Bewilderment, panic, dismay at times, seized hold of employer and employed alike. The machinery of social and industrial life has been thrown greatly out of gear. Under such a condition of things, some degree of confusion, distrust, and dereliction of obvious common-sense, became perhaps inevitable. But the working classes, as a whole, have been fairly loyal, up to a certain point. Content with the issues of arbitration, they have suffered reduction after reduction in their wages with Spartan-like endurance and fortitude. It is true that there have been large exceptions, but these have only proved and confirmed the rule. In almost every staple industry throughout the country, arbitration, in these perilous and disheartening times, has won triumphs that can never fade.

It is right that these triumphs and successes should be put on record, as much for the guidance of the future as for the honour of the past. The time for writing a really complete history of arbitration has not yet come : nor will it perhaps have arrived until some other expedient, more simple, certain, and satisfactory, has taken its place. The present volume

---

* *Novum Organum*, Book I. Aphorism cxiv.

makes no pretensions to being either a full or a connected history; it is written with the sole purpose of helping on the good work, in its hour of greatest need. For it must have struck all who have watched the recent course of industrial events, that much ignorance still prevails as to the methods and issues involved, and that there is not a little prejudice still to be overcome.

CHAPTER II.

THE PROBLEM OF TO-DAY.

It is hardly likely to be disputed, by any one who has given consideration to the subject, that the great problem of the present day, as we have argued in the previous chapter, is that of harmonising the relations of capital and labour.

This problem has been before the world for centuries, and each succeeding century has but served to increase its urgency. The nineteenth century has brought the problem more prominently to the front than any other, simply because the modern constitution of industry and of society has forced it more directly upon public attention.

Underlying this great fundamental problem of the distribution of the results of the products of industry, and the social amelioration of the masses, there are many minor problems that now and again find articulate expression in movements and demands on the part of great masses of the working population of our own and other countries.

The movements known and distinguished as Socialism, Nihilism, Collectivism, and many others, are all the outcome of dissatisfaction with the industrial organisation of society, and especially with the general conditions and rewards of labour.

The more beneficent and admirable movements distinguished as Profit-sharing, Co-operation, Industrial Partnership, and others, are the expression and the symbols of efforts on the part of the ranks of labour to emancipate themselves in some degree from the thraldom of labour, so as to enjoy the fruits of industry on a larger scale, if not in a different form.

Unhappily, however, these fruits have been growing more

and more rare, and consequently more and more difficult to realise. The modern manufacturing system has introduced a revolution in all the essential conditions of industry. The small producers and the independent workmen, who carried on manufacturing operations on a small scale, have practically disappeared before the much more economical system of production, of which the modern cotton factory, blast-furnace, rolling mill, or machine shop are but common types. The tendency for more than half a century has been to displace the small capitalist, and to substitute large aggregations of factory workers for the home industries that were in vogue before the factory system became the rule of the land.

This movement has witnessed its most signal and significant manifestation in our own day. Within the present generation, production on a larger and yet larger scale has been carried out in reference to every important industry. A modern cotton factory will produce as much as a dozen factories would have done thirty or forty years ago. By increasing the speed of the spindles from 4,000 to 8,000 or 9,000 revolutions per minute, a much larger quantity of cotton is got from the same machinery with much the same amount of labour. By increasing the size of the blast furnaces, applying a higher pressure of blast, and introducing various mechanical improvements, the typical smelting plant will now produce three or four times as much iron as it could have done a generation ago. A Bessemer converter at that period was thought to have done great things if it turned out 10,000 tons a year, but it is now no uncommon thing for a vessel of this description to produce over 50,000 tons a year. A modern rolling mill will produce 1,500 tons of rails or plates in a week, where 300 or 400 tons would have been deemed a large output at the time we speak of. Until a comparatively recent date few collieries produced more than 10,000 to 20,000 tons of coal in a twelvemonth, but modern collieries often produce half-a-million tons in that period. A modern steamship will carry 8,000 to 10,000 tons of cargo, where one-third of that quantity would have been deemed almost an achievement less than half a century ago. A modern locomotive engine will weigh well on to a hundred tons, and pull over 2,000 tons of dead weight on a level road, where earlier locomotives could not have done more than one-tenth of that amount of duty. And so with nearly every other process and appliance used in modern manufacturing or distributing industry.

All this has had the effect of inducing over-production and a keenness of competition that was not known in the days of our forefathers. Competition leads to the cutting of prices, and thereby to the cutting of profits, until those who are engaged in it are compelled to either give up the race, or endeavour to make some sort of arrangement that will save themselves from ruin.

Those who have given attention to the recent phases of political economy, especially in reference to production and distribution, have remarked that capital has been receiving a less, and labour a larger share of the proceeds of their joint industry. In the older countries of the world, and especially in our own—which occupies a unique position in respect to free trade—the profits that have been earned in the chief industries common to all have become more and more attenuated, until in many cases they have almost, if not quite, disappeared. The iron trade presents a chapter in the history of industrial disaster to which there are happily few parallels. In all the leading centres of that industry—in South Wales, Cleveland, Staffordshire, and Scotland—the records of the last twenty years are dismal, disastrous, and depressing in the last degree. In some cases, more than one-half of the original firms established to carry on this industry have gone to the wall, even after many of them had previously made large fortunes, and the strongest and most virile firms have found the utmost difficulty in saving themselves from a like fate.

It is natural to ask, why should capital incur such risks? If legitimate manufacturing business is so full of dangers and pitfalls, why should capital not be withdrawn from it and put into something else?

There are two answers to hand. The first is that when

capital has once been invested in a manufacturing enterprise it is not so easy to withdraw it. The second is that every manufacturer and capitalist hopes, and probably believes, that in seasons of prosperity he may succeed in recouping himself for the losses incurred when industry was unprofitable.

Although the most irrefutable testimony has been given to the fact that in our principal industries—including iron, coal, and cotton—the average rate of profit on the capital invested over the last twenty years has not been higher than—if so high as—it would have been had the money been invested in Consols, and not nearly so much as if it had been invested in ground-rents, or even in railway securities, yet the average capitalist is always hoping for large dividends, and now and again—although of late years at much rarer intervals than formerly—he finds his hopes realised. Three such periods have happened since 1870—the first in 1872-73; the second in 1880-81; and the third in 1889-90. Most of the intervening periods have been marked by unremitting and not generally successful efforts to avoid more or less serious loss.

Bad as the condition and prospect have been for the great industries on which Great Britain is so much dependent, capitalists might have gone on in the old groove, hoping for the occasional rewards of patience that they have hitherto met with as a set-off to the troubles of the average period, due to over-production and competition, or, in other words, to their own course of action. But of late years they have been called upon to face another, and an even more formidable danger, which, if not entirely new, has at any rate assumed new phases that invest it with a dread and a power for evil that it had not previously exercised to anything like the same extent.

It need hardly be added that this new terror is the increasing restlessness of labour, and the exercise of the power possessed by that force to deprive the capitalist of the fruits of his anxious years of watching and waiting, when at length there is a prospect that the fat kine will eat up the lean.

A suspension of labour at a time when industry is depressed and profits are low is bad enough, but it may then be borne with equanimity, because employers would probably not lose much in the form of unrealised profit. But that work should be stopped,—that collieries, factories, and furnaces should be laid idle when there is every possible inducement to work steadily, alike in higher profits for employers and higher wages for employed,—this is the self-immolation, the modern Juggernauth, with which we have now to reckon, and to get rid of which we are all so anxiously concerned.

The problem of the hour is, then—(1) How is capital to be protected against the menacing power of labour unions, now or recently so disastrously exercised for its destruction; and (2) how is labour to be protected against itself?

In thus stating the problem, we do not stop to argue the question whether capital or labour is more tyrannical, unreasonable, and selfish. We do not seek to ascertain whether capital has an undue share of the products of industry— whether labour should have a higher rate of remuneration, whether the one interest is always sufficiently conciliatory and considerate towards the other. The fundamental question is—How are the parties concerned to be got together to discuss their differences, with a view to amicable settlement? In other words, how are strikes to be avoided, and capital to be conserved? The solution of this problem lies at the root of our manufacturing supremacy, because it is not to be denied that if the prospect for capital in relation to the attitude of labour does not improve, we shall be likely to witness a movement that will end in the transference of capital, in so far as it is convertible, to other channels, where the terrible experience of the ironmasters of Cleveland and West Cumberland, owing to the Durham strike of 1882, and the not less memorable difficulties of the great industries of Lancashire and Yorkshire, consequent upon the Midland coal strike of 1893, are not likely to be repeated.

The struggles of capital against the evils and the dangers which it has itself created against the modern Frankenstein which it has found it so much more easy to establish than to control — are sufficiently formidable, but in one way and another they may be endured. But labour does not yet appear to have sufficiently realised how important it is that these evils and dangers should not be increased by springing upon capital unknown and unexpected conflicts with influences that are incomparably more serious than any adverse results brought about by hostile tariffs abroad, or financial panics at home, although, unlike these, easily within our own control.

CHAPTER III.

ATTEMPTS AT SOLUTION OF THE PROBLEM.

So long as the problem that has been stated in the preceding chapter remains unsolved, so long will industry be exposed to the risks and dangers attending the use of force and physical endurance as a means to overcome one party or the other.

It is clear on the face of it that a trial of brute strength can settle nothing satisfactorily; at the most it can only prove that one party can hold out longer than another. But even this does not prove that either is less exhausted than the other, or that the one party has larger resources than the other. The one that has most at stake is likely to give in first, but the other may easily be much more *in extremis*.

When industrial war has once begun, the parties concerned have a sentiment of *amour propre* that renders it much more difficult to settle a dispute afterwards than it would have been if the dispute had never been allowed to go so far. An army in the field may be desirous of capitulating, and may be unable to continue the struggle without incurring terrible sacrifices, but this does not prevent the continuance of the war until "peace with honour" can be claimed.

It is therefore of the first importance that no dispute should be allowed to proceed so far as an open rupture. Every possible precaution should be taken to provide for a conciliatory and friendly consideration of the question at issue, before it is allowed to breed an open sore.

This fact has been recognised in most of the principal industries of our own and other countries, by the establishment of Committees of Conciliation, Councils of Experts, Arbitration Boards, Sliding Scales, or other machinery, designed either to bring the disputants into close touch with one another, or to refer the matter at issue to a competent tribunal to be composed of one or more parties whose decision is generally accepted as final.

One of the first organisations established with this end in view was the French system of *Conseils des Prud'hommes*, or Councils of Experts, which was created under the Napoleonic code in the early years of the present century, and has since then been developed on a considerable scale, until it has become the recognised medium for the settlement of all differences between employers and employed, not in France only, but in Germany, Belgium, and other countries as well. The objects, scope, and constitution of the tribunal are explained in another chapter (*vide* chap. xx., p. 154).

These Councils of Experts have now been in existence for well on to a century, and they have done a remarkable amount of good. Their machinery is simple, inexpensive, and readily accessible, but their scope is limited. Their functions are akin rather to the County Court of England, or the so-called Small Debt Court of Scotland, than to the wider functions and broader aims of an Arbitration Board. Their machinery is, however, suited to a much more ambitious programme than they themselves carry out. They are really composed of two Committees,—the first the Committee of Conciliation, before whom the disputants appear with their witnesses, but without lawyers, and who have a right to call for documents or industrials products relating to the case. If this Committee does not effect a settlement satisfactory to the parties, the issue is submitted to the Committee of Judgment, which deliberates with much of the formality, and with most of the powers, of a duly constituted legal tribunal. A very large number of cases are brought before these councils. Generally speaking, more than one-half of the total number of cases brought up are not settled by the Conciliation Committee, and have consequently to be referred for judgment.

The *Conseils des Prud'hommes* are not, however, suited for the purpose of arranging the larger matters that eventuate in important differences between employers and employed. Their very constitution renders them unfitted for this purpose. They are only intended to solve more or less trifling quarrels, and they have certainly not succeeded in preventing strikes on a large scale in any Continental country. They correspond, indeed, rather to the old Trade Guild or Corporation, which they were originally designed to supersede, than to the much more free and independent procedure of Arbitration Boards of modern growth.*

It is difficult to see how the system which they administer could be applied to the general regulation of the rate of wages, of the hours of work, or of the many other matters that nowadays are liable to provoke a general suspension of labour; and it is against these that society and the combatants themselves specially require to be protected. Even in France their unsuitability for dealing with large questions has been virtually acknowledged, by the passing of the new law of December 1892 providing for conciliation and arbitration in collective disputes between employers and employed.

One of the first attempts to substitute conciliation for the "might is right" system of settling differences that previously prevailed, was that made in the carpet industry, mainly at the instance of the late Mr William Henderson, of Durham. In

---

* "The origin of these Councils is interesting. The silk manufacturers of Lyons in the last century possessed a *Tribunal Commun*, for settling trade disputes which worked within the limits of their guild or corporation. It fell, with the latter, under the law of March 1791. The manufacturers, feeling the disadvantages and costliness of the more cumbrous machinery of the Law Courts in settling their disputes, took advantage of a visit from the Emperor in 1805, to petition for an institution similar to their old *Tribunal Commun*, in which men pronounced sentence who understood the trade. It was granted in the law of March 18, 1806, and worked so well that it served as a model for the Councils which were rapidly formed at Rouen, Nîmes, Avignon, and other towns. The decree of June 11, 1809, defined the procedure for creating future Councils. The first Council formed in Marseilles was for the soap factories, in 1810. In the beginning of 1892 there were in that town 149 Councils for all sorts of trades."—*Royal Commission on Labour, Foreign Reports*, vol. vi., p. 49.

that industry, previous to the year 1839, "not a year passed without the occurrence of strikes, and the bitterness of feeling between masters and workmen was most lamentable." This suggested to several leading employers the formation of an association, "which, ignoring all past ill feeling, should set itself, in the first place, to do justice and even more than justice to the operatives, and, in the second place, to convince them by its acts that the Association was their best and truest friend."

This difficult and, as many at that time were disposed to regard it, Quixotic measure was, however, not carried out on modern lines, and its methods would now be likely to be regarded as one-sided and even archaic in character. Periodical meetings of the employers were arranged for, to which, during a part of their sitting, deputies from the different works were admitted. But the object in view rather appears to have been to call the employers to account in the presence of each other, than to arrange differences mutually with their workmen. The principal feature of the system was stated to be, that "masters disposed to tyrannise over their workmen would not dare to do so when liable to be periodically called to account for it in the presence of their fellow-manufacturers;" and it was hoped that "the paid delegates of the workmen, whose object had generally been to prolong mischief, would cease to have power," when the workmen were given to understand that their special grievances were being inquired into with a view to redress.*

Up to a certain point, this system appears to have succeeded. Mr Henderson, in the communication from which we have already quoted, states that "every strike in the carpet trade of the United Kingdom has ceased on the appeal" of the Association thus constituted; and he adds his conviction, "that the organisation succeeded, because the first step towards improving the social condition of the working classes, is to convince them that they will always meet with justice at the hands of their employers."

---

* *Reports on Paris Exhibition of 1889*, vol. vi., p. 105.

No doubt the Association had excellent aims, and did good work so far as it went. But it would not nowadays be regarded as going nearly far enough. It was reserved for others to follow in the direction taken, by more modern arrangements designed to secure industrial peace. No one is entitled to more credit for discernment and tact in anticipating and providing for the requirements of the altered condition of things, as between capital and labour, than Mr Mundella, who was one of the first to recognise the justice and the expediency of calling in the workmen to discuss matters of difference with their employers, and thereby giving them the previously unknown consciousness that they had a voice in the settlement of their own affairs. This new sense of power was naturally somewhat warily exercised at the outset, and the concessions made by the employers were regarded with suspicion and distrust. But, by-and by, the workmen came to feel that their employers had nothing "up their sleeve" when they sought conference with them, but were honestly anxious to arrive at understandings just and honourable to all parties.

Many subsequent attempts were made to introduce the principles of conciliation and of arbitration into the settlement of disputes in the chief industries of Great Britain. In the silk trade of Macclesfield, a voluntary Court of Arbitration, suggested by the *Conseils des Prud'hommes* of France, already referred to, was established as far back as 1849, in consequence of a strike of the *employés* in that industry. The board consisted of twelve representatives on each side, with a chairman and a secretary; but it did not succeed in obtaining legal sanction for its awards, nor could it have done so, because, as Mr Crompton has pointed out, "it aimed at the settlement of future prices, as well as the enforcing of subsisting contracts."* In the printing trade, again, arbitration in one form or another has been common from early times, and about 1853 a Court of Arbitration was constituted, with a barrister as umpire; but the court was

---

* *Industrial Conciliation*, p. 125.

broken up, because the workmen, while accepting the award as a decision in an actual dispute, refused to accept it as a decision binding in all other cases arising out of past contracts and involving similar questions.*

About 1860, a Conciliation Board was established, mainly through the mediation of Mr Mundella, in the Nottingham hosiery and lace trades, which did good service for many years; and in 1865, Mr (afterwards Sir Rupert) Kettle was instrumental in forming a board for the building trade of Wolverhampton. In 1869, the Board of Arbitration and Conciliation was formed in the North of England iron trade, on the suggestion of Mr David Dale, and since that date the progress of the one system or the other has been rapid, if somewhat chequered.

The later and more recent attempts at introducing more or less modified systems of conciliation, and the diffusion of its spirit and principles throughout various industries in our own and other countries, will be found dealt with in succeeding chapters. We need not, therefore, further pursue the historical vein here, but turn our attention to some of the more prominent and commanding aspects of the question, as elicited by the experience and commended by the judgment of those who have made the matter a special study. This we shall now undertake in succeeding chapters.

---

* *Industrial Conciliation*, p. 131.

CHAPTER IV.

INDUSTRIAL CONCILIATION.

THE most competent judges are greatly divided in opinion as to whether conciliation alone, or arbitration alone, or conciliation plus arbitration, is to be preferred as a means for the adjustment of labour disputes. There is much to be said for both systems; and probably when all has been said that can well be said on the whole matter, it comes to this that each has its own special mission and function, suited to its own special circumstances.

Conciliation has been described as the system of "the long jaw," as the "higgling of the market," and as a friendly discussion over the matter at issue. But however it may be described, and whatever form it may take, it resolves itself into an informal attempt to come to an agreement without calling in any outsider, or making any formal appeal to a formally-constituted tribunal.

The great merit of conciliation is, that when it is successful the parties agree upon the spot, and there is an end of the matter; whereas in the case of arbitration, they have no knowledge of what the issue may be, and if it is deemed to be unjust and arbitrary there is a danger of the award being rejected. Mr Crompton says that he "cannot but sympathise with the feeling that the men must often have, that if the arbitrator could have had their knowledge of the details and the situation the result would have been different." [*] In the case of the Board of Conciliation established in the Nottingham hosiery trade, the chairman had originally a casting vote.

---

[*] *Industrial Conciliation,* p. 134.

Mr Mundella has stated that the exercise of that vote has twice got the Board into trouble, and after that it was decided that the parties would not vote at all. The rules of the Board still gave the chairman the casting vote, but it was never exercised. Both sides know the fatal consequences of disagreement, and they consequently agree by coming to the best arrangement possible under the circumstances.*

Arbitration, as commonly understood and practised, is of course a much more formal and stately process. The essential principle of this system is, that the matter in dispute shall be referred, and that the decision of the referee shall be accepted. But thereby hang not a few difficulties and complications. The parties to the dispute are left entirely at liberty to make their own arrangements. They agree upon the constitution of the court, upon the number of arbitrators, upon the form of procedure, upon the lines within which evidence or pleadings shall be admitted, and finally upon the umpire or referee. As, however, the system is usually followed, the employers appoint two or more of their own number as arbitrators, and the men do the same, so that those who nominally hold the position of arbitrators are really more like advocates, and in ninety-nine out of every hundred cases referred, the ultimate decision rests with the umpire.

It becomes, therefore, a matter of very great importance, both for the satisfaction of the parties, and for the competency of the award, that the umpire should be qualified for his responsible post. But what are the qualifications required? Should the umpire be like the *Prud'hommes* of France and Belgium, an expert in the special industry affected? or should he be an outsider, with no local knowledge, but high character? This is really the crucial point —perhaps a more important point than all the others put together.

Every now and again cases occur that one of the parties concerned refuses to submit to arbitration. This may be partly due to the stiff-necked obduracy of the party, or to a

---

* *Industrial Conciliation*, p. 38.

lack of confidence in their own case, or to a fear that the umpire will not be a sound man, or to some other cause. In the case of the great strike of 1893 in the Midland coal trade, the miners refused to submit the matter at issue to arbitration, although ultimately they agreed to such a reference. In the result Lord Shand was appointed to act as umpire by the Speaker of the House of Commons, who was requested to make the appointment. It is to be presumed that this choice was primarily made because of the legal acumen of the selected jurist, which would of course enable him to sift evidence, and to bring inconclusive matters to the test of proof. But an umpire must not only be fair and unprejudiced, he must be able to convey the impression that he has these qualities in a high degree, or the result may be dubious.

One obvious argument in favour of conciliation, as contra distinguished from arbitration, is that under the former system there is at least every probability that the parties will not decline to come together with a view to a settlement. Conciliation implies that they are ready and anxious to settle, and it does not commit them to any irrevocable or foregone issue. But in reference to arbitration, cases have again and again occurred where both employers and employed have declined to submit to a referee, so that an absolute deadlock of negotiations was involved. The cases in which such refusals occur appear to be infrequent, but they are sufficiently numerous and vital to prove that conciliation should first be resorted to, whenever practicable, and that a more formal reference should only follow upon a declaration that a settlement cannot otherwise be arrived at.

So far as we have already gone, we have spoken of arbitration and conciliation as if they were two distinct systems having no necessary connection with each other. And so indeed they are. But this has not interfered with the adoption of both systems simultaneously, or almost so. In most of the leading trades conciliation is now practised in the appointment of a joint-committee of employers and employed, who are called on to investigate, and if possible to settle, all matters in dispute. This system is carried on in the Durham and Northumberland coal trade, in the North of England iron trade, and in many other leading industries. The existence of a joint committee is necessary for the settlement of minor disputes, of which many are liable to arise; and the functions of the committee are much akin to those of the *Prud'hommes*, excepting that the decisions arrived at have no binding character, and must be satisfactory to the parties interested before they can be accepted.

The principle of industrial conciliation is so well understood that it can hardly be necessary to define it in any very precise form. It means, in effect, that the parties concerned in any dispute that may occur are prepared to meet together for the purpose of discussing the whole subject, if possible, in order to arrive at a friendly settlement without having the question at issue submitted to any formal tribunal, or arranging for placing the determination of the issue in the hands of any third party.

Conciliation must always of necessity precede any attempt to settle a dispute by a reference. There must at any rate be the conciliatory attitude implied in a readiness to have the dispute referred; and when the parties have proceeded so far, it would appear to be desirable that they should at least meet and try to arrange it between themselves.

The obvious advantage of conciliation, and the claim to adoption that it possesses above and beyond any other system, is that it makes an end of the matter to the satisfaction of both parties. In the case of an appeal to arbitration, the issue is invariably left in the hands of a third party, who has no further direct interest in it. The award may be just, or it may be unjust. In either case, the one side or the other is liable to think that it has a tendency to place them at a disadvantage; and as they have had no voice of their own in it,—beyond their share in the choice of the umpire who makes the award,—they are sometimes disposed to look upon both the umpire and his award with disfavour, and now and again to revolt against them. All this is avoided by conciliation, which leaves the issue absolutely and entirely in the hands of the parties concerned.

The "long jaw" is a happy phrase invented by Mr Mundella to express the essential feature of the discussions that took place between employers and employed, in the hosiery and lace trades of Nottingham, with a view to the settlement of labour difficulties and disagreements. It is indeed the fundamental basis of conciliation, inasmuch as it implies a friendly business talk between the parties interested in the question under consideration. As a general rule this is one-half of the whole trouble in labour questions. Until the system of bringing employers and employed face to face was introduced into the hosiery and lace trades of Nottingham, the building trade of Wolverhampton, the lace industries of Nottingham, and other centres of industry, which showed an early appreciation of the importance of getting over the great gulf that formerly separated capital and labour, and led the one to take up a continuously antagonistic attitude towards the other, there was not much chance of making solid progress towards a satisfactory settlement of matters in dispute. But, directly the parties were brought face to face, they began to understand one another, to appreciate each other's difficulties and arguments, and to display a mutual forbearance and concession that would otherwise have been impossible.

Mr Mundella has himself borne testimony of a very emphatic kind to the success of the system of conciliation adopted in the hosiery and lace trades of Nottingham. During the whole sixteen or seventeen years that he was president of the board, "there had only been two or three cases where the men had been recalcitrant." Where the workmen set themselves against the board, they alienated the sympathy of the intelligent section of their fellows, and deprived themselves of Union support.

The Joint-Committee in the coal and iron industries is an outcome of the Committee of Inquiry, which was adopted nearly thirty years ago in the Nottingham hosiery trade, as part of the system of conciliation. In the latter case, the committee consisted of four members of the board—two employers and two operatives; and the committee made an attempt to settle every dispute brought before it, but without the power to make an award. The functions of the committee are in point of fact modelled on those of the Committee of Mediation or Conciliation in the *Prud'hommes* system, although in the latter case the committee usually consists of only two members,—one an employer and the other a workman,—who are supposed to be of different industries.

In some of the most "advanced" industries, as, for example, the engineering trades, conciliation is not only approved of, but regularly adopted in preference to arbitration. It has been held that in the case of the latter system, the issues between the parties are so direct that only a trial of strength can settle a question on which they have once agreed to differ. It is also said that "when trade is good employers will not accept arbitration, and the workmen will not do so when trade is bad,"* although that has not, of course, been a rule of invariable application. And the argument used by labour leaders is, that "arbitration is not so sound in principle as conciliation, owing both to the weakness of its sanction generally, and to the fact that that weakness is more marked as against the men than as against the employers."†

---

* *Royal Commission on Labour, Group A*, 23,681-2.
† *Ibid.*, 25,348-54.

CHAPTER V.

INDUSTRIAL ARBITRATION.

ARBITRATION may be defined as a means of settling a question in dispute by a reference to a third party, when the contendants have failed to agree between themselves. It therefore comes into operation as a kind of *pis aller*, after conciliation has been tried and failed.

Generally speaking, in practice, conciliation is applied to the settlement of small disputes through the medium of a joint committee of employers and employed; and arbitration is applied to the adjustment of larger questions, such as the general rate of wages, when these are not provided for by sliding scales or in some other way.

Sir Rupert Kettle has pointed out that it is not merely as a means of settling a scale of wages that boards of arbitration and conciliation are useful. The contract of hiring and serving involves other matters besides prices,—such, for example, as hours of work, Saturday half-holidays, and weekly reckonings. Then, again, there are such questions as "walking time, artificial light, and overtime in the building trade; the quality of the metal and Sunday 'fettling' in the iron trade; the speed of machinery and dampness of the yarn when weighed in the cotton trade; 'good from over' in the potteries. Such subjects as these boards of arbitration can not only settle between the individual employer and his workmen, but can lay down rules upon, by which being 'as fair for one as another' the whole trade is willing to abide. So that individual masters cannot, under the pressure of competition, impose upon workmen terms more onerous than of the trade, nor can workmen have excuse, even when they change service, for refusing to fall into the routine of trade obligations."

"'The duty of a board of arbitration," remarks the same authority,* "does not end with the making of a contract of hiring; it affords important assistance in carrying out that course. Many intelligent persons will think that when an agreement is settled and reduced to writing, a course I advise in all cases,

that it will then be quite easy to interpret it. This is, in practice, found not to be so. Even Acts of Parliament, upon the wording of which so much care is bestowed, are often ambiguous, or, in the technology of my profession, 'insensible.' Indeed, since that much discredited science, pleading, has fallen into disuse, we seem to have lost the art of making our written instruments 'certain to every intent.' Both employer and workman have confidence in their contracts, when they know there is an impartial and popularly informed tribunal which can be called upon to put upon them a binding interpretation. When minor differences arise, such as do not affect great trade interests — differences often commencing with a personal quarrel between a workman or body of workmen and an overlooker or foreman, it is well that some judicious conciliator should step between the disputants, and by authoritative advice prevent these small bickerings growing into a trade strife a taking of sides, to be followed by the proverbial consequences of the letting out of troubled waters. It is then—(1) As an open market, in which the fair wages for a fair day's work can be determined; (2) To prevent misunderstanding as to the meaning of hiring contracts; and (3) To pacify quarrels when they arise in the execution of such contracts, that I think boards of arbitration and conciliation are required."

It goes without saying that no stereotyped system of arbitration can be adopted that would be equally suited to the circumstances of every industry, nor even in all probability to any considerable number of industries. There are, to begin with, some two thousand or more industries carried on in the

---

* Paper read before the Social Science Congress in 1871.

United Kingdom, each differing from all the others in some more or less characteristic and essential particulars. Then, again, not only has every industry its own special features and conditions, but every district has its own special rate of wages, and its own special customs and usages, even for the same industry; so that a basis or system that might be admirably suited to one would be quite ill adapted to another, and any attempt to bring about unity and conformability might lead to serious disagreements.

Very great importance is attached by both employers and employed to the choice of an umpire. The umpire should be, like Cæsar's wife, "above suspicion." He should be neither a strong partisan nor a man of intemperate and one-sided judgment. As a rule, it would probably be better that he should have no interest in labour questions as an employer. There have, no doubt, been many cases where an employer was trusted by workmen to deal with questions affecting the rate of wages to be paid. In the North of England, Mr David Dale, himself one of the largest employers in the country, has often been called in to decide knotty points involving questions of wages, and he has for many years been the umpire chosen by the unanimous suffrages of the Board of Arbitration and Conciliation in the manufactured iron trade of the north; but Mr Dale's is altogether an exceptional case, as he is also an entirely exceptional man.

The umpire should be a man who is accustomed to weighing and sifting evidence, and if not actually a lawyer, he should at least have some judicial powers and experience. In what is called "open arbitration," all sorts of matters, relevant and irrelevant, crucial and trivial, fundamental and remote, are liable to be introduced. This may, of course, be done in perfectly good faith. But in handling the mass of materials submitted, the umpire should be able, with trained judgment and intelligence, to separate the essential from the non essential, the incidental from the fundamental, the immediate from the remote. If he fails to do this—if he commits an error in not assigning to fundamental facts their due importance,

C

and if he magnifies the value of non essentials, he is likely to do injustice to the one side or the other.

Such an injustice does not produce only a temporary effect. If either side is fully persuaded that a just award has not been made, the whole system suffers, because the injured party loses confidence in its merits. This is the worst thing that could befall it. The basis of arbitration, or of any system of a voluntary character designed to redress the balance between capital and labour, is faith in its efficacy and in its results. If that faith is in any degree shaken, the parties whose confidence has been damaged are less likely to accept the system in the future, and this result has happened again and again to the extent of an absolute refusal to have anything to do with it.

Another very important consideration for both parties is that the arbitrators should if they are charged with the duty of naming an umpire fix upon a man in whom both sides have the fullest confidence. He should, as a rule, be neither a master's man nor a man's man. He should not be too pronounced a politician, lest it be thought that his politics might warp his decision. He should not have made himself too conspicuous on behalf of any interest or shibboleth affecting the relations of capital and labour. He should, if possible, be one who knows something of the local conditions influencing and perhaps controlling the matters at issue. If he is an employer, he should at least be noted for fair-mindedness; and if he is known to have a specially sympathetic feeling towards labour, it will probably not do any harm, although there is a tendency on the part of extremely conscientious men to strain in the other direction, in order that they may not err on the side to which their sympathies are understood to lean.

Arbitration has, of course, been called into frequent requisition for other purposes than the determination of the rate of wages, although that rate has generally been thereby affected, directly or indirectly. A case in point may be noted, the more so that it was a case to which a good deal of importance was attached at the time, as calculated to fix the future customs of an extensive industry. In 1891 the Durham coalowners and the men employed in their coke yards decided to refer to arbitration a basis of work and wages suited to the various classes of cokemen, for the guidance of the joint-committee which usually determined all matters of pending controversy. The unusually large number of five arbitrators were appointed to represent each side, and Mr Robert Spence Watson of Newcastle-on-Tyne was requested to act as umpire. This was essentially a case that called for the mediation of an expert, which the umpire could not pretend to be. He had to decide what should be considered the standard oven, what amount of work each class of workmen should be expected to do in a given period of time, what should be the basis of payment, and what was the correct definition of an average "bench." The umpire, in the absence of any expert knowledge of the trade, required certain returns bearing on the points at issue to be furnished to him, and these he had examined by accountants, who prepared tables of general averages, which guided him to a decision which was generally satisfactory, care being taken to insist that the award did not in any way affect the right of any parties to show cause why, in this case, the details of the award should not be departed from.

It is not perhaps unnatural that with the workmen and their leaders in all cases, or at least in the great majority, the first question that is submitted, in considering the matter of whether arbitration or conciliation should be adopted, is the crucial one of the probable effect on wages. If the workmen had an assurance that wages would be favourably affected by arbitration, they would not be likely to hesitate long about its adoption. If, on the other hand, the adoption of either system were likely to lead to a lowering of wages, the readiness to adopt it would probably not be quite so apparent.

It is hardly necessary to remark, that the spirit of the system is not, in either case, primarily to either raise or lower wages, but to do justice between the employers and their employed. Sir Rupert Kettle was pressed, some years ago, to say whether, in his opinion, arbitration boards would raise wages. His reply was excellent. He answered that "these boards will fix, with business like accuracy, the market value of a given kind of skilled labour at a particular place and time." It is no necessary part of their business to either inflate or depress labour, and this cannot be too clearly understood.

Much, of course, depends upon the special conditions affecting the particular description of labour under consideration. If the labour is badly paid in relation to its market value and the prices paid for labour of a kindred character in the same district, the tendency will necessarily be to raise the price to be paid by the employer. If, on the other hand, the reward of labour is unduly high, the tendency will unquestionably be to level it down. Much must depend upon the particular and special circumstances of each individual case, and much also upon the view that may be taken of them by the umpire, in whose hands the final decision will usually ultimately rest.

At an early period in the history of industrial arbitration, and indeed up to the present time, the question has constantly arisen—What security are the leaders of the workmen prepared to offer that any award arrived at shall be duly carried out? No doubt, when the unions had less power than they now have, guarantees on the subject would not be readily forthcoming; and the history of arbitration has shown that the influence of their leaders has not always been powerful enough to keep the workmen from repudiating an adverse award. But of late years the unions have got more hold over their members, and they have introduced a number of very useful provisions into their rules, specifying that support shall be withheld from men who enter upon a strike without previously making an offer to submit the matter in dispute to arbitration, and withholding support also from men who do not faithfully abide by an award under an arbitration deliberately accepted, no matter how adverse the result may be.

It appears to be a fundamental pre-requisite of the adoption of conciliation and arbitration, though not perhaps to the same extent of sliding scales, that there should be strong unions of both employers and employed, and for all practical purposes the stronger the better, as the representatives are thereby enabled the more fully to pledge the various parties concerned to carry out whatever regulations or awards are decided on. Generally speaking, advanced employers have frankly and fully recognised this fact, and have hailed the workmen's unions with considerable favour. Every now and again, however, cases have arisen where a policy of repudiation has appeared to be expedient. If the whole of the *employés* engaged in a particular industry or work are members of the same union, there would be little or no difficulty; but of late years unions have shown a tendency to multiply, so that an employer may have to undertake separate negotiations with any number of unions before he knows exactly where he is. For this reason employers have properly discouraged dealings with more unions than one for the same sort or description of work. Thus, for example, in the making of pig iron, it is manifestly of advantage to all parties that the whole of the men employed about blast furnaces including mechanics, enginemen, and boilermen should belong to the same union, and should be considered and dealt with in one operation; but in some cases the men have claimed that they had separate unions, and that their wages should be made the subject of a separate negotiation. It is desirable that a limit should be imposed upon claims of this kind, otherwise the whole time of an employer may be taken up with fruitless negotiation, first with one body of men and then with another, although the same considerations and prices may equally govern the wages of all.

The *rationale* of the system of arbitration was thus clearly and concisely laid down by Mr Rupert Kettle, in his remarks at the meeting of the Social Science Congress in 1870:

"Whether an award should be capable of being legally executed, was a very moot point. In the present state of arbitration it was wise that both parties should be perfectly at liberty to go freely into arbitration or to withdraw from it; but while they remained together they ought to be bound, the being bound by the award being essential to the success of any system of arbitration. In its present state of development, practical means by which it could be carried out were almost infinitely varied. One was the placarding of bills in the masters' offices, so that all parties—both employers and men—might be fully conversant with the basis of the contract existing in any particular establishment. It had been said that the result of the arbitrations of last year had been to reduce wages; but all that the board could do was to ascertain exactly what was the market value of the labour at the time that the meeting took place. If an arbitration board made a decision which took wages out of capital, it would be most unjust; and, on the other hand, if the board took profit out of wages, that would be equally unjust. But it afforded the means of ascertaining exactly what the value of the labour was at that particular time; in fact, it was a mart and a market where both parties were independent dealers, where the market price was arrived at by discussion by the board; and if a dispute arose as to what was the market price, by discussing the grounds upon which the two parties based their respective claims the true value was ascertained. But the decision must be just and equitable at the time, and not based on what might be at the time forced from one side or conceded by the other."

In pointing out the difficulties that have had to be overcome in the establishment of the Board of Arbitration in the North of England iron trade, Mr Jones (then Secretary to the Manufactured Iron Trade of the North), in his paper read before the Social Science Congress in 1870, alluded to the fact that the ironworkers of that locality included a large number who had only recently come into the district, and who therefore lacked the ties of attachment that bind men to older establishments—the operatives being drawn from all iron manufacturing centres, and being largely augmented by Irish labourers, who could not be expected to act in unison so well as if they had more in common with each other. The nature and historical associations of the industry were also against arbitration. The great majority of ironworkers were very indifferently educated; their labours were exceedingly trying to the physical strength, but required no high degree of intellectual powers ; the whole traditions of the trade were largely made up of strikes, and the men had grown up suspicious of their employers and distrustful of their statements. Manual labour entered very extensively into the success of each operation in the iron trade ; the nature of the materials to be operated upon caused all classes of workmen to be mutually dependent from one end of the works to the other; and hence, even a small number of men who declined to work in harmony with each other, could influence the labour of many hundreds of workmen.

Every now and again cases occur which show that extraneous circumstances may have a great influence upon the rate of wages—or at any rate upon the ability of the employers to pay a certain rate of wages—as well as the mere variations of realised selling prices. A case that strongly brought out this fact occurred in the iron trade of the North of England in 1873. The employers claimed a reduction at that time of 12½ per cent., on the following grounds : —

" I. That in consequence of the high prices of coals, and of pig-iron (the price of which depends so much upon that of coal), they are unable to sell iron with a profit with the present rate of wages.

" II. (Though this argument is not so much insisted upon as the first.) That the rise of wages in the finished iron trade has been greater than in any analogous industries, except the coal trade.

" III. That it is expedient to lower wages, as an inducement to coalowners to reduce the price of coal, and so bring down to a price that will induce purchasers to deal."

Here we find that two arguments at least are more or less independent of the ordinary relations of prices to wages. The first is, that the high prices of materials made it impossible to produce manufactured iron at a profit with the then rate of wages in the latter industry, but this is not by any means equivalent to saying that the rate of wages in relation to realised prices is higher than it should be, or higher than it usually had been. In point of fact, circumstances are easily conceivable, if they have not actually occurred, in which it would be practically impossible to manufacture at a profit, even if the prices were exceptionally high and the wages the lowest on record.

The next consideration urged upon the arbitrator in the case above-named is also one that has no necessary or direct relation to the selling price of the commodity which the wages immediately affected are employed upon. It was proposed that the wages of the ironworkers should be lowered as an inducement to coalowners to reduce the price of coal, and so bring down iron prices. This may not only be a most desirable and necessary thing, but it may be a thing absolutely indispensable in the interests of capital and of labour alike, and yet it is one that has no direct bearing upon the relationship of immediate wages to immediate prices. The point was very fully and very fairly discussed by Mr Kettle, who, in making his award, held that "although the price of fuel ought not directly to affect the rate of wages . . . it must indirectly affect it from the inevitable tendency of high prices to check consumption."

In some cases the workmen have demanded that they should be allowed to examine the books of the employers, in order to be able to fix the amount of profit and loss, implying, if not directly asserting, that the amount of the profits earned by employers should be an essential element in the determination of wages. In other cases, the employers have readily agreed to allow the arbitrator to examine their books, with a view to the ascertainment of the financial results of their business. In the first case, as well as in the second, the proposals have generally been declined. The Durham coalowners gave a most emphatic denial to the claim of the workmen to know their profits; and Sir Rupert Kettle, as arbitrator in the manufactured iron trade of the North of England in 1873, declined to avail himself of the offer of the employers to see their books, in these terms :—

"If I had accepted this offer to go over the books for the purpose of ascertaining profit and loss, I should, by implication, have admitted the right of the employer to ask his workmen to participate, directly or indirectly, in their employers' losses ; and I do not see how the employers could, with logical consistency, have refused the workmen at any future time the examining of the same accounts, that they might participate in profits."

The logic of these remarks is obvious. Apart, however, from the reasoning of Sir Rupert Kettle, it is clear that the ascertainment of the average profits would be extremely invidious and difficult, even if it were to be admitted. No two mines, and no two works or factories, would be likely to show quite the same profits, and there would be a danger of opening a door that it would not be easy to shut.

Cases have occurred again and again where the employers have gained and the workmen have lost by open arbitration having been substituted for a sliding-scale. In the finished iron trade, for example, the upward movement of prices between 1869 and 1873 was very rapid and considerable, and would, under the operation of a sliding-scale, have given very high wages in 1873, when the general average price of the four descriptions of manufactured iron relied upon for a basis in the North of England rose to nearly double the average price of three years before. If the old so-called Thorneycroft standard or scale had then been applied, the wages of puddlers would have been doubled, and the wages of millmen would have been raised about sixty or seventy per cent. But Mr Rupert Kettle, in his award under the arbitration of September 1873, stated that although, if the scale were then in existence, wages would be higher, yet the rate was then "as high as they (the workmen) were entitled to, or as it is prudent of them to require"; and he added, that "there are some finished iron makers who can barely afford to pay the present rates, and therefore a change would be likely to lessen the demand for labour"; but as it did not appear that there was strong evidence that the lessened demand had already set in, the arbitrator did not therefore give the employers the relief they asked for.

The precise manner in which the one party should speak of

or address the other, although apparently a matter of trivial importance, is one that has really much to do with the maintenance of that conciliatory spirit that is so essential to the keeping up of harmonious relations. The day has gone past when the old terms of masters and workmen were deemed to be satisfactory, inasmuch as the former is held to imply an undue degree of servitude on the part of the latter. "Employers" and "employed" are no doubt much better, and more exactly describe the true relationship of the parties concerned. In the Durham coal trade arbitrations, the use of the term Association was introduced when speaking of the Coalowners' Association, and the term Executive was employed to describe the Executive of the workmen's Union.

The question has often been put, both by workmen and by outsiders, Does the adoption of arbitration tend to increase the rate of wages, or to reduce it? This would be a very interesting economic problem if it could be accurately solved, but it does not admit of easy solution. In an arbitration which is not encompassed by specific restrictions, and in which it is competent for either side to submit any evidence that may be deemed relevant, the employers are often able to show that there are considerable discrepancies as between one set of wages and another, and that the rate of wages paid all along has been exceptionally high relatively to the wages paid for similar, or approximately kindred, work in other industries. This has been the case to a large extent in the matter of puddling. Owing to the arduous and disagreeable character of the work it was at first difficult to persuade men to take it up, and their labour had to be bought by the inducement of a specially high rate of wages. But in course of time the necessity for this special inducement was not so urgent. Men were drafted into the trade from other industries, until there was an abundance of labour, and hence wages tended downwards towards an average level.

CHAPTER VI.

MATTERS PROPER FOR ARBITRATION.

THERE are many matters that are not suitable for arbitration, and for the determination of which any resort to arbitration would be a waste of both time and money. Arbitration, therefore, should not be lightly resorted to. It is not, of course, so expensive a remedy as a regular legal tribunal; but it usually involves the assemblage of witnesses, the preparation of evidence, the employment of a certain amount of clerical labour, and other financial outlay, that often makes up a considerable sum. It involves also the expenditure of a large amount of valuable time, by men who can usually ill spare it; and this, of course, is more especially true of the umpire, who is generally a public man of high standing, and who would not be likely to give up the time needed to settle a trivial question which concerned only a handful of men.

It is for this reason, as much as because of the uncertainty that always attends the issue of an arbitration, that the system has recently been superseded, or supplemented to a large extent, by sliding-scales, which are automatic in their action, and involve a minimum outlay of time and money.

Substantially, arbitration is usually called in to determine what shall be a fair day's wage, having regard to the conditions of employment, the current prices of the commodities produced, the amount of skill required, and other circumstances of a more or less determining character.

Whether a fair day's wage, as thus defined, answers to the modern demand for a living wage, is a matter that we shall not attempt to settle here. But there is a standard to which this matter can always be submitted.

On the question of the determination of a fair day's wage, we may profitably quote the following words of Sir Rupert Kettle :*

"The economist would say, a fair day's wages is the price which the day's labour would then and there bring in the open market. I concur fully and freely in the answer—it is sound all fours. I see great difficulty in practically applying it under existing arrangements to fix the rate of payment for skilled labour ; and it is because I have found these difficulties otherwise insurmountable, that I advocate the establishment of boards of arbitration. I say we have no open market for skilled labour. What is a market? and what is meant by a market being open? By market we do not mean any number of transactions of buying and selling, each conducted separately, and each without either of the contracting parties having knowledge of any other bargains. By market I understand something equivalent to a mart—a coming together of numerous buyers and sellers, who by their dealings communicate incidentally to each other, and thereby to the assembled traders, the state of supply and demand, upon which variations in price depend. You cannot ascertain the proportion supply bears to demand by a single transaction; nor can you upon any number of transactions conducted secretly. In order to work out a trustworthy result of the operations of supply and demand, you must derive your information from a sufficient number of instances to give the absolute mean power of each of these forces. . . . There is no open market in which the buyer and seller of skilled labour can meet and determine what is a fair day's wages; no means of obtaining that openness and publicity to both buyers and sellers—that talk of the market founded upon authentic information which biasses, if it does not actually control, the negotiation upon which market price is properly founded. I say that a board of arbitration affords a good substitute for such a market. A given kind of skilled

---

* "On Boards of Conciliation and Arbitration between Employers and Employed." Paper read before the Social Science Congress, 1871.

labour, quality for quality, bears a nearly uniform value for a long period as compared with other marketable articles, and the fluctuations in price are never sudden."

Ab initio, the problem is complicated by the question of what constitutes a "fair day's wage." There is the further problem of what constitutes a fair day's work. These two considerations are intimately bound up with one another. If the work provided is precarious and irregular, the rate of wages to be paid will be expected to be higher. If work is constant and steady, the wage rate may be lower. It does not, of course, always happen that these are determining facts. In the case of dock labourers, for example, the work is unusually precarious and uncertain, and yet the rate of wages is exceptionally low. In the case of men employed by municipal corporations for occasional work, the same rule prevails. But in cases of this kind, labour is not, and cannot very well be, organised, and this circumstance often practically compels the workers to accept what they can get.

As an example of the differences that prevail as between one district and another, the matter of overtime may be quoted. Returns collected some years ago by the Iron Trades Employers' Association (Manchester), showed that in Barnsley, Bradford, Bristol, Halifax, Leeds, and other towns, 54 hours must be worked as a week's work before overtime rates are paid. In Barrow-in-Furness, Hull, Liverpool, London, Manchester, Newcastle-upon-Tyne, and other towns, the practice is varied more or less, but where each day is declared to stand for itself, the men have to make up the lost time of that day before they can claim overtime rates. In Sunderland, however, overtime commences at five o'clock, and the men have the extra rates paid on each day, whether they have lost time or not.

Similar differences were found to obtain in the number of hours beyond nine per day that were paid at time and a quarter; in the hours when time and a half rates begin to be payable; and in the customs prevailing as to the duration of the higher rate, which continued in some cases until starting-time next morning, and in others ceased after a certain number of hours, the remainder being charged double time. Differences also prevail as to the rates paid for night work when done by a night shift, as to the rates paid for work done on Saturday afternoons, and as to other similar customs and conditions of employment. Manifestly it would be impossible to make all these different customs subject to precisely the same treatment and award, just as it would be impossible to reduce the rates of wages paid all over the country for the same character of work to one uniform level. It is not, indeed, desirable in the interests of either employers or employed that such a dead level of uniformity should be attempted. In some cases the conditions are greatly different to others, as, for instance, where one employer is near to, and another remote from, shipping facilities or coalfields, or where one commands cheaper materials than another, and so on.

As an example of the difficulty found in applying precisely the same rules and conditions to the settlement of so apparently simple a matter as the standard rate of wages, reference may be made to the differences that obtain in the rates of wages paid in the principal industrial centres of the country for work that is in almost every particular identical. A recent official return of the wages paid in engineering shops, foundries, boiler shops, and shipbuilding yards in England, exhibited variations that were very difficult to account for on any other hypothesis than that of the custom of the trade. Fitters in machine shops were found to be receiving 27s. in Huddersfield, 30s. in Halifax, and 31s. in Barnsley, while in London their wages ran up to 38s. Ship platers were receiving 31s. at Barrow-in-Furness, 36s. at Liverpool, and 42s. in London. When, however, we come to boiler-riveters, we find that whereas they were receiving 28s. at Bradford, they were being paid 33s. in Belfast and in London, and 34s. in Newcastle-on-Tyne and Sunderland. For boiler caulkers, again, the rate of wages paid in Sunderland was 4s. 6d. more than in the neighbouring city of Newcastle-on-Tyne, and 4s. more than in London; while Barrow-in-Furness paid to strikers in boiler shops 1s. a week more than they were being paid on the Thames.

The fact is, that the rate of wages is usually fixed according to various standards, and by different considerations, that cannot very well be made the subject of arbitration, such as the average of the district, as determined by usage and the amount of labour of a particular description available at the moment. Thus it is natural that the average rate of wages paid on the Thames should be above that paid in provincial centres, and so it invariably is for ordinary unskilled labour, but it is not always so for particular descriptions of skilled labour, if the supply is in excess of the demand. The return that has already been named showed that, in the principal engineering and ship building works, the average rate of wages paid to labourers for ordinary unskilled work was usually higher in proportion to the average of other districts than that paid to certain descriptions of skilled hands, but that was no doubt because the latter were generally glad to get employment at less than what might be deemed the district rate.

It might be supposed that the higher rate of wages paid in a particular district would attract workmen to that district until there was a glut of labour, and that the rate of wages, following a well-known economic law, would then fall to the level of other districts. But the excess of one district over another is not always a permanent one. As a matter of fact, the migration of labour does take place to a certain extent, and with precisely the consequences that might be expected. In other cases, however, the district average is permanently higher, and is kept so by usage of the trade, whether the amount of work available is greater or less; and in such districts, if there is an excess of workmen through migration or other causes, they must take their chance of being more or less unemployed, and of finding their work exceptionally precarious.

Many disputes have arisen between employers and employed, where either party has declared that they decline to go to arbitration because they "have nothing to arbitrate." In other words, this means either that the party refusing to submit to arbitration is determined to have its own way in any case, or that it has made up its mind to refuse to treat with the other party for reasons of its own. In such cases it is difficult to know how to proceed. The most certain course would appear to be to enforce an appeal to arbitration by statutory enactment; but to do this would be to strike at the root of voluntary arbitration, and to introduce a system of compulsion that would probably in the long run do much more harm than good.

It may at once be taken for granted that there is a *prima facie* case against the party that declines to have a matter in dispute fairly and fully considered by an unprejudiced and judicial tribunal. It is not, however, by any means a foregone conclusion that this is, or must be, always the case. Circumstances are not only conceivable, but are of constant occurrence, in which the employers find it practically impossible to continue to pay a certain rate of wages without grave injury to themselves in which workmen are fighting for a principle which they deem fundamental, as, for example, the limit of a day's work, or the existence of their organisation or in which concessions on one side or the other have proceeded as far as they can be carried without involving sacrifices that are not to be thought of.

When, however, the matter in question is a matter of wages, the refusal to submit to the award of a properly constituted board of arbitration is generally to be regarded with disapproval, if not with suspicion. It was a refusal of this sort by the workmen that really led to the great Midland coal strike in 1893, with its attendant tremendous losses; and the action of the miners in taking up this attitude was probably the worst feature of the strike, both because it was its real origin, and because it did not involve any question of principle that the workmen could justify, seeing that in the final event the refusal to adopt arbitration had to be departed from, and the adoption of that system of settlement became the ultimate basis of the compromise under which work was resumed.

On the other hand, it is clear that no legal compulsion can well be brought to bear upon either party to a dispute to compel a resort to arbitration. This is quite a different matter from that of compelling obedience to an award after both parties have agreed to accept it. In the latter case, the previous agreement amounts in effect to a contract, a breach of which might fairly enough entail certain specific penalties. But if either employers or employed, at the outset of a dispute, declare point-blank that they refuse to admit the principle of arbitration at all, it is difficult to see how they could be coerced into its adoption, without an infringement of that personal liberty which the law secures to every man to buy and sell labour, as he buys and sells other commodities, in the market that suits him best.

One resort is, however, always left open to the party that is prejudicially affected by the refusal of the other to submit to arbitration. It may be difficult and inexpedient to invoke the aid of the law, but it is neither the one nor the other to make an appeal to the force of public opinion, which is often more powerful and more greatly feared than even the terrors of the law. When, therefore, there is a refusal to resort to arbitration, the other party can always place itself right with the public by publishing an official statement of the circumstances that have led to the dispute, and this in the long run is likely to have a strong influence in the direction of bringing about a settlement.

CHAPTER VII.

INDUSTRIAL SLIDING SCALES.

At an early period in the history of the relations of capital and labour, the advantages of having the remuneration of workmen regulated by some such determinant as the prices realised for the products in which their labour was employed, became obvious. This advantage became more manifest as the independence and freedom of labour became more pronounced. The original applications of sliding-scales would probably be difficult to trace, but it is certain that they were used to some extent in the last century. Both the ryot system of India and the metayer system of Italy, supply the crude conception of a sliding-scale, —as applied, not to wages, in the ordinary sense, but certainly to the remuneration of those who are engaged in a particular form of industry.

As now applied to the fixing of the rate of wages, according to the results brought out by an ascertainment of selling prices, the sliding-scale is quite a modern institution, and may be regarded as almost in its infancy.

A recent writer on the system under consideration has stated that a sliding scale is an arrangement by which wages move up and down from a certain standard with the price of coal. The formation of such a scale is as follows :—A period of time being taken, the price of coal ruling over that period is ascertained, and is thereafter known as the " standard price." Then the parties fix what is mutually agreed on as a fair wage as the basis of the standard price, and this becomes known thereafter as the "standard wage." When coal is being sold at the standard price, the standard wage is payable. The next thing is the graduation of the relationship between prices and wage. It is agreed that when prices rise or fall by a certain amount from the standard, wages shall rise or fall by a certain percentage from their standard. Periodical revision is agreed to, usually from one to four months. The books are put into the hands of two accountants, one chosen by each side, under pledge of secrecy. At the end of the revision period, these accountants find if the average price of coal— usually taken as the price realised for the entire output, large and small together—has risen or fallen, and, according to their finding, notice is issued that the wages for the coming period will be raised or reduced by the agreed percentage.

The sliding-scale is not a cast-iron system by which one unvarying tonnage rate is paid. Every one knows that rates vary, and must always vary, from colliery to colliery, and even within the same colliery from seam to seam, according to the ease or difficulty of working. Thus there is necessarily considerable "give and take." All the same, the "average wage" of a good hewer is quite definite enough to establish a standard. If the miner finds the seam too hard to make the average at the rate offered him, he lifts his tools or claims a higher rate. If the manager thinks he is making the average too easily, he reduces the rate, and so on. Practically there is no difficulty in adjusting tonnage rates or the "darg," as it is known in Scotland—to the recognised day's wage over the district.

The wages of puddlers and millmen in the forges of both the North of England and Staffordshire have virtually been controlled by a sliding-scale ever since the year 1863. In other words, they rose or fell according to the ascertainment made for the employers, or from data furnished by them, of the net average realised selling price of iron. Until 1872 there were not such very large fluctuations in that average as there were at a later date. In 1868 the lowest point was reached with an average of £6. 5s. 5d.; and in 1864 the highest point was attained with an average of £8. 11s. 7d. The highest price paid for puddling in the North of England between 1862 and 1871 was 9s. 6d. per ton, this rate having coincided with an average realised selling price of £8. 11s. 7d. But in 1873 the ascertained average price rose to £11. 19s. 3d., and this brought about an average puddling rate of 13s. 3d. per ton, which was continued from the 31st day of May to the 30th of November 1873. From that point both prices and wages again fell, until early in 1875 the average realised price was only £8. 14s. 3d., and this rate has since then almost continuously dropped to the lowest point known in the history of the trade, alike for prices and for wages.

In the cases of the North of England and South Staffordshire the rates paid for puddling have not been so high over the last few years as they were thirty years ago, relatively to the realised prices of iron. Thus, we find that in 1864 the price paid for puddling relatively to a realised selling price of £8. 11s. 7d. was higher than the rate paid in 1875 relatively to a realised price of £8. 14s. 3d., and it has been much the same since the latter date. But this does not prove that arbitration has prejudicially affected the wages of the men, or that they would have been better off had there been no sliding-scale to determine what their wages ought to be. It was part of a general movement, which has tended to establish a certain equilibrium of wages, levelling up those that were specially low, and levelling down those that were specially high.

One of the principal objections to sliding-scales, from the workmen's point of view, is that they do not act with sufficient alacrity. When prices are going up, the men are, perhaps not unnaturally, desirous of sharing in the improvement as soon as they possibly can. Under a system of conciliation, they may make an immediate demand upon their employers, which is likely, in the ordinary course, to be at once considered. Under the system of arbitration, such an application would perhaps be entertained less quickly, but still it would be likely to be dealt with in a limited time. But under a sliding-scale system, the workmen have to wait for the advance of wages, if there is to be one, to be effected by the regular periodical ascertainments of realised selling prices provided for under the scheme, and this they have often declined to do. Numerous cases might be cited where strikes have occurred owing to the impatience of the workmen in reference to this matter.

A principal witness on behalf of the miners of Scotland informed the Royal Commission on Labour * that "a sliding-scale was adopted in 1863, but was stopped by a strike against an impending reduction of wages, after it had been twelve months in existence." The same witness stated that there had been several readjustments of wages affecting the whole Ayrshire coalfield, and that they had "been brought about by restricting the output, and so raising the price of coal, and enabling the coalowners to pay a higher wage." †

A recent writer on sliding-scales, who appears to have something more than an ordinary smattering of the rules of political economy, has stated that "a sliding-scale formulates the system which is already followed in the coal trade, though with much friction, that wages follow price. It thus substitutes a clear principle for seemingly arbitrary or half-informed action. It tends to steady trade, not only by avoiding the disastrous dislocations of a strike or lock-out, but by giving coalowners a basis for calculating their labour cost some little time ahead, and so protecting them from any irrational claim for advance of wages at times when falling prices are likely to sweep away profits. It tends to steady wages, not only by promising continuous work, but by preventing those sudden rises which experience shows are not always well used, and those sudden falls which make the collier lose grip of what it is most important he should hold, his standard of comfort. It tends to promote peace and good feeling between masters and men, not only by assembling them round a table and forcing them to look at things through each other's spectacles, but by giving large wages to the colliers at times when the masters can best afford to do so, and taking the strain off production in times when falling prices demand relief in cost.

---

* *Group A*, q. 13,263-6.
† *Ibid.*, q. 12,432-8.

In short, a good sliding scale so unites the interests of both parties, as to make them realise that capital and labour make as good allies as they make bad enemies."

One of the grievances to which the workmen attach importance, in the installation of a sliding scale, is that it leaves the employers absolutely free to reduce prices as they may think fit, and that competing manufacturers are tempted by the knowledge that prices and wages must fall together to reduce their quotations more recklessly than they would otherwise dare to do.* The men argue that they have thus, under a sliding-scale system, surrendered to their employers the right to determine the price of their labour. But this argument overlooks two important considerations, the first, that wages, after all, only constitute a part, and in many cases a relatively small part, of the cost of producing a given commodity; and the second, that it is always the interest of the employer to obtain the very best price that the circumstances will allow.

Professor Munro has described the principle of the sliding-scale as "the greatest discovery in the distribution of wealth since Ricardo's enunciation of the law of rent." We shall see in succeeding chapters how this discovery has been applied.

---

* *Royal Commission on Labour, Group A*, q. 13,966-75.

CHAPTER VIII.

THE COAL-MINING INDUSTRY AS IT WAS.

For a number of years past the coal-miners of the United Kingdom have pre-eminently distinguished themselves by their repeated suspensions of labour, and by the serious inconvenience and loss that they have thereby inflicted upon the rest of the community, and more particularly upon the great industries of the country. This movement is not by any means a new one. It has been more or less characteristic of the coal trade for some thirty years past, but it reached a culminating point, first in the great strike of the miners of the county of Durham in 1892, and next in the strike of miners in the Midland Counties in the year 1893. The effect of these two suspensions of labour—whether strikes or otherwise has been very serious, not only to the parties directly and immediately concerned, but to the general commerce and industry of the country, so that thoughtful men of all parties and sections are anxiously seeking for means to render their repetition difficult, if not impossible.

It is natural that the question should repeatedly be put Why have suspensions of work, and especially in the coal industry, become so much more frequent and serious of late years? In order to a proper understanding of this matter it is necessary that we should take a short retrospective view of the rise and progress of coal-mining, and of the men employed in that great staple industry.

Until the close of the last century, a system of serfdom or bondage prevailed among the colliers, who on entering a coal-mine became bound to labour therein during their whole lifetime; and in the case of sale or alienation of the ground, the right to their services passed to the purchaser without any special grant or agreement. The sons of the collier could not follow any occupation save that of the father, and could labour only in the mine to which they were held to be attached by birth. The Act which put an end to this state of things was passed on the 23rd May 1775, and its preamble was as follows:

"Whereas many colliers, coal bearers, and salters in Scotland are in a state of slavery or bondage, bound to the collieries and saltworks where they work for life, and are sold with the mines; be it enacted that

I. No person shall be bound to work in them in any way different from common labourers.

II. It shall be lawful for the owners and lessees of collieries and saltworks to take apprentices for the legal term.

III. All persons under a given age now employed in them to be free after a given day.

IV. Others of a given age not to be free until they have instructed an apprentice."

But this Act did not succeed in effecting the complete relief of the colliers, who were still exposed to the greatest hardships, and had few means of improving their rough and cheerless lot. A return published some years ago stated that the wages paid a hundred and twenty years back to the men employed at Newbottle Colliery were as follows: Grieve, 7s. per week; overman, 10s.; banksman, 6s. 7½d.; bottom-man, 6s. 7½d.; and miners, from 7s. to 8s. 4d. After making the most liberal allowances for the greater value of money in those days, it is obvious that these wages could only have kept the workmen a single remove from absolute starvation. Men's wages were so inadequate that married women and children of tender years entered the pit along with their husbands and fathers, and worked there from twelve to fourteen hours daily. Lord Ashley, afterwards the Earl of Shaftesbury, obtained the appointment of a Parliamentary Commission to inquire into the employment of children generally in 1841. The disclosures made by the Commissioners led to the passing of a Bill on the 7th June 1842, prohibiting the employment of boys under ten years, limiting the period of apprenticeship, and putting a stop to the employment of women in pits. It was stated that in some of the Durham and Northumberland pits infants under six years were employed, ventilation was almost entirely disregarded, and the precautions against danger were so slight that fatal accidents were of daily occurrence. The Act of 1843 led to a marked improvement in the moral and social condition of the miner. He still, however, stood upon the lowest rung of the social ladder, his wages were barely sufficient to keep the wolf from the door, little or nothing was done by outsiders to alleviate the hard terms of his lot, and his position and prospects were altogether so unsatisfactory, that Parliament had to interpose every now and again with rules for the regulation of coal mines, restrictions of different kinds, the appointment of inspectors, and penalties for the non-observance of the Acts.

During this time, however, the miners were not only a disunited and helpless, but they were also a relatively insignificant body of men, from a numerical point of view. Up to the beginning of the present century, the total production of coal in the United Kingdom was not much over ten million tons a year, or one-eighteenth part of the average annual output of the last five years. Bailey gave the total number of hands employed in the coal trade of the county of Durham in 1830 at 7,393, whereas in 1890 the same county employed over 130,000 men in the same industry.

Even in those days, as in these, there was an occasional scarcity of men, and wages consequently rose. The prevalent custom was to secure the services of the miners for a year certain, just as agricultural labourers were engaged, and they were required to sign a bond on being paid 2s. to men and 1s. to boys as binding or bounty money. In 1804 an extraordinary demand for coals led to a scarcity of hands, and the apprehension that pits would be stopped for want of men led the coalowners to offer twelve and fourteen guineas per man on the Tyne, and eighteen guineas on the Wear, as bounty money. " Drink," we are told, " was lavished in the utmost profusion, and every sort of extravagance was perpetrated," and not only so, but wages were increased to the extent of from 30 to 40 per cent. Here we have a reproduction of the conditions that obtained during the coal famine of 1873, and this little bit of history has quite recently been reproduced again under different conditions.

The first pitmen's union, of which we have any record, was founded in the neighbourhood of Newcastle-upon-Tyne in the year 1826. The ostensible purpose was that of obtaining a higher rate of wages. For some years previously the rate of wages had been very low. The extravagant binding-money paid in 1804, and the great increase of wages that coincidently took place under the apprehension that the pits were to be undermanned, brought into the trade a large number of agricultural labourers and others who had had no previous experience of mining. These men had now become skilled miners, and a glut of hands was the result, the demand having failed to respond to the increased resources of production. The first general strike of pitmen took place in the year 1831, when the underground workmen employed at forty-seven different collieries assembled on Newcastle Town Moor, to protest against the penalties contained in their annual bond. Energetic attempts were made to coerce the employers, who, in the long run, conceded the demands of their men. In the following year another strike on a larger scale took place, this time for an advance of wages; and as the employers not only refused to meet the demands of the miners, but threatened, on their failure to resume work, to eject them from their dwellings, riots took place, and it was found necessary to protect the strangers brought in to fill up the places of the strikers by locating police and soldiery at several collieries. In spite of the discouragements placed in their way by the men on the spot, large numbers of people left their homes in Wales and elsewhere to work in the north. It is said that "the northern stage-coaches were crowded with adventurers, and the stage-waggons were filled with their bedding and boxes." Many from the shorter distances of Staffordshire or Yorkshire walked or hired light vehicles; and certainly to see the numerous haggard pedestrians, or the cart-loads of squalid women and children, in and about the town of Newcastle, going and returning, was a grievous sight.

The " bond " or contract to which the miners of that day took such decided objections was not a new thing, but many of its provisions had been found increasingly irksome. The men were not furnished with copies of the bond, but they were simply called together, and had to sign it after hearing it read out. The principal objections had reference to the time of lying idle, to the amount and method of collecting forfeits for sending up short measure, or mixing the coal, and to one or two other matters.

This bond was the occasion of another serious strike in May 1844, when the men demanded weekly pays, a six months' engagement, a guarantee of five days' work a week at 3s. per day, hewers not to be called upon to " put " (that is, to move the coal), the men generally to be furnished with particulars of their earnings and deductions, the day's work to be limited to eight hours, and in case of accident 10s. per week with medical attendance to be given, no fine for " foul " coal beyond the labour price of the tub, an arbitration clause, and a week's prior notice, with a specification of the charges to be brought against them in the case of being summoned before the magistrate. The owners, on the other hand, submitted counter-proposals, providing for fortnightly pays, with some running-on days (that is, keeping a part in hand), a twelvemonth's engagement, but terminable by a month's notice on either side, no guarantee of regular work, and hewers to " put " and do other work when required.

It might be supposed that the majority of the claims brought forward by the miners would be conceded as a matter of course. And so they are, when reasonable, at the present day. But in those times the employers were unwilling to make concessions not previously known, and more especially to the new force of coercion then being brought against them. In the long run, however, they were compelled to yield to a large extent to this then unfamiliar force, although on that occasion, as on many others, the men did not gain a bloodless victory.

Between 1846 and 1870 there were many strikes in the principal colliery districts. About the latter year, however, questions of difference between coalowners and their men began to be referred to arbitration very generally; and this was followed by the adoption, in the principal districts, of a self-adjusting scale, that accommodated wages to selling prices with automatic precision, and to which further reference will be made.

The most immediate cause of the revolution in wages and in the hours of labour, that have formed such prominent features of the coal industry within recent years, was the adoption by Parliament of the Coal Mines Regulation Act of 1872. This Act compelled the coalowners to undertake a large capital outlay in providing additional houses for their workmen, who had to be largely increased in consequence of the limitation of the average *per capita* output resulting from the shorter hours of labour prescribed. The consequence was that in the county of Durham—and the result would be much the same in other districts—the yield of a miner's day's work fell from 4.67 tons in 1871 to 4.02 tons per shift in 1873. This movement had a great deal to do with the coal famine of 1873, during which the wages of the miners rose to a point they had never known before. But this was not the only serious part of the business. In one of the arbitrations that were held in 1874, as to the wages to be paid to miners, it was stated that in the county of Durham not only had there been an increase of wages to the extent of 58.7 per cent., as compared with 1871, but the staff of off-handed men in the pits had been increased to such an extent, owing to the requirements of the Act of 1872, that the cost of this labour alone had been increased by 92.2 per cent. as compared with 1871. This was quite independent of the higher market value of metal, wood, iron, and all other commodities that come under the head of colliery stores, which in the same collieries had been increased by 80 per cent. upon the ton of coal sold.

During the greater part of this period prices ran up and down in the most extraordinary manner, largely owing to the fears and apprehensions of consumers ; and in most of the colliery districts, wages followed prices rapidly and largely, until in not a few cases colliers were receiving nearly 100 per cent. more wages for a reduced amount of work, or at any rate for a shorter working day.

From these events, and from this period, may be dated the modern movement of unrest and demoralisation which has made coal-mining industry so notorious within recent years. The upward course of prices and wages did not present a great deal of difficulty. Employers perhaps made concessions reluctantly, but they were generally made in the long run, when prices were high. It was when reductions of wages had to be insisted upon in the face of a falling market that the real trouble began. The men were, not perhaps unnaturally, unwilling to give up the advances that they had received while prices were still rising, and they had not been sufficiently schooled in the elements of political economy to understand that no amount of resistance can keep up either prices or wages in a falling market. The process of adjustment was a slow, laborious, and painful one, but it was ultimately accomplished, and that too without many serious strikes. In the county of Durham, then as now the principal coalfield of the country, the claims of both employers and employed were referred from time to time to arbitration, and nothing could be more creditable to the workmen than the loyalty with which they accepted one adverse award after another, until the old level of wages had been practically restored. But they could hardly be expected to be quite satisfied with a system that generally worked against them, and ultimately they decided in 1877 to substitute a sliding-scale for the previous resort of open arbitration, under circumstances that are referred to in the following chapter.

CHAPTER IX.

SLIDING-SCALES IN THE COAL INDUSTRY.

THE county of Durham furnishes, in the coal industry, an example of a case where conciliation, arbitration, and sliding-scales have all been tried, and where all—or at any rate the two last named—have been thrown over. It is natural that so serious an indictment against both of these systems as is involved in this fact, should challenge the attention, and court the inquiry, of all those who are interested in them. This is quite apart from the fact—which, however, is not without its due measure of importance—that the Durham coal industry is the most important in Great Britain.

Wages were regulated by agreement in the Durham coal industry until about 1874, when arbitration was resorted to on the application of the employers for a reduction. Several similar arbitrations followed, all of them ending in favour of the employers, who were compelled to obtain relief in a steadily falling market. The miners were not therefore averse to adopt a system that guaranteed to them a certain fixed wage in relation to a certain ascertained price, and under which they were assured that their wages would not fall below a prescribed minimum.

The first scale in the Durham coalfield was adopted in 1877, for two years, as between the Durham Coalowners' Association and the Durham Miners' Association. The standard price was anything between 5s. 8d. and 6s. 4d. per ton, the price being determined, at the hands of two accredited accountants, as the "average net price realised for all coal raised at the pit-mouth" during the four months preceding.

When prices fell below 5s. 8d., but above 5s. 4d., wages for the next four months were reduced 5 per cent. for underground men, and 4 per cent. for surfacemen; when prices rose above 6s. 4d. and under 7s., wages rose 5 per cent. and 4 per cent., respectively; and so on, rising 5 per cent. and 4 per cent. for every 8d. But if prices fell below 5s. 4d., wages fell only an extra $2\frac{1}{2}$ per cent. and 2 per cent. This scale had a minimum wage of 4s. 8d. It was terminated by the employers. Trade was bad, many of the pits were stopped, great numbers of miners were on the union funds, and "the scale worked too well for the men," to quote their representative. In the next scale, accordingly, we see the influence of the "market price of labour" on the determination of the standard wage.

The second sliding-scale was entered on in 1879. The standard price was now reduced, on the award of Lord Derby, to 4s. 2d. (to 4s. 6d.) per ton, and moved up or down $2\frac{1}{2}$ per cent. for every 4d. A notable innovation was the "double jumps." When price touched 5s. 6d., wages rose 5 per cent. for every 4d. of advance in price, resuming the former progression from 6s. 2d. upward. In the case of surfacemen other than engineers, mechanics, and cokemen, 2 per cent. was to be substituted for $2\frac{1}{2}$ per cent. all through, and 4 per cent. for 5 per cent. in the "double jumps." This agreement was signed for two years, and was terminable then at six months' notice.

The third sliding-scale dates from 1882. The wages now varied for every 2d. per ton variation of price. The standard price is still further reduced to 3s. 10d. per ton. Each 2d. makes a change in wage of $1\frac{1}{4}$ per cent., except in the case where price touches 5s. 10d. (to 6s.) and 6s. (to 6s. 2d.), when the advance is $2\frac{1}{2}$ per cent. for each 2d. For surfacemen, as before, 1 per cent. is substituted for $1\frac{1}{4}$ per cent., and 2 per cent. for $2\frac{1}{2}$ per cent. The revision period was four months, and the agreement was from 29th April 1882 till 30th June 1883, terminable on six months' notice thereafter. There is the following addition:—"'That the quantity of all coals disposed of otherwise than for colliery purposes, be ascertained and priced at the average selling price of coal of a similar description, and that the sum thus arrived at be added to the sales."

The fourth sliding scale is dated June 1884. At that time the price of coal at the pit mouth seems to have been 3s. 10d., and the average wage 1s. It is the same as the third scale, and was established for two years, but actually lasted till 1889. At that date it was terminated by the men. They considered that the standard wage, as compared with the standard price, had been fixed too low, and demanded that a higher proportion should fall to wage when coal rose to a certain point.

There is now no sliding scale in Durham. Wages are arranged by negotiation, and local questions are settled by a joint-committee of six masters and six men, under the chairmanship of the County Court Judge, who has a casting vote. But the miners' secretary, when asked at the Labour Commission, "Can you suggest any means of avoiding or arranging strikes, and promoting cordial relations between capital and labour?" answered: "The best means that has come under my experience is the sliding-scale. I have always believed, long before it was introduced, that it was the safest and most beneficial to all parties concerned,—that is, providing you can get an equal and fair basis." And again: " I have not the slightest doubt in my mind, but what an equitable sliding-scale could be arranged that would give equal justice to the owners and the men."

In a recent article in a leading Glasgow journal, it was pointed out that the principle that the worker should not suffer by a fall to the same relative extent as the capitalist finds marked expression in the Durham scale, where above a certain point the advance is $2\frac{1}{2}$ per cent. for every 2d., while below the same point the fall is only $1\frac{1}{4}$ per cent. for every 2d.; and in the Cumberland scale, where above a certain point the advance is $1\frac{1}{4}$ per cent. for every $1\frac{1}{2}$d., while below it the fall is $1\frac{1}{4}$ per cent. for every 2d. In the light of what has been said, a plausible argument might be made out for the slower progression downwards as subsistence level is neared.

"At the same time, it should be clearly understood that this principle obtains even in the ordinary sliding-scale. Take, for instance, the Lanarkshire scale, where wages advanced 2½ per cent. for every 1½d. in price. Suppose the standard wage per day were 5s., the standard price 5s., and the usual 'darg' three tons. Then a rise in price of 6d. per ton would give the masters an extra 18d. per day per man, against which they would be paying 10 per cent. extra wage, or 6d. per day. Here the masters' gross gain is 1s. per man, against the man's net gain of 6d.; and although there is a great deal to come off the 1s., owing to the simultaneous rise in wages of all the oncost men, and the advanced price of coal consumed in the colliery, the masters will gain a greater share of the advance than the men. But a fall in price of 6d. per ton from the standard would show exactly the converse of this. The master would lose 6d. per ton per day, while the man lost only 6d. per day. Making similar deductions for reduced oncost, &c., the masters would bear the greater share of the reduction."

In the Northumberland coal industry there have been three different sliding-scales since November 1879, when the first came into effect. The first scale lasted for about three years and a month, the second for three years and about ten months, and the third for about seven months only. The last scale was given upon a very short trial, principally because, as the price of coal was very low, and showed a tendency to fall still lower, the men were liable to have repeated reductions of wages, instead of having their wages either maintained or increased, and they had begun to despair of again seeing prices so far improve as to allow of their wages being fixed at what they regarded as a fair and proper level.

Of the scales adopted in Northumberland, dated 1879 and 1883, the former gave 2½ per cent. change in wage for every 4d. in price, the latter giving 1¼ per cent. for every 2d., with "double jumps" at 6s., 6s. 4d., 7s. 2d., 7s. 8d., 8s. 6d., 9s. The masters terminated the scale in 1887, when prices went down to 4s. 6¾d., asserting that they must shut the mines unless they got some relief in wage. They consider the re-establishment of a scale "highly desirable," but at present the men fight shy of it. Since the great strike of that year, however, there has been scarcely any suspension of work, even at single collieries. Matters are regulated by mutual agreement between the two associations, meeting once every two months, and the working of the joint committee is said to be most satisfactory.

In Cannock Chase collieries there were several sliding scale arrangements up till 1883, showing a graduation of 3d. in wages for every shilling variation of price. The Masters' Association still approves of the scale.

In the Ocean collieries scale, the standard price being 10s. to 10s. 9d., there was a minimum wage when price fell to 8s. 6d.

In the Bedworth collieries scale of 1879 (now abandoned) the revision took place every month; wages rose 1d. per day for every 3d. per ton, and there was a minimum wage of 3s. 4d. per day when the price was 5s. 6d.

Under the Somerset scale of 1876 (also abandoned), the standard price being 10s. and the graduation at the rate of $7\frac{1}{2}$ per cent. for every shilling, there was a minimum wage at the price of 9s. 4d. per ton. Accompanying this was a provision for a maximum wage when the price touched 18s. 4d.

There is no sliding scale in North and West Lancashire, in Leicestershire, in Derbyshire, or in Yorkshire, although the employers generally express themselves as favourable to its introduction.

In Scotland, the first sliding-scale was one proposed to the miners in 1873 by the coalowners of Ayrshire. The basis of this scale was that when coal was selling at 6s. per ton the wages should be 4s. 6d. per day, rising 6d. per day for every 1s. of advance in price. The scale held for only a year, when it came to grief over a dispute whether the price of coal justified a reduction of wages or not.

In 1879 Mr James S. Dixon had circulated in the Lanarkshire coal industry a proposal for a sliding-scale, by which the "nominal daily wage was to be the average net price per ton at the pithead got for the coal, dross, and triping despatched from the enrolled collieries." This proposal had the great merit of simplicity, and even yet commands attention by the closeness with which wages, if regulated by it, would have approximated to the wages actually realised since. In 1886 and 1887 came disputes and restrictions of work, as a consequence of which the Coalmasters' Association came into existence, with a membership of forty-nine firms and sixty-four collieries. In March 1887 a two days' conference between sixteen miners and sixteen masters was held, under the presidency of Sir James King. A sliding-scale was proposed, but as the miners made it a prior condition that an advance of wages should be given unconditionally no arrangement was come to. The owners, however, seem to have been struck, during the conference, with the idea of the sliding-scale, and on 27th June adopted it on their own account, the Larkhall owners at the time, with one exception, falling away from the Association.

The standards were taken from the month in which the scale was adopted, the standard wage being payable when coal was anything between 4s. 4d. and 4s. 5½d. Wages were to advance 2½ per cent. for every change of 1½d. per ton in the net value of triping that is, large and small coal together—at the pithead. The revision period was monthly. Unfortunately the men would not be parties to the scale, and left themselves free to accept or reject its ruling. The practical result was that the scale decided the wages which the Association from time to time intimated. The unassociated masters followed the scale, and for over two years it worked well. In their report for the year 1888 the Association declared their satisfaction with the scale, and their confidence in its principle. "This rational mode of regulating wages must," they said, "commend itself to all concerned." But in September 1889 coal rose fast. The men grew dissatisfied with the slow operation of the scale. This, however, might have been got over, but as some of the unassociated masters gave an independent advance, the Association was forced to abandon the scale and do likewise.

It has been claimed that this scale, in case of a rise, was

much more liberal than the English scales. It gave an advance of 10 per cent. for every sixpence, while the average of the others gives 10 per cent. for every shilling. On the other side, however, it made a correspondingly sharp reduction when prices went down and below the standard. It did not last long enough to pass the ordeal of many reductions. The complaint was that its advance, even on this liberal scale, was not rapid enough to satisfy the men.

The Cumberland mines have been under the sliding-scale since 1879. In that year the selling prices of July, August, and September—viz., 4s. 6.19d.—and the wages ruling in October of that year, were taken as the standard. The revision period was four months. For every advance of 4d. in coal, wages were to advance 2½ per cent., with "double jumps" at the third and sixth fourpences.

In the second scale, of 1832, the standard price remained the same, but the standard wage was increased 2½ per cent. For every advance of 2d. wages were to rise 1¼ per cent., with "double jumps" at third, sixth, ninth, and twelfth twopences.

The third scale, of 1884, was unchanged, except that the rate of advance became 1¼ per cent. for every 1½d. above the standard, till the price went above 6s. 6.19d. per ton, when the 1¼ per cent. was given only for every 2d. For every fall below the standard, on the other hand, wages went down 1¼ per cent. for every 2d.

The fourth scale, of 1887, repeated the same provisions, except that the standard price is raised from 4s. 6.19d. to 4s. 6.50d.

CHAPTER X.

THE COAL INDUSTRY OF SOUTH WALES.

No sliding scale hitherto adopted in the coal-mining industry has been exposed to greater strains, or has stood the test so well, as that which continues to govern the rate of wages to be paid to miners in the collieries of Monmouthshire and South Wales Coalowners' Association. This organisation comprises seventy colliery companies, owning 207 collieries, which produced in the year 1890 more than 21,000,000 tons of coal, and employed about 70,000 men.

It must not, however, be supposed that the scale has been an unqualified success, or that it has not had to undergo considerable modification from time to time. As a matter of fact there have been five different scales introduced since the first one was adopted in May 1875, and each new scale has represented concessions of one kind or another to meet the views or demands of either side.

The scale at present in operation was adopted in January 1892. It provides that wages shall be regulated by the average net selling price of coal delivered free on board at Cardiff, Newport, Swansea, and Barry; that the wages and prices at December 1879 shall be taken as the standard; that both the workmen and their employers shall be bound to observe and fulfil all customs, provisions, and conditions existing in December 1879; that wages shall be advanced or reduced at the end of each period of two months by additions or reductions of $1\frac{1}{4}$ per cent. upon the mean monetary result found by the joint-auditors as between the scale of 1882 and that of 1890; that there shall be no maximum or minimum wage; that any contract for the sale of coal for a period of more than twelve months shall not be taken into account for more than six successive audits of two months each; and that anthracite coal shall not be taken into account.

The agreement contains, moreover, the following very useful provision, which is worthy of being copied in all similar documents and understandings:

"Both parties to this agreement pledge their respective constituents to make every effort possible to avoid claims or disputes at the collieries; and that in case of any unavoidable differences, the owners and the officers, together with their workmen, shall endeavour to settle all matters at the collieries; and only in case of failing to effect a settlement shall an appeal be made to the joint-committee. It is also hereby agreed that in such cases no notice to terminate contracts shall be given by either employers or their workmen before the particular question in dispute shall have been considered by the joint-committee, and they shall have failed to arrive at an agreement."

In South Wales the last general strike of coal-miners took place in the year 1875, and lasted for nearly five months, during which a very great deal of damage was inflicted upon the trade of the district, not to speak of the loss sustained by the parties directly concerned in the struggle. In the end the matter was settled by the adoption of a sliding scale, which has continued to operate without intermission, though with occasional revisions, since that time.

During the whole of this period the local disputes that have arisen have been referred for settlement to the sliding-scale committee, which is established on much the same lines as the similar committees in Durham and Northumberland, and really discharges the functions of a conciliation board. During the six years ending 1891 eighty cases have been adjudicated upon by this committee, nearly all of them in an amicable way. About 90 per cent. of the cases have been brought forward by the workmen, and many of them are stated to have been very trivial.*

---

* *Labour Commission Report*, A, 11,652-11,717.

The South Wales and Monmouthshire sliding-scale was primarily the result of the great strike of 1875. The first scale dates from May of that year. Its revision period was six months. Here also we have a minimum wage, fixed for each colliery at 5 per cent. above the several hewing prices paid at the same colliery in the year 1869. The standard price of "screened large coal" corresponding to this standard was fixed at 12s. per ton for steam coal, and 11s. per ton for bituminous coal f.o.b. at Cardiff, Newport, and Swansea. For every extra 1s. per ton, the wage for the next six months was advanced by $7\frac{1}{2}$ per cent., till prices reached a maximum of 21s. and 20s. respectively. It is significant that in 1878 the workers consented to a reduction of 5 per cent. below the minimum, which however was made up to them by a special bonus for one year in the succeeding scale. In the second scale, accordingly, dated January 1880, we find that both minimum and maximum have disappeared. It was a two years' agreement, and shows a revision period of four months. The standard wage was made up from the rates actually paid at the several collieries in December 1879. The standard price was 8s. 6d. per ton for collieries in group 1, and 8s. for collieries in group 2, the coal, as before, being large colliery-screened coal f.o.b. at Cardiff, Newport, and Swansea. Wages were to advance by gradations of $2\frac{1}{2}$ per cent. for every 4d. per ton of advance, or reduction in the net average selling price in each group. There now appears a provision that when the selling price in groups 1 and 2 reaches 13s. 2d. and 12s. 8d. respectively, there shall be an extra advance of $2\frac{1}{2}$ per cent. on the standard wage for every 16d. of advance in price, similar reductions being made as prices fall to these figures.

The third sliding scale came into operation in June 1882. It was substantially the same as the second, except that the two groups were merged in one, that wages were now made the equivalent of a standard price falling between 7s. 8d. and 8s., and that the "double jumps" at 13s. 2d. and 12s. 8d. were abolished. There were several changes in the scale between times, but it may be sufficient to give the present sliding scale, which came into force on 1st January 1892. It repeats the previous conditions, with the following changes: The revision period is two months. The standard price is between 7s. 10½d. and 8s. Wages move up or down at the rate of 10 per cent. for every shilling, viz., 1¼ per cent. for changes in price which approximate to 1½d. per ton. This arrangement is said by the miners' agent, Mr Isaac Evans, to have "given greater satisfaction than any arrangement that was ever made previously."

In December 1891 the sliding-scale in the South Wales coal trade was exposed to a severe strain, under which it appeared likely to give way. The parties quarrelled as to the basis of the scale, which, as settled in 1890, was as under:—

"The average net selling price shall be taken as for large colliery-screened coal delivered f.o.b. at Cardiff, Newport, Swansea, or Barry. For coals sold into waggons or otherwise at the collieries, the cost of transit to the ordinary port of shipment shall be added in calculating the average net selling price. Workmen's coal to be excluded.

"The standard of wages upon which future advances and reductions are to be made shall be the several rates actually paid at the respective collieries in the year 1879, and such wages shall be equivalent to a standard average net selling price of 7s. 10½d. and under 8s. per ton. Provided, that at the collieries where the standard or basis upon which the wages are regulated is the rate of wages paid in the year 1877, that shall continue to be the standard for those collieries.

"The wages shall be advanced or reduced at the end of each period of three months by additions or reductions of 1¼ per cent. upon the standard wage rates for every increase or reduction of 1½d. per ton in the average selling price of coal, in accordance with the following scale; and in no case shall the wages due to the workmen be less than would be due to them at the same average selling price under the sliding-scale agreement dated 6th June 1882, as modified by the agreement of 7th November 1887."

The scale follows in the agreement. It was concerning the basis of the scale and the small coal question that employers and men found themselves differing. Happily the difference was patched up, and the scale remains.

A recent writer * has stated that the strongest buttress of the sliding-scale committee has been the body formerly known as the Monmouthshire and South Wales Collieries Association, and known now as the Monmouthshire and South Wales Coalowners' Association. "This Association, which included sixty-seven of the most important coalowners and coalowning companies in July 1890, and possessed at that time a very large balance in cash, which has been increased to £100,000 at least, is practically a society for mutual assurance and indemnity against loss from strikes. Each member subscribes beforehand—and this is important—in proportion to his output, and the function of the Association is to regulate the action of members as to wages. In other words, and in order to escape a tedious description of the practice in given cases, if the men employed by a member ask for an increase of wages, the member asks advice of the Association. If the Association tells him to yield, then yield he must, or be content to lose his share of the benefits of the Association ; if the Association tells him to resist, then he may resist in the full knowledge that he will be indemnified against loss of profits upon an agreed scale so long as the funds of the Association last, and that the members of the Association are under a legal liability to increase, if necessary, their already large funds. Moreover, no member may withdraw from the Association without giving six months' notice, and the net result is that an employer who is supported by the Association has immense reserves to fall back upon. This the men know well, and they also know that, when any considerable strike is threatened or pending, it has been arranged that 'no workman employed at a colliery immediately before a strike or stoppage thereat takes place shall during such strike or stoppage be employed by any member.' Now, the Association possesses precisely half the representation on the sliding-scale committee, and it is obvious

* The *Times*, December 29, 1891.

that the case must be, and in truth the fact is, that the sliding scale committee fixes the rate of wages from time to time; and that, if masters or men are refractory, the Association is able to enforce the judgment of the sliding scale committee. To the master it says, 'If we ratify your resistance to a demand, you shall be no sufferer by that resistance; but if you will not make concessions which you ought to make, we can and we will deprive you of the indemnity which you have purchased on terms.' To the men it says, 'We cannot make you work at a given colliery on given terms; but if you will not work at that colliery on those terms, we will take tolerably good care that you shall not be employed by any of us, for we have considered the terms in the light of the decision of the sliding-scale committee, and we think them just to you and to your employer.' Of course there is room for a dispute between the two parties, in which the employers' section of the sliding-scale committee takes one view and the men's section takes another. Even in such a case, however, there is comfort in the thought that there can be no delay caused by refusals to negotiate and so forth, since the sliding-scale agreement provides for six months' notice on either side, and for a meeting of joint committee at least once in every month, so that there can be no strike without ample preliminary discussion."

In the coal trade of South Wales three variations of wages took place under the scale of 1875; three others under the scale of 1879; fourteen under the scale of 1882; six under the scale of 1890; and five under the scale of 1892 to the 1st August of that year. It can hardly be maintained, therefore, that these scales did not respond with sufficient alacrity to price movements. The ascertainments being made every two months, the rate of wages may be changed six times a year. Sometimes, however, they are not changed for considerable periods, owing to the stationary character of prices. So little movement took place in the price of coal between December 1886 and April 1888, that the average rate of miners' wages for the whole of that period remained at $2\frac{1}{2}$ per cent. above the standard; but when prices did begin to advance, wages went up in sympathy with them, until in March 1891 they were 57½ per cent. above the standard of 1879, which was a higher wage than the scale made provision for, the details of the scale going no higher than 52½ per cent.

Previous to the establishment of the sliding scale in South Wales, the coal trade of the Principality had been seriously harassed and disturbed by strikes, so much so indeed that it made probably less progress than any coalfield in the country. The *Mining Journal* of 15th March 1873 had the following remarks on this subject :

" Instead of being developed, production has actually retrograded, and constant strikes have led to a decrease in the output of coal. This is all the more to be regretted, seeing that, being the largest of our coalfields, where the minerals are unusually easy to work, the production ought to have increased in a much greater ratio than in any other district in the kingdom. If we look back for only six years, we find that there has been a very large increase in the quantity of coal raised in all our leading mining centres excepting in South Wales, so that the output, which in 1866 was 101,630,544 tons, had increased in 1871 to 117,352,028 tons. But of that increase South Wales was in no way a partaker, although it had advantages superior to most other districts. That the constant strikes which have taken place in it have been a curse to the workmen and their families is thus easily traced from the progress of the coal trade for some years past, and the figures given cannot but be surprising to themselves and their leaders, should they see them. Thus we find that in 1866 South Wales, which may be taken to comprise Glamorganshire, Pembrokeshire, and Carmarthenshire, produced 9,376,413 tons of coal ; in 1867 the output had fallen to 9,092,300 tons ; whilst in the following year, 1868, it was still further reduced to 8,959,500 tons. During the next year (1869) the quantity raised was 9,179,650 tons. In 1870 it had advanced to 9,299,770 tons; but in 1871 another strike brought the yield to 9,120,600 tons.

" From the above figures it will be seen that more coal was

actually raised in South Wales in 1866 than in any year since. Not only that, but whilst it appears that in 1866 there were 29,300 male persons connected with the collieries in South Wales, who raised 9,376,443 tons, or equal to 320 tons for each person employed, in 1871 there were 37,960 persons employed in raising 9,120,000 tons, or equal to about 240 tons per person. Surely these facts are sufficiently suggestive in themselves to cause those men who have the slightest amount of common-sense, and who have some little particle of independence left, to well consider their position, and what they have gained by their long seasons of idleness, which show them to such a great disadvantage when compared with any other body of miners in the kingdom; or whether it is any credit to them to be told, that for the last six or seven years at least they have been the idlest body of colliers in the country, and that they have preferred living on the charity of others, to maintaining themselves and their families with respect and credit. These are plain truths, that cannot be disputed, and must be felt by every man who gives a moment's consideration to the actual position of the great body of the coal-miners of South Wales at the present time. It may, then, well be asked how long is South Wales to monopolise the reputation it has enjoyed for the last six or seven years, as being the only mining district in the kingdom which has made no progress in increasing the production of its valuable coal seams, but just the reverse? Or how long will the thousands of hearty workmen agree to become constant paupers, relying upon others for a miserable support of themselves and their families?"

CHAPTER XI.

SLIDING-SCALES IN THE PIG-IRON INDUSTRY.

SEVERAL more or less successful attempts have been made to introduce the principle of the sliding-scale in the determination of the wages of ironworkers, both of those employed at blast furnaces and of those employed in rolling mills.

Probably the most important, and certainly the most extensively applied, of these scales is that which regulates the wages to be paid to ironworkers employed by the Cleveland Ironmasters' Association, which is composed of seventeen firms, owning 108 blast furnaces.

The wages of blast furnacemen in the Cleveland district have been regulated by sliding-scales for more than twelve years past, with the exception of one period of eighteen months, and some shorter intervals. In these twelve years there have been six different sliding-scales.

The latest scale is dated the 8th April 1891, and provides that 24s. to 34s. 2¼d. per ton for No. 3 Cleveland pig-iron shall be considered the standard, and that below that figure deductions shall be made from the rates and wages prevailing immediately prior to the sliding-scale agreement of 7th November 1879, while corresponding additions shall be made to the wages paid for any variation of price above the standard. Thus, when the price of No. 3 Cleveland pig-iron is between 29s. and 29s. 2½d. per ton, a deduction of 6¼ per cent. shall be made from the standard rate; and if the price of pig iron goes up to 60s. per ton, there shall be an addition of 35 per cent. to the standard rate of wages.

The fundamental questions presented for settlement in this and in all similar sliding-scales is, first of all, that of whether the basis of the scale is satisfactory and reasonable as between employers and employed; and next, whether the method to be adopted for the ascertainment of the average prices, on which wages hang, is likely to give accurate and reliable results.

As regards the first of these points, the most important fact to be remembered is, that wages alone do not come into the account when the price of a commodity is increased. In the special case of the Cleveland iron trade, the North Eastern Railway Company claims to have a finger in the pie, inasmuch as it gives concessions when prices are low, and expects to have them returned in the form of higher rates when prices are high. Usually, also, when the price of pig-iron, or of any other commodity, rises to an exceptionally high figure, it carries with it, or perhaps is carried along by, many other items that determine the cost of production, such as royalty rents; the prices of coal, coke, limestone, and iron ore; the rates of shipping freight; the cost of standing and maintenance charges, and so on. Hence it is readily conceivable, that a manufacturer may, with a low scale of costs, be making more profit when his realised prices are low than when they are high. And hence, also, the extreme and obvious difficulty of arranging a scale that shall merely take into account the relation of wages to prices, seeing that the latter give no index to the cost of production or to realised profits.

Every care is taken to ensure that the method of ascertaining realised selling prices shall be fair, impartial, and equitable. In the case of the Cleveland Ironmasters' Association, the average is based on returns obtained from eight selected firms out of a total of seventeen; but it is provided, that " if for any reason either party to this agreement desire to omit any of the firms named, or to add thereto, the matter shall, in case of difference, be referred to" a committee consisting of not more than six on either side, " who, if they cannot agree, shall appoint an umpire to settle the matter."

The ascertainment of realised selling prices takes place every three months, and is " confidentially ascertained by two properly accredited and certificated accountants, one chosen by the ironmasters and the other by the blast furnacemen, and at their respective charges."

In West Cumberland, the wages of twelve establishments, employing about 2,500 men at blast furnaces, are regulated by a sliding-scale, which is very much on all fours with that adopted in the Cleveland district. The main points of difference are, that the standard is fixed at a higher price, and a minimum wage is specified.

In the pig-iron industry of Cleveland, wages have been regulated by a sliding scale for upwards of twelve years. The scale cannot be terminated without giving three months' notice. Since the first scale was introduced several modifications have been adopted, one of them being what is known as a "double-jump," or, in other words, the pace at which wages advanced in relation to prices is doubled, with a view to giving men an earlier relief when prices begin to rise.

One very material difference between the sliding scale adopted in the Cleveland district, and that adopted in West Cumberland, for the pig-iron industry, is found in the method of the ascertainment of prices whereby the rate of wages is regulated. Under the Cleveland scale wages are regulated by the ascertained average selling prices of the previous quarter, whereas the Cumberland scale is based on the prices declared on the Glasgow Exchange. There is, however, often a difference between realised and quoted prices, and the latter are generally subject to much greater variation than the former. One case has been quoted, in the first quarter of the year 1880, when the realised price of pig iron was only 42s. 8d., whereas the quoted price was as much as 58s. 11d.[*] Not unnaturally, perhaps, the workmen employed in and about blast furnaces have generally been anxious to have the quoted prices taken as a basis; but this cuts both ways, if they only knew it. For if quoted prices are often higher than realised prices when trade is improving, the realised prices are

---

[*] *Report of Royal Commission on Labour*, Group A, cf. 14,517 et s/.

often higher when trade is declining, being generally based on contract rates taken over a more or less considerable period.

The conditions of blast furnace labour may be cited as illustrating the difficulties of framing a sliding scale for the regulation of wages over a large area of operations. On the first blush, it might appear as if nothing could be more simple than to fix a scale rate for the remuneration of the labour of men employed about a blast-furnace. The labour is not of a character that seems to vary much; it is pretty constant; the requirements to be met do not involve a high degree of skill; and the product is always substantially the same. And yet there are no fewer than twenty-six different classes of workmen employed about blast-furnaces, who are paid under the scale at rates varying according to the nature of their occupation. The question that has to be determined, is not alone the relation of a particular wage to a particular price, but the relation which the wages paid to one class of workmen shall bear to the wages paid to twenty-five other classes, and the relation of each to the realised selling price of the product.

CHAPTER XII.

ARBITRATION AND SLIDING-SCALES IN THE STAFFORDSHIRE COAL AND IRON INDUSTRIES.

SOME valuable experience of the working of both arbitration and sliding-scales is supplied by the iron and coal industries of South Staffordshire. In this busy district wages have been regulated in a manner that is highly creditable to both employers and employed for a long series of years. Much of the success of the system adopted in the Staffordshire industries is due to the painstaking and conciliatory disposition of Sir Benjamin Hingley, M.P., who has for the greater part of the time that sliding-scales have been in use acted as chairman of the Board of Arbitration under whose auspices and control they have been applied.

According to evidence submitted to the Royal Commission on Labour, the first effort to form a wages board in the Midlands was made in 1872, when twelve employers chosen by the masters' association met twelve representatives of the men's union to discuss and settle wages. Their proceedings, however, were quite informal. No rules were formulated, no special times of meeting were fixed, and no president was appointed. About two years later an attempt was made to form a united board for South Staffordshire and the then new ironmaking district of Middlesbrough. Meetings were held at Derby, London, and York, and they resulted in the adoption of the "Derby scale," which lapsed in June 1875, after continuing in operation for one year only.

In January 1876 the employers and workmen of South Staffordshire came to an agreement concerning the formation of a new board, to be called the South Staffordshire Mill and Forge Wages Board, and to consist of twelve employers, twelve operatives, a chairman (viz., the chairman of the Ironmasters' Association for the time being); two secretaries (one chosen by the employers and the other by the workmen), and a president. The last named officer corresponded to the referee not to the president of the North of England Board, his function being to arbitrate when the Board came to a deadlock, rather than to preside over its deliberations. He was to be altogether outside the trade, and his award was to be final. Mr J. Chamberlain was the first president; and at the same time Mr J. R. Hunt became chairman; Mr D. Jones, employers' secretary; and Mr J. Capper, operatives' secretary. The Board, thus constituted and officered, was, from the first, successful in arranging the rate of wages without conflict or serious disagreement.

When the Board was established, there was a distinct understanding that it should as closely as possible follow the lines of the similar board in the North of England. But in 1886, when Sir Thomas Martineau, the Mayor of Birmingham, was made president, it was reorganised upon a wider basis, so as to include the whole iron-making district of which Birmingham is the chief centre. The actions and decisions of the Board had gradually become recognised, not only in South Staffordshire and East Worcestershire, but also in the iron districts of North Staffordshire, Shropshire, Lancashire, South Yorkshire, and Derbyshire. A formal alliance was therefore arranged at this time between the Board and the firms outside its original sphere, whereby the latter paid contributions to the former in return for the benefits they had already begun to derive from its action. Its title was at the same time altered to the Midland Iron and Steel Wages Board. With the steel trade, however, it still had very little connection. At a recent date there were forty-two firms that were directly, and about eighty that were not directly, represented on the Board. The former are subject to the jurisdiction of the Board in general, and to its standing committee,—consisting of three representatives of either side and the two secretaries,—in local wage questions. The latter recognise its authority in general questions only.

Employers that are represented on the Board, without being actually members of it, are not so completely in touch with their men as those that have the opportunity of meeting the men's representatives in council.

In the iron trade of the Midland district the first scale was established in 1872; and before retiring from the post of president of the Board of Conciliation, in 1880, Mr J. Chamberlain recommended its re-adoption. The experiment was accordingly tried when Mr Richard Chamberlain was president and Mr Hingley chairman; but in 1862 the employers in the North of England, under pressure, conceded an advance in wages greater than that under the scale in the Midlands. The South Staffordshire men accordingly insisted upon a similar advance, and the scale lapsed in consequence. It was subsequently re-established upon the basis of 1s. per ton for puddling to 1s. realised price. About the year 1881 the men had an extra 6d. per ton, which is, roughly speaking, equivalent to a 5 per cent. premium. In 1890 they demanded a higher premium, which caused the scale to be once more abandoned, and it still continues in abeyance. Both employers and employed, however, are said to approve of the system.

In the South Staffordshire and East Worcestershire coal trade, wages have now been regulated by a sliding scale since 1888. To trace the history of its formation, it is necessary to go back to 1874, when, in consequence of the outbreak of a strike, the matter was referred to the arbitration of Mr Joseph Chamberlain, who made an award settling payments on the following principle: For "thick" coal colliers, 5s. 6d. per day was fixed as the maximum, and 3s. 6d. as the minimum rate. When "thick" miners' wages stood at 4s. 6d. a day, "thin" miners were to be paid 3s. 3d., and they were to experience a rise or fall of 3d. as the rate for "thick" coal varied by 6d. Under this award the miners worked till November 1877, when there was a considerable depression in the industry, and the work could no longer be carried on at so high a minimum rate for "thick" work as 3s. 6d. per day. A conference accordingly took place between masters and men, and an agreement was made abolishing minimum and maximum rates, fixing the scale of payments at 3s. per day on a standard price of coal of 9s. per ton (this being the price at which Lord Dudley's coal was at that time being sold), and providing for a rise and fall of 3d. per day for every variation of 1s. in the Earl of Dudley's price. The "thin" wages were to be 2s. 6d. when the "thick" were 3s., and the former were to rise and fall 1½d. in correspondence with each change of 3d. in the latter. This arrangement was guaranteed a continuance of six months, after which time it was to be terminated by a three months' notice from either side. At the end of December 1881, this scale underwent a slight modification. When the price of Lord Dudley's coal was over 9s. per ton, the wages for thick coal were to rise and fall 4d. instead of 3d. for every 1s. variation, the relation between the rate for "thick" and "thin" coal remaining undisturbed. On 2nd May 1883, the men gave notice to terminate the agreement, in consequence of Lord Dudley having lowered the price of his coal by 1s. a ton. The arbitrator to whom the matter was referred decided that during the three months that the scale remained in force, wages should continue at the same rate as if the price of coal had not been reduced. The settlement of a new basis he left to the consideration of the then proposed Conciliation Board.

In the month of August 1883, a wages board was constituted in the South Staffordshire coal trade. The men's representatives on the board at once proposed that wages should be calculated on the basis of a minimum rate of 3s. 8d. per day; and upon the objection of the employers to accede to this, they refused to submit to any arbitration that would not endorse their claim. Mr Haden Corser, the president, refused to make an award under such conditions, and the matter was shelved till 4th June 1884, when Mr Rowlands was called in to arbitrate. This gentleman made an award to the effect that "the rate of wages should be reduced from 3s. 8d. to 3s. 4d. a day, and that such reduction should take place from the 14th day of June 1884 and continue until the 27th day of December 1881, and thereafter until the Board should agree upon some alteration, or until a new award should be made." This decision, however, was repudiated by the men's representatives on the Board; and a disastrous strike, lasting from 28th of June to the 13th of October 1884, was the result, after which the men accepted the award, and returned to work at the reduced rate of wages.

In 1888 the Wages Board, which had been broken up by the strike in 1884, was reconstituted on similar lines to that existing previously, but without a president. Its first act was to draw up an automatic scale, not based, as before, on the price of one class of coal at one particular colliery, but upon the average selling price of all qualities of coal throughout the district. That price was to be ascertained by submitting the books of twelve employers — six selected by the representatives of their own body on the Board, and six by those of the men — to the examination of a firm of accountants approved by both parties. Alterations in the scale could take effect only after three months' notice.

Subject to a few minor modifications, effected without friction by mutual agreement, the scale adopted in 1888 still continues to operate, and is said to be giving perfect satisfaction.

Every alteration, however, hitherto made under it in the rate of wages, has resulted in a gain to the men. The ascertained prices for February, March, and April 1889, fixed the wages for "thick" coal at 3s. 10d.; those for June, July, and August at 4s.; those for September, October, and November at 4s. 4d., and those for January, February, and March 1890 at 4s. 8d. Since that date no further ascertainment of prices has taken place, and there has consequently been no further change in the rate of wages.*

In the South Staffordshire mining district the basis of the scale has been varied at different times; but it has usually been

---

* Evidence submitted to the Royal Commission on Labour (Group A).

a minimum of 3s. 4d. per day for thick coal and 2s. 8d. per day for thin coal, when the average selling price was 4s. 9d. per ton or less, and it has varied wages to the extent of 1d. per day for 2d. per ton rise or fall in average selling price of thick coal, and 1½d. per day for a rise or fall of 2d. per day in thick coal miners' wages. In March 1874, the miners of South Staffordshire came out on strike against the sliding-scale system, which gave them 5s. 6d. per day for thick coal and 4s. for thin coal when the price of the former was 16s. to 19s. per ton. In July 1874 the sliding-scale was altered as regards its minimum, which was raised to 3s. 6d. per day for thick coal. In March 1877 six months' notice to alter the sliding-scale was given by the employers, and the minimum was then dropped, with the result that in May 1879 the thick coal miners were only receiving 2s. 9d. per day with coal at 8s. per ton. In November 1881 the workmen gave three months' notice for an alteration of the sliding-scale, which was afterwards made to vary by increments or decrements of 4d. to 1s. of realised selling price, instead of 3d. as before. This, however, did not appear to suit the employers, who, in May 1883, gave three months' notice to terminate the scale, and a little later gave fourteen days' notice for a reduction of 4d. per day in wages all round.

As the Staffordshire scale is now arranged, the wages of thick coal miners would advance from a minimum of 3s. 4d. for an average selling price of 4s. 9d. per ton to 4s. 8d. for an average realised price of 7s. 5d. per ton, and any alteration in the scale is subject to three months' notice.

CHAPTER XIII.

ARBITRATION AND SLIDING-SCALES IN THE FINISHED IRON INDUSTRY OF THE NORTH OF ENGLAND.

No industry has supplied a more remarkable testimony to the merits and advantages of both arbitration and sliding-scales than the finished iron trade of the North of England, where a Board has been in uninterrupted operation since 1869, and where wages have for the greater part of the intervening period been regularly varied according to the ascertainment of selling prices. All this has been accomplished without any serious dispute, and without any suspension of labour worth speaking of, in an industry where disputes were previously both frequent and disastrous.

There were special difficulties in the way of regulating, without conflict or trouble, the wages of the ironworkers of the North of England. The iron industry of the Cleveland district may be said to have been created between 1850 and 1869.[*] To meet the demand for labour in the ironworks that were growing up on all hands, men had to be imported from other districts, and many of them were not of the best class. With no special tie to the locality, and attracted only by the prospect of a higher rate of pay than they had previously enjoyed, large bodies of the workmen in and about the ironworks of that time were probably less moderate in their demands than they would have been under other circumstances. At any rate a

---

[*] There were a number of comparatively small works in existence previous to the earlier of these years.

great strike took place in 1865, which was followed by a lockout in the following year; and for a considerable part of the time between 1865 and 1868 the whole district appeared to have been given over to disputes and demoralisation. Very serious losses were incurred by the employers, and it appeared as if a district that had all the essential elements of a successful career were about to be ruined by industrial war.

Such was the position of affairs, when Mr David Dale, on the 25th March 1868, communicated to the North of England Iron Manufacturers' Association the particulars of a plan which he had devised for establishing a standing local committee for the consideration, from time to time, of questions affecting their mutual relations. Mr Dale said:—

"The theory of each master bargaining with each man is no doubt a sound one; but when experience has proved the desirability of conducting a business on the principle adopted by iron manufacturers of paying, for all the leading branches of work, tonnage rates common to the general body of manufacturers within a certain iron-making district, such prices being as a general rule varied at all works simultaneously, there comes to be felt the need of some organisation enabling the employer to communicate and to discuss matters with the class, as he would, in the primary conditions of things, have done with the individual.

"The employed, whose interests are similarly and simultaneously affected by any change in tonnage rates, must naturally be expected to seek some machinery by which their common interests can be represented. This, as we know, frequently takes the shape of a union, hostile and distrustful in its attitude towards the employers, and having an executive whose leading men are not themselves affected by the matters which they are called on to deal with on behalf of the general body. This machinery being entirely unsuited to free and friendly communication between the employers and employed, each remains in ignorance of the others' feelings, and incapable of looking at matters from the other's point of view.

"There is a general desire to see a remedy provided for

this state of things. The time is favourable. There are no questions now at issue to give any proposal the appearance of being suggested in the interest of any particular party.

"But this state of things cannot be expected to be permanent. It seems therefore very desirable to be prepared with some organisation, by which the questions, certain before long to arise, may be fairly considered and discussed by the two parties interested in their settlement.

"Subject to reconsideration, and to the suggestions of others, I would propose that such iron manufacturers in the North of England as may approve the establishing of a 'Standing Local Committee of Employers and Employed' should bring the subject under the notice of their men, and invite them to elect two workmen one from the forge, and the other from the finishing mills to represent their fellow-workmen on the committee. The firm should nominate two of its principals, and the committee would then be constituted of two principals and two workmen from each of the works which come into the arrangement.

"The primary functions of the committee would be to consider and discuss general questions affecting the body. Its conclusions would have weight as recommendations only, save where any question between an individual employer and his men might be voluntarily referred by both parties to the committee.

"All questions simply affecting the men at any one works would be dealt with (as it is best they should be) by the parties immediately interested; but if they failed to agree, it would be most convenient to be able to consult a body like the committee, whether the parties agreed to abide by its decision or not.

"All general questions, however, affecting the relations of the two bodies, or any considerable part thereof, to each other, would be, as its principal function, considered by the committee, the views of both parties would be heard, incorrect impressions as to facts (which lie at the root of most trade misunderstandings) would be removed, and in the majority of cases I am sanguine enough to believe fair conclusions would be come to by the committee, and acquiesced in by those they represent."

On the 7th April 1868, at the quarterly meeting of the Iron Manufacturers' Association, a standing committee was appointed to take such steps as they might deem desirable for the realisation of Mr Dale's ideas. After carefully inquiring into the various plans adopted in different industries for discussing, in a friendly manner, questions affecting capital and labour, and for the avoidance of misunderstandings and strikes, the committee, on the 12th January 1869, reported that, "Should the men be favourable to the experiment, they would recommend that the Association should take steps for the establishment of a local standing committee of masters and men, directly associated with ironworks."

For the first time the representatives of the Ironworkers' Union and the Iron Manufacturers' Association met together, at Darlington, on 1st March 1869, "to consider the question of wages, and the establishment of Courts of Arbitration for the settlement of trade disputes and the regulation of prices." The workmen, however, did not enter upon this new era without some misgivings. They had been so accustomed to regard their employers as their natural enemies that they were afraid of being made the victims of some conspiracy, or of suffering some disadvantage that was too esoteric for their comprehension. To guard against possible harm, however, they demanded from the employers "personal guarantees that we shall not be interfered with, deprived of our labour, or made marked men, like others have been beforetime." The guarantee was readily accorded, and the workmen thereupon proceeded to enjoy the novel, and probably, at the outset, rather uncomfortable, sensation of meeting the employers on terms of equality, and discussing without reserve or constraint of any kind questions affecting their mutual interests.

On the 22nd March the Board was formally established, with Mr Dale, of Darlington, as its first president, and Mr Edward Wood, a workmen's delegate, as its vice-president.

At this meeting a code of twenty-two rules for the guidance of the Board was formally adopted.

The first rule set forth the formation of a "Board of Arbitration and Conciliation for the Manufactured Iron Trade of the North of England."

The second rule declared "that the object of the Board shall be to arbitrate on wages, or any other matters affecting their respective interests that may be referred to it from time to time by employers or operatives, and by conciliatory means to interpose its influence to prevent disputes, and to put an end to any that may arise." The next rule provided that the Board should be composed of "one employer and one operative from each works joining the board; and any works more than five miles apart, though belonging to the same firm, may claim to be treated as separate works." A standing committee was appointed, consisting of four employers and four operatives, in addition to the president and vice-president; and it was provided that "all questions shall in the first instance be referred to the standing committee, who shall investigate and endeavour to settle the matter so referred to it, but shall have no power to make an award. In the event of the committee being unable to settle any question, it shall, as early as possible, be referred to the Board." In case of the Board being unable to agree on any question submitted for its adjudication, provision was made for the appointment of an independent referee, whose decision shall be final and binding on all works which have joined the Board." At this meeting the Board also resolved "that pending the preparation by the standing committee of a permanent financial scheme, arrangements should be made, as early as possible, by which one penny per month shall be stopped off the wages of each man earning 2s. 6d. per day or upwards who may not send in any objection to such deduction."

When the Board was established there were in Northumberland, Durham, and Cleveland twenty-eight ironworks for the manufacture of finished iron, *i.e.*, for the conversion of pig-iron into rails, plates, angles, and bars. These twenty-eight works employed about 12,000 men and boys. No less than eighteen firms joined the Board at once, and nearly all the others afterwards followed.

Very soon after the establishment of the Board a statement was issued on its behalf, setting forth the facts of its origin and objects. The auspicious circumstances under which the Board entered upon its career were referred to in hopeful and encouraging terms. We are told that, having been formally established, " the Board was at once called upon to consider an application from the operatives for a general advance of wages, or tonnage prices for the work done by piece. It has investigated the grounds for such an application fully, deliberately, and with a manifest desire on the part of all its members to arrive at an accurate knowledge of the facts. The matter is not yet disposed of, but there is every reason to believe that the means provided by the rules will bring it to a satisfactory issue. Meanwhile, instead of misunderstanding and bitterness being created, and the original question being obscured by partisan statements, each party has come to know and to respect the feelings of the other, and the way has been cleared for an impartial judgment on admitted facts. To ensure the success of the system just described, it is important that it should be fully understood and approved by all the operatives. Whether or not they are members of the Ironworkers' Union, as hitherto constituted, or as it may hereafter exist, they are free and are invited to consider themselves as belonging to the Board and entitled to take part in the election of its members, and they should all feel that they are bound by the decision of the Board or of its referee. In similar manner, employers, whether members of the Iron Manufacturers' Association or not, are invited to join the Board. Half the members of the Board being men to whom every attendance at a meeting involves the sacrifice of a day's work, and consequently a day's pay, as well as the expense of a journey to and from the place of meeting, it becomes needful to provide for this expense, as also for the secretaries' salaries, hire of meeting room, &c. It is therefore proposed that every man earning 2s. 6d. per day or upwards shall contribute 1d. per month or 1s. a year, and that each employer shall contribute as much as is contributed by all his workmen. It is believed that if this be generally agreed to, a sum will be raised more than equal to the expenses of the Board, and that probably there may be a surplus available for such purposes as may be thought fit. The employers have, at the request of the operative members of the Board, agreed to facilitate the collection of the men's contributions by arranging for their being deducted from the wages of each man who may not object thereto. It now remains to be seen whether the system which has freed the trades of Nottingham from the bitterness and strife which formerly distinguished them, can be successfully applied to the great iron industry of this country."

As the Board failed to come to agreement on the application for an advance of wages, already referred to, it became necessary to appoint an umpire, to whose judgment and final decision the matter might be referred. By common consent, Mr Rupert Kettle, of Wolverhampton, was called in to act in this capacity. On Saturday, 1st May 1869, the Board held a meeting at Darlington, when the whole facts relevant to the question of the proposed advance of wages were laid before the referee, who ultimately awarded—"That the wages of ironworkers be from Monday next as follows: the puddlers to have 6d. per ton advance upon present prices, and the millmen an advance of 5 per cent. on present prices; that these prices shall not be altered until the end of this year; and that this arrangement shall include all classes of workmen in mills and forges who subscribed to the last reduction of wages in December 1867." In making this award Mr Kettle made a rather important statement as to the facts and figures on which it was based. It was suggested by the vice-chairman (Mr Wood) that a verbatim report of the whole proceedings should be published, in order to show how the arbitration was conducted. The arbitrator, however, pointed out that some of the papers submitted for his perusal contained information which, if it had fallen into the hands of any ironmaster in Wales, Belgium, or any other district directly in competition with the North of England, would have afforded him the opportunity of knowing the exact dealings of the firms by whom the information was supplied, the names and addresses of their customers, and the dates and prices of every contract, executed and unexecuted, ranging over several years. Since then the meetings of the Arbitration Board have without exception been conducted in private, only the results of its deliberations being allowed to transpire. On the occasion of this initial arbitration, Mr Kettle declared that the masters had laid before him tabular statements based upon nearly the whole of the actual business transactions of the Cleveland district from the year 1863, and embracing every ton of iron from five-sixths of the works. These tables the arbitrator declared to be "so comprehensive and so minute, both upon the subject of prices and of wages, that they completely exhaust the question." As might have been expected, Mr Kettle's first award was made the subject of a good deal of adverse criticism; and as the advance which it sanctioned was one-half that asked for, the question was put, "How has this arbitration resulted in a mere compromise, in which both parties have, upon a give-and-take principle, arrived at an amicable conclusion?" Anticipating a question of this sort, Mr Kettle answered it by pointing out that he had been supplied with figures based on an estimate of the prospective as well as the present state of the market; that although the present state of prices did not justify any advance of wages, it was quite clear that the time would soon arrive when the masters would be called on by the men to reopen the wages question, upon the prices obtained from the date of the award to the close of the rail-making season: and that upon this he had founded a negotiation in the nature of conciliation rather than of arbitration, which would render it unnecessary to have another arbitration, and a consequent disturbance of trade, in a few months afterwards.

Early in 1869 Mr Thomas Hughes, Q.C., was called in to arbitrate on another application—this time by the men for an advance of wages; and the second award, like the first, was faithfully observed by both parties. When, however, the period of its currency drew to a close at the end of 1870, the trade was in a most uncertain position, owing to the unsettled state of affairs on the Continent of Europe. No one could possibly foresee whether the decline in prices which had already taken place would continue, or would be more than recovered by a considerable rise. It was under these very difficult circumstances that the wages question had again to be dealt with, and once more under the arbitration of Mr Hughes. Early in 1871 he decided that wages should be reduced 5 per cent., and that they should continue so reduced till 31st March 1872 (a period of fifteen months), subject to one revision at the instance of either party, to take effect not earlier than July 1871. At the end of the six months for which the reduction was thus made absolute (i.e., in July 1871), the men exercised the option reserved to them of calling for a revision for the remaining nine months. This was just at the period when the settlement of affairs on the Continent was opening out the prospect of a large trade and better prices. Mr Hughes awarded the restoration to the men of the 5 per cent. he had deducted at the beginning of 1871, thus re-establishing for the nine months ending March 1872 the wages which had prevailed during 1870.

This award did not give satisfaction to the men, because of their belief that, whilst the arbitrator had, in reducing wages at the beginning of 1871, been influenced by the probabilities of a decline in prices, he had not taken account, in his award of July 1872, of the probabilities of an advance in prices. Hence the men asked for a reconsideration of the award on that ground. The arbitrator was unable to appoint a meeting for hearing this appeal till the middle of October 1871. Meanwhile considerable further improvement in the trade had taken place, and advances of wages had been given in other iron-making districts. The men had therefore their obligation to abide by the arbitrator's decision put to a strong test, and that test they stood to until the hearing of their appeal by the arbitrator in October 1871. Mr Hughes did not feel justified, on that appeal, in reversing his former decision ; but he expressed a hope that the employers would voluntarily modify the contract, because all parties had become satisfied that a mistake had been made in extending it for so long a period ahead, especially when the trade was undergoing an unusually rapid improvement owing to the settlement of affairs on the Continent. Whilst the men's representatives and leaders stoutly maintained the obligation of their clients to adhere to the confirmed award up to March 1872, if the employers did not see fit to modify it, it is undoubtedly the fact that a not inconsiderable body of the men held language implying that they would not be so bound. Whether they would have carried out this view was not brought to the test, because the employers accepted the suggestion of Mr Hughes, and gave an advance of 5 per cent. for the remaining period of the original term, obtaining at the same time the assent of the men to a scheme for adjusting wages in future by a sliding-scale of prices.

Some interesting evidence as to the constitution of the Board of Arbitration and Conciliation in the finished iron trade of the North of England was given before the Royal Commission on Labour (Group A) by Mr Whitwell, the chairman of the Board. Mr Whitwell stated that a representative of the employer and a representative of the men are sent from each works in membership to sit on the Board. According to this constitution, a large owner will have as many representatives as he has works. The men's representatives are chosen by ballot every December. Their appointment holds good for one year only, but they are eligible for re-election.

Except for a special purpose, the Board holds only two meetings a year, viz., in January and July. At the January meeting it elects its officers, *i.e.*, a referee, a president, a vice-president, two secretaries, two auditors, and two treasurers. They all hold office for a year, and are eligible for re-election.

The Board also appoints a standing committee at the same meeting. The employers nominate ten of their body, exclusive of the president, and the operatives five of their body, exclusive of the vice-president. The double representation of the employers was introduced by mutual consent, for it appeared that the employers' nominees were not able to attend so regularly as those of the operatives. It is provided, however, that only five of the former are to vote, speak, or otherwise take part in the proceedings at the same meeting of the committee.

The standing committee deals with local, the full Board with general, questions. Should the former fail to agree, the matter is laid before the referee annually elected by the Board; but should the latter so fail, an arbitrator must be specially appointed. There is, however, no objection to the appointment of the referee for this purpose. Most of the questions that have come before the standing committee have related to wages or to modes of working. The committee meets as occasion requires, generally about once in every month. The average number of cases it has dealt with per annum during the last ten years is 18.7, the total number since its formation being 161.

Only four cases have come before the referee since February 1883, when the office was instituted. He is guided in his decisions by well-established rules of practice, though he has full scope for the exercise of his common-sense. With him the settlement of local questions terminates. Owing to the small number of cases that come before him, his duties are chiefly advisory. The number of cases dealt with by the Board and the standing committee tends to decrease. A larger proportion of them are settled at home, without coming before the Board at all. The men do not make complaints and force appeals to arbitration simply in order to gain something by the compromise likely to result. It would be very inconvenient not to have arbitration as an ultimate resort. The arbitrator is guided in settling general questions, just as the referee is guided in settling local ones, by certain fixed rules of practice, supplemented by his own common-sense.

Awards are loyally respected by both parties. The men respect their leaders, and allow themselves to be guided by their advice.

For the last three years, the average income of the Arbitration Board has been £994. 13s. 11d., and the average expenditure £1,076. 18s. 2d. Employers and employed contribute to its funds in equal proportions, the subscriptions of the latter being deducted from their wages. The representatives of both parties are paid the same amount for attendance at the meetings of the Board and the standing committee, except that the operative members are paid a double fee for meetings held on any day other than Saturday and Monday, if they are employed on the night shift.

The membership of the Board was at its highest figure in January 1874, when it included thirty-five works; it was at its lowest in January 1888, when only ten works belonged to it. At present there are twelve works in membership. The number of operatives subscribing has varied between a maximum of 14,867 in January 1873 and a minimum of 3,127 in January 1886, and now stands at 4,270.

This diminution in its membership is chiefly due to the fact that the trade is passing from iron into steel. Twenty of the ironworks, formerly in membership, have been wholly dismantled, and three ceased to belong in consequence of their adaptation to steel. The Board was originally established to deal exclusively with iron, and has only recently opened its membership to steel works.

The transition from iron to steel has still further affected the membership of the Board, because fewer men are required to produce a given quantity of the latter than of the former. In fact, the diminution in the number of operatives subscribing to the Board represents the difference between the amount of labour required to produce a ton of steel and that required to produce a ton of iron. Again, a large number of employers prefer, by standing outside the Board, and following its decisions, to reap all the benefits without bearing any of the burdens of membership; and where the employer holds aloof, the men are ineligible. The diminished membership of the Board must not be taken as a measure of reduced production. It is true that the annual "make" of finished iron has fallen since 1873 from 650,862 to 251,471 tons; but, owing to the increased production of steel, the tonnage of the two commodities combined, viz., 750,000, is quite as high as it has ever been since the Board was established.

Nor must it be taken to imply dissatisfaction on the part of the men. On the contrary, their confidence in the Board is now greater than ever. In the report made by the standing committee to the Board at its twenty-first annual meeting, 28th January 1890, reference was made to the immense benefit conferred on the district by the Board in preventing labour disputes, which under its *régime* have occurred only under circumstances of special irritation and excitement.

Before the Board was established it was impossible for employers and employed to come to terms upon questions of reduction or advance in wages without a stoppage of work. The Board has effected a great improvement in the relations between the two parties. Only two or three short stoppages have occurred since the Board was formed. They were all merely sectional, and the operative members of the Board did their best to check them.

Since the Board was established, there have been sixty wage settlements—seven by mutual arrangement, twenty by arbitration, and thirty-three by sliding-scales. The rates have varied between the 13s. 3d. per ton, long weight, paid for puddling on 2nd April 1873, when other work was paid for at $27\frac{1}{2}$ per cent. above the standard, and the 6s. 3d. per ton, short weight, paid for puddling on 31st October 1885, when the wages for other work were $27\frac{1}{2}$ per cent. below the standard.

In making settlements of wages, regard is had to the capability of the works to produce cheaply, the quality of the machinery, and the ability of the men employed. The quality of the machinery is an important element in determining the rate of wages an employer can afford to pay. According to this mode of judgment, it may happen that two workmen of equal ability are earning different wages because one of them is so fortunate as to be employed at works possessing better machinery than those at which the other is working. The Board, however, endeavours to secure uniformity of wages only in connection with uniformity of conditions.

Sliding-scales for the automatic regulation of wages for iron workers, by the net average realised selling price of manufactured iron, have been drawn up five times during a period of five years and ten months. The first scale was adopted in 1871, but it was operative for three months only. The next, which was introduced in 1874, and lasted twelve months, was that known as the Derby scale, on account of its details having been settled at a conference at Derby. Under this scale, an arrangement was made with the South Staffordshire iron trade for basing a uniform wage on the average net selling prices in the two districts. The third scale came into force in May 1880, and continued in operation until the end of January 1882. It was known as the "Dale" scale, because the settlement of its basis had been placed in the hands of Mr David Dale, as arbitrator. It was revised for a short time in 1883, but notice was given by the operatives for its discontinuance after one settlement had taken place. The scale at present in force was adopted on 1st July 1889. Its basis was fixed at a meeting of the board held on 15th April 1889, on receipt of the report drawn up by the committee which had been specially appointed to consider the matter. It had an original binding force of two years.

In the manufactured iron trade, which was of much greater relative importance twenty years ago than it is to-day, the principle of a sliding-scale was adopted many years before the formal details were put into mechanical shape. Mr Thomas Hughes, who had on several occasions been called in to act as arbitrator, thus stated the principle as existing in 1870 in both Cleveland and Staffordshire :—

"Already a custom would seem to have grown up in the trade which is acknowledged within certain limits both by employers and workmen, namely, that for every rise of £1 in the selling price of manufactured iron, wages should be advanced 10 per cent. in mills and forges, and 1s. per ton for puddling. It will be only necessary as a first step that the Board should formally acknowledge this scale by resolution, declaring that it is to be adopted in future, and adding, perhaps, a proviso that in no case shall any reduction or advance be made unless the selling price shall have varied 5s., so as to be equal to 3d. a ton for puddling and 2½ per cent. on other wages."

In some quarters exception was taken to the principle here laid down, on the ground that it would be difficult to regulate the wages of the ironworkers mechanically, according to the selling price of iron, because iron did not simultaneously suffer increase or reduction all round, nor were the prices of the raw materials to be purchased at the same unvarying price. In other words, one leading description of iron might move up largely and rapidly, while another might remain stationary, and a third—although this would be a very exceptional case—might even suffer a decline.

This difficulty was met at an early stage of the sliding-scale movement in the North of England in a very effective manner. Profits earned in any industry—even if accepted as a proper determinant of wages—would involve enormous difficulty and trouble, inasmuch as no two firms make quite the same rate of profit, and would involve punishing one set of employers in consequence of the misfortunes or incapacity of another.

CHAPTER XIV.

CONCILIATION AND ARBITRATION IN OTHER INDUSTRIES.

ALTHOUGH the experience and applications of conciliation and arbitration so far recorded have been mainly confined to the coal and iron industries, it must not be supposed that other industries have not been equally ready to adopt the systems described, or that their application to other industries has not been equally successful.

The original applications of either system were not made in the coal and iron industry, but in the hosiery and lace industries of Nottingham, in the building trade of Wolverhampton, and in other trades more or less referred to in other sections of the present volume. The system has, however, had a wider and more general application in the coal and iron trades; and as these are the principal industries of the country, and are on the whole the most subject to fluctuations of price, they present the most interesting and varied experience.

In the nail and bolt trade of the Midland counties, a board of conciliation or joint-committee has existed since 1890, composed of representatives of employers and employed, for the purpose of dealing with questions of wages. It has prevented the outbreak of strikes, which would otherwise have occurred during the past year or two owing to the depression of trade. Indeed, no dispute has arisen since the board was formed. There is no longer any provision for arbitration; but before the board was formed, a workman was himself appointed permanent arbitrator, at the suggestion of the largest employer in the trade. Mr R. Juggins told the Royal Labour Commission* that he acted as such from 1872 to 1877, during which period he successfully dealt with about two hundred questions, chiefly relating to wages. Upon the outbreak of a strike, however, in 1877, Mr Chamberlain, who was appealed to to settle the dispute, struck out of the agreement between employers and employed the clause providing for arbitration. As a matter of fact the necessity for arbitration has been materially reduced by the establishment of a standard rate of wages. This reform was carried out by the conciliation board, which fixed the rate at 32s. for a week's work of fifty-four hours. Owing, however, to the depression in the trade, the men often do not manage to get employed the full time, and so the average sum earned per week probably does not exceed 20s.

Among the chain, nail, bolt, and lock-makers, however, there appears to have been halting progress made in the direction of conciliation. Two witnesses on behalf of these industries, before the Royal Commission on Labour, expressed themselves strongly in favour of the establishment of boards of conciliation which should refer matters to arbitration on failure to agree, and one of them stated that he had made an unsuccessful attempt to arrange a meeting with some of the larger employers with a view to constituting such a board. He explained that it would be very difficult to persuade the employers to meet together on a board of conciliation or on joint-committees, because the more respectable members of their body would object to associate for this purpose with the smaller men, who are really middlemen or sweaters, and are a curse to the whole trade. There is no sliding-scale, but there is a standard rate of wages, which the workers endeavour to maintain, and with this object they have always applied for an advance when trade has been improving. In 1889 the employers agreed to establish a uniform list of wages, but the men have charged that they have ever since endeavoured to effect reductions in individual cases, and to evade the rule by making the workers

---

* Group A, cf. 17,781-94.

in the domestic workshops contractors. To stop this, one witness suggested that employers should be compelled to give their men a note of reckoning, stating the size of the iron and the rate of payment per cwt.

Mr E. Jones, representing the South Wales Iron and Steel Workers and Mechanics' Association, stated to the Royal Labour Commission, that in his district wages had been regulated by a sliding-scale for nearly two years. He produced a copy of the original agreement. It is dated 18th September 1890, and signed by employers' and workmen's representatives from the Dowlais, the Ebbw Vale, the Blaenavon, the Tredegar, the Rhymney, and the Cyfartha ironworks. It is based on the average net selling prices of steel rails and bars as ascertained every three months by professional accountants. Its terms were settled after a thorough discussion between the parties; but the men have now become somewhat dissatisfied with the basis, though they for the most part continue to approve of the principle.

Mr J. Hodge, representing the Steel Smelters' Amalgamated Association, stated that there was no sliding-scale, though, in making readjustments of wages, regard was had to the course of prices. The witness was not in favour of the system. Sliding-scales, he held, are often unjust, for they disturb the relationship that ought always to be preserved between wages and profits. They may sometimes give low wages when profits are high.

Mr Lougher, representing the same association, stated that generally speaking the men did not approve of the system of sliding-scales. Such a scale is indeed in operation at five works in the South Wales district, but of these only one employs members of the union. Among the men at this works the scale is very unpopular—in the first place, because, being Siemens-Martin men, they object to have their wages regulated on the Bessemer steel basis, which steel is made at the other works, and is practically a different trade; and in the second place, because their union was not recognised in the negotiations by which the scale was established.

Mr Anson, representing the Rotherham branch of the same association, said that wages were not governed by a sliding-scale. In regard to this matter some firms accept the adjustments made in the West of Scotland and the North of England.

An association, known as the British Iron Smelters' Amalgamated Association, was founded in 1886, and the secretary of that organisation, in giving evidence before the Labour Commission in 1892, stated that "Conferences have been held with regard to the establishment of a board of conciliation, which would be a more satisfactory means of settling wages than exists at present. It was agreed to constitute such a board, and a committee was appointed to draft rules. The employers' representatives, however, desired to frame a rule to the effect that half the expenses of the board should be deducted from the men's wages; whereupon the men's representatives proposed as an amendment, that the men's share of the contributions should be paid through their union. The employers would not agree to this, because it would oblige every member of the board to be a union man. But it would be quite necessary for the union to have control over all the members of the board, for otherwise the men's delegates could not be responsible for the decisions being obeyed. The proposal of the employers was objectionable, as involving a virtual breach of the Truck Acts. Negotiations were suspended in consequence of this disagreement, and so the relations between employers and employed remain unembodied in a printed constitution."

Several attempts have been made to introduce the principle of arbitration into the cutlery trade of Sheffield, but hitherto it appears without satisfactory results. About 1890 a board was composed of four representatives of the Trades Council and four of the Cutlers' Company and the Chamber of Commerce combined, for the special purpose of discussing certain proposed amendments to the Merchandise Marks Acts; but, when approached by the secretary of the Trades Council, with a view to the establishment of a permanent board to deal with disputes, the two corporations representing the employers are stated to have firmly refused to entertain the proposal.*

In the engineering trades, as in most others, there appears to be a considerable difference of opinion as to the best mode of procedure. Some approve of conciliation after Mundella's system; others prefer conciliation, plus a chairman with a casting vote; and others arbitration, in its most formal and binding shape. Difficulties urged against arbitration have been that it is difficult to agree upon the exact terms of the reference, and to procure as arbitrators men that are at once impartial and possessed of the requisite technical knowledge. It has been suggested that where an arbitrator was appointed by the State, as in the case of Lord Shand and the Midland coal trade, the absence of technical and local knowledge might be got over by the appointment of expert assessors; and this really seems to be a very excellent suggestion.

The most important trade union in Europe is probably the Amalgamated Society of Engineers, which drew up a scheme some years ago of the formation of a board of arbitration. This scheme provided that, "pending a settlement of any question by the board, there shall be no stoppage of work, and the wages, piece-rates, hours of work or over-time, shall, until settlement, remain as when notice was given." Some of the details of the proposed scheme were not, however, acceptable to the workmen, and hence it did not come into effect.† In the engineering trades, consequently, although there have been negotiations at different times between employers and employed, no general scheme of arbitration or conciliation has yet been established.

In the shipbuilding trade of the Wear, where conciliation has been in operation since 1885, a reference to arbitration has only been found necessary on two occasions; and on each, "the registrar of the Sunderland County Court was selected as third referee or umpire, partly because he was capable of weighing

---

* *Report of the Royal Commission on Labour.*
† *Ibid.*, Group A, 23,100-8.

evidence, and partly also because he was profoundly ignorant of the technicalities of the trade." *

While there are many points of difference between employers and employed in reference to the principles and methods that should guide the settlement of trade disputes, there is one matter on which almost all of them appear to be agreed, and that is a profound distrust of a State board, which has been recommended in some quarters as the true, if not the only, effectual solution of the problem. The prevailing view of employers on this subject has been very well stated by Mr James Laing, the Chairman of the Board of Conciliation for the Wear Shipbuilding Trade, when he informed the Royal Commission on Labour that "local boards of conciliation are more valuable than a universal arbitration board established by the State, for members of the latter would be unable, probably even with the aid of technical assessors, to secure a proper adjustment of the various interests concerned in the manufacturing industries of the country. A State board would, no more than any other board, be able to interfere with the free action of either party, and secure the enforcement of its awards." †

The rules of a number of trade unions contain provisions empowering the executive council to refer disputes to arbitration, subject to the approval of two thirds, or some other determined majority, of the members. Other provisions, which are now freely introduced into such codes, contain clauses inviting the men to put the question of a reference to arbitration to the vote before resorting to a strike.‡ In the shipbuilding trade of the Wear, with its board of conciliation of which an arbitrator or umpire is a fixed adjunct—it has not been uncommon for the leaders of the men to make provision for the establishment of a system of conciliation when rearranging the rates of wages.§

---

* *Royal Commission on Labour,* Group A, 25,712-25.
† *Ibid.,* Group A, 26,050-72.
‡ *Ibid.,* Group A, 20,486-504.
§ *Ibid.,* 22,051-5.

One prolific source of dispute in certain trades, and especially in the engineering and shipbuilding industries, is that known as demarcation differences. As a means of preventing such disputes, it has been suggested that boards of arbitration should be formed in every industrial district, the members of which should be, not men engaged in the rival trades, but of other workmen and employers. In one case, where the line of demarcation could not amicably be drawn, the joiners on the Wear suggested that the employers should intervene, but the dispute was ultimately settled by Mr Burt, M.P.

Among other boards that have at different times been constituted for the settlement of disputes between employers and employed, mention may be made of one in the nail trade of Staffordshire in 1880, which collapsed within a year because some manufacturers refused to join it, and others neglected in consequence to adhere to the prices which it fixed;* of another in the shipbuilding trade on the Wear, which is often called upon to settle disputes as between one trade and another, as well as between employers and employed,† and which has been described as being "not so much a board as a system of boards—one in connection with each trade in the district—all of which are governed by the same constitution, and are compelled on failure to agree to refer the disputed matter to a court of three referees, chosen from among a pre-arranged list of names, one by each party, and the third by the two thus selected." ‡

---

* *Royal Commission on Labour*, Group A, 20,249-51.
† *Ibid.*, 22,022-3, 20,038-41.
‡ *Ibid.*, 25,712-25.

CHAPTER XV.

THE ATTITUDE OF EMPLOYERS.

THE whole history of the movement that has resulted in the adoption over a wide area of conciliation and arbitration as means for the settlement of industrial disputes, proves that the more liberal and advanced employers have usually recognised the principle as a rational and suitable one to be applied to difficulties of the kind stated.

This sympathetic attitude towards conciliation and arbitration was manifested in England many years ago, long before it became so general as it now is among employers elsewhere. The Trades Union Commission took a great deal of evidence from employers during the period that they were making their valuable and elaborate inquiries, and in a large majority of cases the leading captains of industry of that time, 1867 to 1869, gave forth no uncertain sound as to their approval and appreciation of the system, which was then deemed to be in its infancy.

The principal witnesses examined on this subject before the Trades Union Commission were Mr Mundella, M.P., who spoke as to the board established at Nottingham for the hosiery and lace industries; Mr Hollins, who gave unequivocal testimony to the success of a board of conciliation of a similar character instituted many years previously in the pottery trade of Staffordshire; and Mr Rupert Kettle, who had taken an active part in promoting arbitration in Wolverhampton and elsewhere. All those spoke strongly on the merits of the system, and recommended its extension. Hence the Trades Union Commission called special attention to the matter in their report. "The great point," they said, "is to bring the masters and men face to face to discuss their differences before their feelings have become embittered, as is apt to be the case when each party is standing out for its own view of what is right, without discussion together."

The most valuable and complete record of the views and recommendations of employers on this subject that has hitherto been made available is that contained in the *Answers to the Schedules of Questions issued by the Royal Commission on Labour*. Arbitration or conciliation is advocated by thirty-eight employers and by eight employers' associations. Some of these answers recommend that boards of arbitration should have power to enforce their awards. Others recommend that when employers and workmen cannot agree over a dispute, either regarding wages or other matters, there ought to be independent arbiters appointed by the Government, each having a separate district, who would be appealed to in such cases. Others again appear to be in favour of profit-sharing and co-operation, while a few are of opinion that sliding-scales are the true solution of the difficulty.

Many variations of procedure are suggested, however, even by those who appear to be most friendly to conciliation.

The Darlington Steel and Iron Company recommend that arbitration be made compulsory, and that neither employers nor employed should be in a position to cause the stoppage of works by strikes or lockouts. The Skinningrove Iron Company favour arbitration, with an appeal to an umpire having power to enforce his award, and appointed either by the Board of Trade or by the local County Council. Messrs John Lysaght & Company recommend " the more extended use of the sliding-scale, and joint-committees of inquiry and conciliation boards, with an ultimate appeal to powerful arbitration boards." Messrs Isaac Jenks & Son believe that " a wages board, similar to the Iron Trade Wages Board, seems the simplest way to settle matters "; and the Steel Company of Scotland believe in making the decisions of courts of arbitration binding on all the parties concerned. Messrs Robert Lloyd, Crosbie & Company of Birmingham believe in the Boards of

Arbitration in connection with Chambers of Commerce, and so with Messrs William Corbitt & Company of Rotherham, the Blainscough Hall Colliery Company, the Claudown Colliery Company, the Radstock Colliery owners, the Aldridge Colliery Company; the Houghton Main and Wodley Colliery Company, and many others.

Testimony of rather a remarkable character was borne by the Thames Iron Works and Shipbuilding Company, whose judgment is thus stated : *—

"There is no arbitration or conciliation machinery in our district. Such means of reconciliation are very desirable, but in the case of a serious strike it is very difficult to find people competent to deal with the highly technical question involved. During our strikes (at their request) I went twice before the conciliation committee of the London Chamber of Commerce, and while I could not but honour the goodness of their intentions, I could not also help realising how entirely they failed to appreciate the point at issue. There is such a thing as crying Peace, peace, when there is no peace, and this is one dangerous tendency of conciliation at any price."

Equally remarkable and interesting is the testimony offered by Palmer's Shipbuilding and Iron Company of Jarrow, who say :—

"An efficient means of avoiding strikes could be found in the principle of conciliation and arbitration, as this offers an effective means of an understanding being arrived at between employers and employed, or between parties representing both. The North of England Board of Conciliation and Arbitration for the iron and steel trades is a good illustration of this. A board of arbitration is formed on the basis of conciliation, that is, endeavouring by compromise, or by reference to a mutually appointed arbitrator as a last resource, for settlement, where discussions of a conciliatory nature which are resorted to in the first instance, both at the board and standing committee, have not been successful. Several temporary arrangements on the

---

* *Royal Commission on Labour : Answers to Schedules,* Group A, p. 358.

same basis have occasionally been instituted for temporary purposes in other branches of our trades. Courts so formed, however, should be legalised and their awards made binding, so that the employer may be protected from the employed, should the latter break away from the award, and *vice versâ*. Resorting to a strike or lockout should be forbidden by law, it being left open to the parties to resort to conciliation or arbitration voluntarily, with power to arrange their court, arbitrators, referees, &c., but with the obligation to register the findings or awards in some public office, the law then taking cognizance of them to superintend their enforcement by penalty or otherwise. Means should, however, be found for providing either party with a legal court of arbitration, or arbitrators, or referees, before which the objecting party should be summoned, and a decision given accordingly. In the event of one side not appearing, the court should have power to satisfy itself as to the reasonableness of the claims made, or the objections of the opposing party to appear, and to give and order accordingly. In the event of the court being satisfied that the party claiming had a fair case, it should have power to call on the other side for evidence, intimating that, if it was not forthcoming, an award would be given notwithstanding, according to the information received. What is intended to be set forth here is the opinion that the difference between employers and employed, and between the different sections of men employed, are destructive of the best interests of the industrial community, and that some means is essential to minimise their differences, and to settle them without impairing the cordial relations that should obtain between employer and employed."

Finally, the large and important shipbuilding firm of Messrs J. & G. Thomson, of Clydebank, submitted the following valuable statement:—

"When employers and workmen cannot agree over a dispute, either regarding wages or other matters, there ought to be independent arbiters appointed by Government, each having a separate district, who would be appealed to in such cases. For instance, there has been a strike of ironworkers on the

Clyde which lasted for six weeks, although the terms of agreement had been arranged between the executive of the men's society and the masters' association ; but the men declined to act on the same. While it is perfectly true that the men favoured this strike, still ironworkers are composed of several classes of tradesmen, and the voting power is in the hands of the most unreasonable and illiterate members, who form the majority. If such an official as above described existed, his services might have been advantageously disposed of in this instance. Even when arranging terms of wages for a period between employers and workmen's executives, this official might be chairman of these conferences. His decision should be final and binding on both parties. Such a system would force both masters and men to formulate reasonable demands only, as otherwise they would be aware that they would not have the slightest chance of obtaining any undue advantage, and thereby bringing trade to a crisis, as they do at present. Whilst the foregoing may not be the best method of solving the strike difficulty, some such measures ought to be adopted for the safety of trade, as strikes are becoming perfectly intolerable, and entail an enormous waste of time and money. Disputes generally ensue when trade is good, and when there is some hope of getting a return for the capital expended, as well as when the maximum amount of wage can be earned by workmen, with the result that disaster is caused to employers and workmen alike."

In previous and in subsequent chapters we shall find ample evidence that the attitude of employers towards the system of conciliation has generally been friendly, and that they have, in not a few cases, initiated the adoption of the system in a particular trade or district. It was the employers who introduced conciliation into nearly every industry in which it is now a feature, and in not a few cases the employers have been anxious to use the system when the workmen have been passive or avowedly hostile. Captain Noble, of the well-known Elswick Works at Newcastle-on-Tyne, quoted a case of this kind in his evidence before the Labour Commission, when he stated that the employers in his district "were in favour of conciliation boards, and, in fact, in the agreement that was come to in the dispute about fifty three hours per week, we agreed that it was expedient to appoint a joint board of conciliation for dealing with all questions which may arise in the future. We have several times asked the delegates that we have met to adopt this resolution, but they have declined to do so."* In Hull, again, according to the testimony of Mr A. E. Seaton, of Earle's Shipbuilding Company, a board of conciliation was formed, on the initiative of the Chamber of Commerce, and the workmen were invited to co-operate, but "we never heard anything further from them." † But while there have been numerous cases of this kind, large bodies of workmen have, on the other hand, ranged themselves on the side of conciliation, and have, as we shall see in the next chapter, been faithful to its mandates; while the cases are by no means rare where individual employers have pronounced against both conciliation and arbitration, and there is a still larger number of cases where they have declared in favour of the former and against the latter.

---

* Evidence taken before Group A, q. 25,240-6.
† *Ibid*, q. 25,632-8.

CHAPTER XVI.

THE ATTITUDE OF WORKMEN.

UNTIL a compulsory system of arbitration has become the law of the land,—and of that there appears to be very little likelihood at present,—it is manifest that the success of both conciliation and arbitration, as well as of any other system designed to diminish friction and promote harmony between employers and employed, must largely, if not wholly, depend upon the attitude taken up towards that system by those who are directly concerned in its adoption.

Generally the proposals for the substitution of some peaceable method of settling labour disputes have emanated from the side of the employers, but this does not necessarily mean that they have always been the best friends of the principle of conciliation. Cases have occurred where the employers have again and again refused to recognise any other solution of the problem to be dealt with than their own will. But if the employers had invariably advocated and stood by the system of conciliation, that would only have been what might be expected from their circumstances. Generally speaking, the employers have a better education and a higher intelligence than their *employés*, so that they are, or should be, capable of acting rather upon reason than upon impulse, and of appreciating the ultimate as well as the immediate bearing of any action that they might undertake. They have also, as a rule, a great deal more at stake. The workman, if he is involved in a strike or a lockout, can pack up his "kit" and seek for work elsewhere. The employer, having once planted himself on a particular spot, has generally come to stay, and he must accept all the direct and indirect consequences of any action in which he is concerned.

Nevertheless, all the evidence that is available as to the attitude assumed by working men towards the systems of conciliation and arbitration, shows that they are generally alive to its importance, and that they have seldom taken up an antagonistic position towards them. Many cases have even occurred where the workmen have proposed conciliation and it has been declined by the employers. Several such cases are on the records of the Royal Labour Commission notably among the cutlers of Sheffield and the miners of Scotland. As a rule, also, the workmen, having once accepted arbitration through their chosen representatives, have faithfully carried out the award of the umpire, however hostile; while cases have occurred where a large body of workmen have raised the funds necessary to recoup an employer for any loss that he may have incurred through the resistance of his men to such an award.

Some light was thrown upon the question of the practical working of arbitration in the evidence given by Mr Edward Trow (a Royal Commissioner), before the Labour Commission, and especially as to the attitude taken by the workmen whom he represents:—"The workmen," says Mr Trow, "truly and honestly believe in the system of conciliation, and faithfully carry out awards. In May 1876, for example, upon the refusal of a small section of their body to obey a decision of the board, the men agreed to pay half the £678, 10s. 1d. which the employers had lost in consequence, and their delegates balloted for substitutes to take over the work of the recusants, because they felt bound in honour to support the authority of the board. Again, in 1882, when a strike took place against a decision of the board, and Mr Trow, in consequence, refused to hold office as their secretary unless the men passed a resolution expressing regret for their action and a determination to be more amenable in future, an overwhelming majority voted in favour of continuing the board. Since that date the system of conciliation has steadily grown in favour, and the witness thought that now there was not a single works in the North of England, where the men would not gladly join the board, if they could only persuade their employers to do so too.

"Ever since the board was formed," adds Mr Trow, "its decisions have been retrospective. In questions concerning an advance of wages, therefore, the men are willing to continue working upon the original terms, pending judgment, for they know that, if the decision is given in their favour, the extra payments will take effect from the moment their claim was filed. On the other hand, when questions concerning reductions await decision, the employers continue to pay the original rate, trusting to the men's honesty to refund the extra amount, if the board finds in favour of the reduction. The only case in which the men abused this trust was that of the Britannia Works, where two men sent in their notices instead of paying. The company took action against them, and the assize judge, sitting at York in May 1875, ruled that they were bound to pay, whereupon they refunded the money."

In some quarters a great deal has been made of the fact that the workmen have sometimes refused to accept an award, and it has been argued thereupon that their loyalty was not to be depended on. No better witness could be cited on this point than Sir Rupert Kettle, who, in addressing the Social Science Congress in 1870, made the following remarks :—"He knew of arbitration boards established in a great variety of trades—the building trade, the textile fabric trade, manufacturing trades of various kinds, contract trades, and the various kinds of productive industries, as well as distributing industries—and he had never known a single instance of a working man breaking his contract. But he was bound to say that he had known of individual masters who had broken the contract. In those cases, however, the public opinion of the district had always been brought to bear for the purpose of supporting the arbitration board. He would tell them further what temptation some of the men were sometimes subjected to to break their contract. He had known instances in the building trade, which consisted of three or four branches, where carpenters, bricklayers, and plasterers consented to abide by the court of arbitration, while the masons positively refused to submit. The result of the award was unsatisfactory to the three trades, but nevertheless, though they did not get an advance, they honourably accepted the decision. A week afterwards the masons struck for an advance, and it was given by the masters; and yet the three bodies of men—the carpenters, the bricklayers, and the plasterers—went on working, and were willing to go on working throughout the whole year, upon the judgment of the court of arbitration, although they were engaged upon the same building as the masons who had got the advance. In another case, he had classified various industries: to consider what should be their relative positions over the coming year. In the arbitration board it was found to be impossible to deal with all the men upon equal terms; it was found that the bricklayers made out a better case for a rise than the carpenters or the plasterers. Though those three bodies, through their representatives, agreed to form one common board for the purpose of discussing the whole question—whether the main drainage scheme would be carried out, whether the town hall would be built, or the new hospital enlarged, and whether certain other works could be executed within a given time; the result was that instead of making a one year's bargain, they made a three years' bargain. They were working now in their third year, and he had not heard a single complaint."

It is, of course, difficult to assemble a considerable number of representatives of two conflicting interests to discuss matters that involve large issues to both without some degree of friction occurring, or being liable to occur. But the first thing that both sides should resolutely strive for is patience, and the next thing is to studiously avoid anything in the form of discourtesy. If the one side ruffles the feelings or excites the temper of the other, there is generated a disposition to retaliate which is more or less inherent in our frail human nature, and this disposition, it need hardly be added, is quite inconsistent with that calm and judicial frame of mind which alone is suited to the trial of such issues.

Few arbitrations have taken place without some display of

temper, and without the use of ill-chosen and hasty words that were afterwards regretted. In the Durham district the two parties have often hit very hard, either in the way of direct assertion, challenge, innuendo, or demur. So far had this proceeded, indeed, that in the arbitration of 1876, the umpire made use of these words: "Each side can now quite feel that they have had their say out. If they choose between this and the printing of the case to meet and mutually eliminate some passages that are mutually hard upon one another, that may be a useful thing for posterity when it comes to read the account." And posterity is likely enough to affirm that it would have been all the better if the umpire's advice on this occasion had been adopted. Hard words are not arguments, reflections and innuendos are not the weapons with which to fight in the presence of an umpire who has a knowledge of his duty. On the contrary, the more courtesy that is shown the more is mutual respect generated, and the more likelihood is there of friendly feelings — which are an almost indispensable condition to arbitration — being maintained. Nor is either side slow to recognise the existence of courteous behaviour on the other side. When the cokemakers of the county of Durham were arbitrating as to the rate of wages that should be paid in August 1876, the cokemen submitted a statement, which the then umpire (the Right Hon. G. J. Shaw-Lefevre, M.P.) described as "a very able paper, very ably stating their case," and which the advocates for the employers described as "very gentlemanly," and deserving of high compliment. It is in this spirit that all cases of the kind should be approached. It is not enough to have full confidence in your own case, but you must be prepared to recognise the merits as well as the defects of the case of your opponents, if you are to arrive at a just settlement of a pending dispute.

In Lancashire several attempts have been made to introduce a sliding-scale for the regulation of the wages of coal-miners, but at the outset of this movement the men appear to have conceived a distrust of the system. At any rate they struck work in 1889, ostensibly against a sliding-scale which had been introduced by the employers, following upon a strike that took place in 1887 for an advance of wages, and which, after lasting for six weeks, resulted in a concession being made to the men. The representatives of the men declared that they do not object to a sliding-scale, "but to one arbitrarily imposed upon them by the employers without discussion, as was the case in 1887."*

An evidence of the earnestness of the workmen is supplied in one very drastic suggestion made before Group A of the Royal Commission on Labour, viz., that whenever a strike occurred with the approval of the executive, the members of the executive should cease to draw a salary, and be put upon the same short allowance as the men on strike. This suggestion was made on behalf of the Associated Iron and Steel Workers of Great Britain, by Mr W. Ancott, the president, who would himself be affected by its adoption. Rightly or wrongly, there is a not uncommon impression abroad that officials have had more to do with strikes than the workmen whom they were supposed to control, but this is certainly not always, and perhaps not often, the case. The workmen are more liable to drive the officials than the officials to drive the workmen, and many recent cases show that strikes have been entered upon against the advice of the responsible advisers of the men.

That the workmen are not unappreciative of the efforts made by those who, their truest friends, seek by conciliation to avoid the ruptures that are otherwise liable to occur in the relations of employers and employed, is evident from many circumstances that have occurred since this system came into general use. But in no case probably has more marked testimony been rendered of this fact than when, in 1870, the representatives of the ironworkers of the North of England met in the Central Hall of Darlington, to present an illuminated address to Mr David Dale—first, for his having been the means of establishing this system in the iron trade of the north, and

---

* *Report of the Royal Commission on Labour*, Section A, *cf.* 9872-8, 10,470.

next, for his unwearied and effective discharge of the duties of chairman of the conciliation board. This address, which was presented by a workman, bore the following testimony to Mr Dale's services :—

"We are deeply sensible of the active part you took, and the valuable services you rendered, in the establishment of this board, and of the kind, courteous, and impartial manner in which you have presided as chairman since its formation.

"Combined with great administrative ability, tact, and judgment, you have brought to bear upon the proceedings and discussions the true conciliatory spirit in conducting the general business, which has not unfrequently been both trying and difficult. The unwearied attention you have bestowed upon the organisation and management of the board has enabled us, on all occasions, to bear and forbear with each other. To your able presidency is mainly due the success that has attended this important movement—a movement which, we trust, will gain strength year by year, and will become firmly established in connection with the northern iron trade."

It is, however, proper to observe that there have been numerous cases where the workmen have recorded emphatic objections to both arbitration and sliding-scales, and some of these may be noted.

Unlike most of the other colliery districts in the country, South Wales does not appear to favour arbitration. At any rate, according to the evidence of Mr Edward Jones of the South Wales Colliery Owners' Association,[*] "Resort has never been made to arbitration upon the failure of the two sides of the standing committee to agree. The workmen's representatives, he says, have generally been in favour of the appointment of an umpire, especially for the settlement of isolated local disputes; but the employers have always objected, because they fail to see any finality in his decision. There would also be great difficulty in obtaining an umpire who possessed the confidence of both parties. Disputes would be greatly multi-

[*] *Report of Royal Commission on Labour*, Section A, 9, 11,679, 818.

plied if the men knew that they could refer questions to an umpire, because his award might reasonably be expected to be of the nature of a compromise, and they would accordingly feel confident of gaining some advantage by every contest. The same objections would apply to the appointment of an independent chairman to settle with the joint committee."

In some cases the adoption of a sliding-scale appears to have been arrived at without a great deal of difficulty; in other cases the negotiations for this end have been fruitless. In West Lancashire, efforts were made at different times during the last ten years or so to arrange a sliding-scale in the coal industry, but no satisfactory basis could be arrived at, and the scale was never introduced.

In nearly every instance where a sliding-scale has been introduced in the mining industry, and abandoned, it has been given up at the instance of the workmen. In West Yorkshire, a sliding-scale was in force for two years preceding 1881, but it was terminated in March of that year owing to the men being dissatisfied with it. In the Durham coal trade there have been four different scales under which wages were fixed according to the ascertained average selling price of coal. Only one of these, however, lasted for more than two and a half years. The first, which came to an end in December 1878, only lasted for a year and seven months. The second, which was concluded in December 1881, only lasted for two years and two months. The third, which came to an end in December 1883, lasted for a year and eight months. And the fourth and last, which was given up in July 1889, lasted for about five years, and was also terminated at the instance of the workmen. This does not prove, however, that the workmen had lost all faith in the system. It only proves that the particular application or basis adopted did not suit them.

CHAPTER XVII.

PENDING PROPOSALS AND LEGISLATION.

DURING the last two years the exceptional frequency and unprecedented magnitude of some of the strikes that have occurred, in the coal and other industries, have suggested and enforced the absolute necessity of attempting some means of avoiding cases of the kind in the time to come.

This necessity has found expression in the introduction of three different Bills, that are intended to secure the end in view, by making more or less binding the adoption of conciliation or arbitration.

In our own country, the Act known as Lord St Leonard's was adopted by Parliament some twenty-five years ago, for the purpose of facilitating the adoption of arbitration, but the Act has practically remained a dead letter. Not that employers and employed have failed to make use of arbitration for the purposes that the Act was designed to promote, but in nearly all the arrangements made for this end the Act itself has been disregarded. The recent serious strikes in the Durham and Midland coalfields, and elsewhere, have forced upon the Legislature the necessity of making some additional legislative provision for meeting cases of the kind, and we are consequently likely to have quite a crop of arbitration Bills, including probably a Government measure, in the ensuing session of Parliament. Two such Bills are already under consideration. One of them, described as Sir John Lubbock's Bill, which is backed by Mr Mather, Mr Howell, and others, proposes to give power to a Board of Conciliation or Arbitration to examine on oath, to issue subpœnas, and to call for the production of documents; and it provides that where the parties have agreed in writing to submit a difference to arbitration, the award made thereon shall be final, and shall be enforceable " in the same manner as a judgment or order of the High Court to the same effect." Sir F. Dixon Hartland's Bill is constructed on different lines. It withdraws the constitution of the arbitration board from the hands of the parties to the difference, and vests it in the County Council, who are to be saddled with the expenses involved; and while it takes authority, like Sir John Lubbock's Bill, to summon witnesses, compel attendance, and administer oaths, it does not provide for giving the same legal sanction to any awards that may be arrived at. This second Bill, in point of fact, appears to be based upon the theory that if a sufficiently full and impartial inquiry is held into the subject-matter of a dispute, and a decision given and published as to the proper mode of settlement, public opinion and its pressure may be trusted to take care that the decision is carried out.

These two Bills open up the whole question of the constitution, procedure, and powers of boards of arbitration, and at the present moment are, therefore, of great public interest. The most important problem involved in any attempted legislation on the question, is that of whether the awards made under a reference to arbitration shall be enforceable by legal process. A hardly less important question is whether the parties to a dispute shall be bound to submit the difference to arbitration. The second of these points is in one sense much more important than the first, because obviously, if it is competent for either party to a dispute to refuse to submit the question at issue,—as was actually the case in the Durham strike of 1892 and the Midland coal strike of 1893,—the giving of legal sanction to the award becomes a matter of secondary importance. In other words, when once arbitration has been resolved upon, the rest becomes comparatively smooth sailing, inasmuch as there have been comparatively few cases where an award has been deliberately set aside by either side. Two aspects of compulsion have therefore to be provided for: the first, compulsion to resort to arbitration; and the second, compulsion to observe the terms of an award - if compulsion is to be adopted at all.

Practically, however, all experience and precedents up to the present time are dead against compulsion in any form. You cannot very well compel a man to agree to submit to reference whether he shall be required to work for a certain employer for a certain wage at a certain time. This must be left entirely to the man's own choice. Nor can you deal differently with a body of men, however numerous, so long as they have broken no laws and rendered themselves amenable to no penalties. Workmen must be continued in the enjoyment of the right to dispose of their labour at whatsoever price they like, and this being so, they cannot be compelled to arbitrate as to what the price of that labour shall be, or as to any other general conditions affecting its value and duration. All that can be done is to endeavour to persuade both employers and employed to agree to submit matters in dispute to arbitration, and failing acceptance of the award made under such reference to impose some sort of penalty. This would be more than any country or any locality has attempted to do up to the present time. The judgment of those who have been most intimately associated with labour movements is, on the whole, adverse to compulsion. The laws adopted with a view to the encouragement and sanction of arbitration abroad are almost wholly permissive. It has not been entirely so in England. The Act 5 George IV., chap. 96 (1824), gives considerable powers of compulsory arbitration on application by either party to a justice of the peace, but the scope of the Act is limited to subsisting contracts; and the formation of permanent boards or councils, or the fixing of future wages and prices, was not contemplated. Lord St Leonard's Act 30 & 31 Vict., chap. 105 (1867)—gives power to the Home Secretary to license permanent councils of arbitration; but their operation was limited to the existing contracts enumerated in Section 2 of the Act 5 George IV., chap. 96. Finally, Mr Mundella's Act of 1872 gives all the powers that can be given for the establishment of permanent boards of arbitration, consistent with freedom of contract. Power is given to fix future wages or prices, and to enforce awards by legal process, as breaches of contract.

Mr Mundella's pending Conciliation (Trades Disputes) Bill (the full text of which is published in the Appendix) places in the hands of the Board of Trade the power (*a*) To inquire into the causes of a difference or dispute, and make a report thereon; and (*b*) To invite the parties to meet together, by themselves or their representatives, under the presidency of a chairman mutually agreed upon or nominated by the Board of Trade, or by some other person or body, with a view to the amicable settlement of the difference. The Board of Trade is also authorised to take steps to establish boards of conciliation and arbitration in cases where they do not already exist, and is required to make an annual report to Parliament under the Act.

It would be difficult to find fault with many of the provisions of Mr Mundella's latest Bill. He does not go so far as some others have done in the direction of enforcing obedience to awards. The whole spirit and tenour of the proposed measure is permissive and voluntary, and this is probably essential in any attempt to legislate on the subject. At the same time, the powers vested in the Board of Trade would enable them to take such a course, in reference to any important dispute, as would cover with odium any party to it that refused to recognise and accept the recommendations of so manifestly impartial an authority. The annual report to be made to Parliament should, moreover, enter into the merits of each dispute, and assign credit or blame where they were deserved, thereby securing sympathy and approval for the one side at the expense of the other.

While the whole subject is still pending, the recommendations of the Royal Labour Commission relative to the settlement of trade disputes have opportunely been published.* The Commissioners find that institutions for the settlement of dis-

---

* *The Times*, 20th April.

putes have grown up within the larger and better organised industries, and are successful in proportion to the excellence of the organisation; that in recent years other institutions, distinguished as district boards of conciliation, have been formed for the settlement of disputes, not in any one trade, but in many small trades within a given area; that both trade and district boards have in all cases been spontaneously formed without resort to certain Acts of Parliament intended to enable them to acquire a statutory basis and certain legal powers; and, finally, that these trade and district boards are highly efficacious where they exist, but do not yet exist in sufficient numbers to cover the whole field of industry.

In these circumstances the Commissioners inquire, in the first place, whether it would be advisable to establish industrial tribunals throughout the country with legal powers to deal with questions arising out of existing agreements. In favour of this course it has been urged that working men are deterred by cost, the character of the tribunal, and other reasons, from bringing questions of this kind before stipendiary magistrates and justices of the peace, who may have jurisdiction under the Employers and Workmen Act 1875; while, as no special tribunals have been established under the Conciliation Act 1867, or other Acts, these authorities are the only ones before whom such questions can be brought. Many witnesses seemed to expect and desire some court that would take cognizance of very technical and local disputes, such as short payment for inferior work, fines and deductions, and the quality of the raw material supplied by the master. While some of these disputes are outside the province of a public tribunal, there is a general impression that workmen have minor grievances for which they cannot readily obtain cheap and summary redress. But, on the other hand, in all well-organised trades they are thoroughly protected; most of the disputes in question would usually be settled by the termination of the engagement rather than by resort to any tribunal whatever; several Acts establishing tribunals of the kind sought have become a dead letter; and if they are to be of real use for very small disputes they must be created in quite impracticable numbers. The report concludes that it would be unwise to institute any general system of industrial tribunals, but that there might be some advantage in empowering town and county councils to establish them in a tentative manner. It would be the function of the councils to take the initiative without directly appointing the members, and any court of the kind, when approved by a public department and established by an Order in Council, would have the statutory powers exercised *in pari materia* by county courts.

These tribunals, it is held, would deal only with disputes arising out of existing agreements or trade customs. But all the greater and more serious disputes affecting large bodies of men, have regard to the future rather than the present, and to the modification of existing conditions rather than to their interpretation. The next question, therefore, is, whether it is desirable to establish statutory boards of conciliation and arbitration. On this point the report concludes that no central department could have the local knowledge necessary to attempt with success the creation of such institutions, and that the intervention of local public authorities cannot be usefully extended at present beyond the experimental action just referred to. The Commissioners hope and believe that the present rapid extension of voluntary boards will continue. At some future time it may be found advisable to give them statutory powers, but at the present stage of progress "it would do more harm than good either to invest voluntary boards with legal powers or to establish rivals to them in the shape of other boards founded on a statutory basis and having a more or less public and official character."

With regard to the promotion of voluntary boards of conciliation and arbitration, the Commissioners report that, though they cannot agree in recommending the direct establishment of such boards of the State, they think that "a central department, with an adequate staff, and having means to procure, record, and circulate information, may do much by advice and assistance to promote their more rapid and universal establishment." It is suggested that legislation such as that proposed by Mr Mundella last year might do much good by giving the Board of Trade a better *locus standi* for friendly and experienced intervention. But care must be taken to guard against any injury to the unique position which the Board of Trade now occupies. Its statistical duties will, in all probability, increase, and " in the collection and preparation of information the importance of absolute and universally recognised impartiality and freedom from any end or purpose except that of exact ascertainment of facts is so great that care will have to be taken that intervention, even of the most friendly character, in trade disputes shall in no degree impair statistical accuracy and credit."

The next point dealt with in the report is the appointment of official arbitrators. When all concerned are willing to arbitrate, there is often great difficulty in finding an arbitrator. " Either the proposed arbitrator or umpire is quite unconnected with industrial work, and then the process of informing his mind is too long and costly, or he is in some way connected with the industrial world, and then one party or the other is apt to suspect him of bias or partiality." The Commissioners think that this difficulty might be got over by giving a public department power to appoint an arbitrator to act either alone or in conjunction with others. If the same persons were frequently appointed, they would become arbitration experts, they would be fairly free from suspicion of bias, their expenses would be paid by the Treasury, and in time, if the system worked well, they might be made permanent instead of temporary and occasional judicial officers, with perhaps power to summon witnesses and examine them on oath.

It will no doubt be very disappointing to those who expected a great deal from the labours of the Commission to find that on this crucial question of the settlement of trade disputes their recommendations are so lame and inconclusive, and their joint wisdom has so manifestly failed to find a panacea for one of the greatest social evils of our time. But men of wisdom and experience must have known better what to expect. There is no "divine afflatus" about a Royal Commission, and it is not necessarily any more easy for a tribunal of this kind to solve a great problem than it is for the individual. The Commissioners, however, indicate one direction in which an improvement of existing machinery is desirable. They hint at the lack of adequate provision for dealing with the minor grievances of workmen. This matter is one that has been taken up and adjudicated upon by the joint-committees that are now at work in connection with most boards established in the iron, coal, and other industries. But such organisations, as we have seen, are relatively few, and it is highly desirable that the system should be as far as possible extended.

SECTION II.—FOREIGN COUNTRIES.

CHAPTER XVIII.

LABOUR DISPUTES AND THEIR SETTLEMENT IN THE UNITED STATES.

The United States of North America are the most important industrial and manufacturing country in the world after Great Britain. It is even probable that they are to-day ahead of the old country from this point of view. But whether their industries as a whole are equally diversified, it is certain that in reference to many of them, such as mining, the manufacture of iron and steel, the working of other metals, the manufacture of railway plant, and above all, the working of railway traffic, the United States are by far the most important industrial nation in the world.

This unique position has been attained within such a comparatively short space of time, that it seems only like yesterday when the United States could make but small pretensions to being an industrial nation, and had little more than a merely agricultural reputation. Even so recently as 1880, only 7.6 per cent. of the total population of the country were employed in manufactures, as compared with 15.3 per cent. engaged in agriculture, while at the same time 23 per cent. of the population of the United Kingdom were engaged in manufacturing industry, as compared with only 7.5 per cent. engaged in agriculture.*

* *England's Supremacy*, by J. Stephen Jeans, p. 16. Longmans.

If we go further back still, we shall find that the percentage proportion of the population of the United States employed in manufactures was relatively smaller, while that of the United Kingdom was not greatly different. Indeed, even in 1861, the industrial population of England was 22.7 per cent. of the whole, as against only 10 per cent. employed in agriculture.*

These facts have a more important bearing on the questions discussed in this volume than might appear at first sight. In the case of a settled and more or less independent agricultural population, such as that of the United States, there is not the same liability to labour disputes that there invariably is where the population is shifting and migratory, and engaged first in one occupation and then in another. Hence the United States have not until quite recently been called upon to face to any extent the great economic problems of work and wages which had at a much earlier period perplexed and disturbed our own country; and hence also we should not expect to find in the United States the same ripe experience of the labour question in its earlier forms and phases, as we must have in Great Britain.

Although in the industrial history of the United States unions of some kind have existed since the beginning of the present century, it is only since the time of the civil war that the labour organisations of that country have attained to anything like their present importance.† The excitement of that period, and the abolition of slavery, gave a strong impetus to the movement in favour of organised labour, and in the ten following years many new unions and so-called brotherhoods were constituted.‡ Of these by far the most important appears to be the "Federation of Organised Trades and Labour Unions of the United States and Canada," which was established at Pittsburg in 1881, and which, ten years later, had a member-

---

* *England's Supremacy*, by J. Stephen Jeans, p. 17.
† *Royal Commission on Labour: Foreign Reports — The United States*, p. 7.
‡ *Ibid.*, p. 8.

ship of 618,000, and claimed to control sixty-two affiliated unions.

Of late years the number of strikes and lockouts occurring in the organised industries of the United States have largely increased. The period 1881-91 appears to have marked their greatest development. Even within the comparatively short period 1882-86, the number of strikes reported for the United States as a whole had more than trebled, and the number of establishments affected had increased more than four-fold.* About 42 per cent. of the strikes reported were attributed to a demand for increase of wages, and 7.7 per cent. to the resistance of a proposed reduction of wages.

Many of the labour disputes that have occurred in the United States have been connected with a reduction of the number of hands employed, or of the wages paid in a particular industry consequent upon the introduction of labour-saving machinery. The rate of wages paid in all manufactures after the Civil War appears to have largely increased, and this fact stimulated the necessity for labour-saving machinery wherever it could be applied. The natural inventive capacity of the American mechanic was thereupon set to work, and within a few years the processes and appliances used in many leading manufactures became more or less revolutionised. The extent to which this movement involved a notable displacement of labour may be estimated from one or two examples. In the Bessemer steel industry, one man in 1890 could do the work, as measured by tons of product, that five men were required to do twenty years before. In the boot and shoe industry, one man in 1885 could do the work that it required ten men to perform twenty years before. And so with most other industries in a greater or less degree.

But while this movement has been carried further in the United States than in other countries, we find that the general causes of labour disputes are much the same there as in Great Britain, and call for much the same mode and conditions of

---

* *Report of Federal Bureau of Labour on Strikes and Lockout.*

treatment. The most serious strikes are those that have occurred in the coal regions of Ohio and Pennsylvania, in the iron and steel industries, and amongst the men employed on railway work. Some of those strikes, and especially those organised by the union or society known as the Knights of Labour, were of great extent, and were marked by violence and disorder of a very serious character.

The Commissioner of Labour, in his valuable reports on American industry, estimated that the total loss to employers from suspension of labour throughout the United States between 1881 and 1886 was thirty-four millions of dollars. Within the same period, the total loss to the workmen concerned is estimated at about sixty millions of dollars. This would mean an average annual loss to both parties of about 3¼ millions sterling a year :* and if this be taken as the average annual loss in the interval that has elapsed since these estimates were put forward, it would represent a total loss to American industry, between 1881 and 1892, of thirty-six millions sterling.†

Having found that labour was becoming more difficult to control, that strikes were becoming of more frequent occurrence, and that the losses and difficulties arising from industrial disputes were becoming increasingly serious, the attention of both employers and employed in the chief American industries was naturally turned to England, as the leading manufacturing country, for a solution of the problem that was being pressed upon their notice.

Several attempts were made between 1870 and 1880 to establish boards of conciliation and arbitration in connection with particular industries, but the success achieved in this direction was not very encouraging. One of the first attempts to legislate on the matter was made in the State of Pennsylvania, where, upon a report presented by my friend Mr J. D. Weeks, of Pittsburg, on the working of conciliation and arbi-

---

* Converting the dollar at 4.80.

† Many very serious strikes have taken place since 1886, especially in mining and railway industries.

tration in labour disputes in England, the State legislature adopted the Wallace Act of 1883. This Act provided for the establishment of voluntary boards of arbitration; but the awards made under it could not be binding unless, and until, they were accepted by both parties. This was virtually the principle adopted by all the boards of arbitration established in England up to that period. Two years later an arbitration Act was established in Ohio, which varied the procedure of the Pennsylvania Act, by requiring that both parties must pledge themselves beforehand to accept the award, whatever it might be. This provision is of course understood, if not distinctly expressed, in every case of arbitration; but it may possibly have a more binding effect on the minds and consciences of imperfectly educated bodies of workmen to have it so stated.

Other boards of arbitration were afterwards established, in the States of Massachusetts, New York, and California; and in 1888, Congress passed an Act, published in the Appendix hereto, " For the creation of boards of arbitration, or commission for settling controversies and differences," between railway companies, &c., and their workmen. In no case, however, has any penalty been attached to the failure of either side to carry out an award, so that "there is no sanction attached to the Act other than such as may be constituted by a dread of public opinion."*

Differences of a more or less important character distinguish the different arbitration boards established in the United States from one another.

The Massachusetts Act of 1886, as amended in 1887, provides for the appointment of a State board of arbitration, composed of three persons, of whom one represents the employers, another the labour organisations, and the third is an impartial citizen recommended by the other two. The California State Board of Arbitration and Conciliation, appointed by an Act of 1891, is similarly constituted. Of the three "competent persons" composing it, "one shall represent the employers of

---

* *Royal Commission on Labour: Foreign Report*, vol. i.

labour, one shall represent labour employés, and the third member shall represent neither and shall be chairman of the Board."

The constitution of the New York Board of Mediation and Arbitration, established in 1887, is somewhat different. One of the three arbitrators is to be elected from the party "which at the last general election cast the greatest number of votes for Governor of this State," another from the party casting the second greatest number, whilst a third is to be selected "from a *bona fide* labour organisation of this State."

In California, the members are elected for one year only; in New York, for three; and in Massachusetts, all the members serve three years, but only one retires every year, so that the persons composing the board are never all changed at once. By an amendment of 1890 to the Act constituting the Massachusetts board, in cases involving special technical difficulties the two parties in dispute may each appoint an expert to serve on the board for the particular case. All three boards, though not nominally compulsory, possess very extensive powers. The Massachusetts board may, upon the application of the employer, or of a majority of his employés, or of their duly authorised agent, open an inquiry, which it may make public or not at its own discretion, and at any stage in the proceedings. Where both parties refuse arbitration, the board may attempt to mediate between them; and, failing that, may, if it thinks fit, investigate the cause or causes of the controversy, and publish a report, finding the causes and assigning the responsibility.

When a decision is given, it is binding upon the parties for six months, or until the expiration of the sixty days' notice of an intention not to be bound by it given by one party to the other. Two instances are recorded in which such notice was given in the report of the Massachusetts board for 1887; but in neither case was the award interfered with at the expiration of the period of notice.

The New York board has a power of investigation which it may exercise when its services as an arbitrator are refused, and after arriving at the facts of a controversy, it may make them public and lay them before the legislature. It is also empowered to suggest amendments to the existing laws touching labour questions. The California board is similarly charged with the duty of investigating all disputes which threaten to end in a strike, and is empowered to publish the results of its investigation. In its report for 1889 the New York board claims that the extensive powers granted to it by the Act deter parties "from making undue exactions or unjust conditions;" but neither here nor in Massachusetts, nor in California, is any provision made in the Act for compelling the observance of the award. The decision of the board is only accepted where the parties are willing to accept it.

The reports of the Massachusetts board for 1888, 1891, and 1892 speak with satisfaction of the number of wage lists drawn up by the board, for which application is often made afterwards by other manufacturers, and which, therefore, serve as a standard of prices. Manufacturers often apply to the board for advice in fixing the rate of wages or the price for a new kind of work.

The report for 1888 states that some firms enter into a written agreement with their employés to submit all differences which may arise to the arbitration of the board, and that strikes and lockouts are thus rendered impossible. The labour organisations view such agreements with distrust, as tending to make their existence superfluous. All the three boards have power in all cases to summon witnesses, and to examine them under oath, as well as to require the production of books containing the record of wages paid. They may also appoint experts to assist the arbitrators in cases which present technical difficulties. A special voluntary board may always be substituted for the State board at the wish of the parties concerned, and this temporary body is endowed for the time being with all the powers which the Act confers upon the permanent arbitrators. Two instances of the appointment of such a voluntary board are recorded in the Massachusetts report for 1887.

The report of the New York board for 1889 states that laws providing for the settlement of disputes between employers and employed by arbitration have been enacted by the Congress of the United States, and the Legislatures of Colorado, Maryland, New Jersey, Iowa, Michigan, and North Carolina, as well as the States previously mentioned. By an Act of 1892, the Governor of New Jersey is authorised to appoint a State board of arbitration to hear appeals from local arbitration boards, as well as to arbitrate directly between employer and employed when the parties in dispute desire it, and to hold an inquiry into the cause of the controversy when they do not.*

Sliding scales for the regulation of wages have been more or less adopted in the coal and iron industries of the United States for many years, but these have been subject to frequent modifications in consequence of the changing conditions of those industries. One of the first scales that was really applied in a practical way was that adopted in 1865 by the Sons of Vulcan. This scale, which was designed to regulate the rate of wages to be paid in the iron industry, only lasted for a few months. Its abandonment was followed by a strike, in which the workmen were successful; and another scale was afterwards introduced, which gave a considerably higher wage for smelting than has since been adopted. This scale was continued in existence for seven years, but it ultimately broke down because it had not a sufficiently low minimum of price. In other words, while it provided for an advance of wages whenever the price of iron varied by one-tenth of a cent. above a certain figure, it did not provide for a fall of prices below three cents. per lb. When, therefore, the price of iron fell below that limit, the employers proposed a reduction of wages to the extent of a dollar per ton. The workmen objected to this, but were willing to accept a reduction of fifty cents. A strike followed, which lasted for four months, and which ended in favour of the workmen.

Since that time the wages paid to nearly all classes of workmen employed in and about the iron and steel works of the United States have usually been regulated by the movements of prices according to sliding-scales. The adjustment of these

---

* *Royal Commission on Labour: Foreign Reports*, vol. i.

scales to the varying circumstances of the trade has from time to time given a great deal of trouble, and has been the cause of some serious strikes, including the memorable strike which took place at the Homestead works of Messrs Carnegie, Phipps, & Co., in 1892. The real and immediate occasion of that strike was a proposal made by the employers to reduce the basis of the scale, in so far as it applied to certain highly paid classes of workmen, from twenty six dollars fifty cents, to twenty three dollars per ton, and to make the scale terminable in January instead of in July. The workmen objected, first of all, to the proposed reduction; but they objected equally to the change of date for the termination of the scale, on the ground that in the middle of winter they would not be able to afford a possible cessation of work, or a possible resistance to any proposed variation of the scale. The strike was memorable for the incident of the skirmish between the men and the Pinkerton detective force; but it can hardly be said to have added anything to our knowledge or experience of the most advisable methods to apply to the settlement of similar controversies, unless it be that of the importance of having the workmen correctly informed as to the real facts of the situation. It appeared, in the course of a subsequent investigation into the facts of the lockout, that the workmen were under the impression that, since the M'Kinley tariff of 1890 had become law, the profits of the employers had increased, and that there was consequently no occasion for any decrease of wages; whereas if the real facts as to profits and prices had been within the knowledge of the workmen, the dispute would probably not have occurred, or would at any rate have ended differently.

Numerous scales have been introduced in the different coalfields of the United States, and more especially in the anthracite region of Pennsylvania, where such a scale was applied to the regulation of the wages of miners as far back as 1869. These scales did not differ much in principle from those that have been adopted in the coal industry of Great Britain. They had in all cases what was known as a basis price, and fixed the weekly rate of wages, or the tonnage price, in reference thereto.

In the United States there has been a constant tendency of late years to a fall of commodities, and consequently to a drop in the prices adopted as the basis of sliding-scales. The original basis price of coal was three dols. per ton at Port Carbon for anthracite mines; but this was reduced, first to one dol. seventy-five cents, and afterwards to one dol. fifty cents, and in both cases the reduction involved more or less protracted and serious disputes. In the case of the anthracite miners, also, as in the case of the ironworkers already referred to, the scale did not provide for a fall of sufficient extent, so that there came a time when coal fell below the basis price, and the workmen refused to submit to the reduction of wages which this movement involved.

The experience gained of sliding-scales in the United States has so far been favourable to their adoption, under certain modifications of the system heretofore introduced. One of the most essential of these is to have a lower limit sufficiently far down to meet any probable movement of prices, and to have the rate of wages fixed to accord with such limits. It is, of course, impossible to provide for all contingencies, and in the United States both prices and the cost of production have moved downwards so rapidly of late years that no one could have anticipated the changes that have actually come about. As an example of this, it may be stated that whereas the first scale adopted in the anthracite coal trade of Pennsylvania provided for a selling price of three dollars as the basis, the actual realised value of the whole anthracite coal product of Pennsylvania in 1891 is stated in the census report for that year at only a fraction over one dollar per ton. Again, on the basis price of 1869, anthracite coal-miners were to be paid fourteen dollars a week as wages, whereas the recent rate of wages has been very much under that figure. In Illinois the miners engaged in the mining of bituminous coal were paid 80.2 cents a ton in 1883, and only 68.3 cents a ton in 1890. The same sort of movement has been apparent in nearly every important coalfield in the United States; and it has been brought about partly owing to the effect of competition in reducing the price of coal, and partly owing to the large supply of foreign labour always available, at relatively low wages, for mining purposes.

CHAPTER XIX.

LABOUR DISPUTES AND THEIR SETTLEMENT IN GERMANY.

GERMANY has for many years been distinguished as the birthplace and cradle of advanced ideas and programmes concerning the rights and requirements of labour. This, indeed, is a prominent feature of the Shibboleth of the Social Democratic Organisation, which has taken so deep a root in the Fatherland; while the Internationalists, the Anarchists, the "League of the Just," and other bodies, secret or otherwise, have either been founded for the purpose of advancing the interests of labour as against capital, or have placed that idea prominently in the forefront of their demands.

In all German labour legislation and movements there may be found traces, more or less palpable, of the influence of the mediæval guilds, which secured large monopolies and privileges for industrial corporations. The guilds practically controlled all manufacturing operations, and decided what new factories should be started, and where, and under what conditions. This exclusive privilege was withdrawn from the guilds and transferred to the State under the Prussian law of 1794. The guilds died hard. They were supported by employers, who, in 1845, demanded the establishment of compulsory guilds, and other reactionary legislation. All this, however, was opposed by the workmen, who in the same year met and demanded, among other things, a working day of twelve hours including meal times, and a fixed minimum wage. To settle the conflicting claims of capital and labour, the Government established district councils of industry, which, however, were not successful. Under the Industrial Code of

1869 all existing guilds were placed on a voluntary basis. In 1881 another law was passed, in the form of additions to the Industrial Code, which was intended to encourage the establishment of voluntary guilds, with a view to maintaining the existence of the lesser industries that were threatened with decay. One of the provisions of this Act was designed to establish harmonious relations between employers and employed, and another was that of deciding disputes between members of the guilds and their apprentices.

As, however, the guilds, even in their modified form, were found to be unsuited to all the purposes of modern industry, and especially unsuited to solve the problem of maintaining harmonious relations between employers and employed, combinations of employers were formed on the one hand, and unions of workmen on the other, for mutual support against the demands and operations of one another. Some of the organisations took measures for the settlement of industrial disputes by conciliation; and one of the first to undertake action of this kind was the National Association of Master Printers, established in 1874 at Frankfort-on-the-Maine.

Germany, however, has been many years behind England and the United States in the assertion of the freedom of contract, in the recognition of the elementary principles of political economy as applied to such matters as the introduction of machinery, in the combination of working-men for trade purposes, and in the disabilities attached to such organisations. German workmen were still struggling to obtain a recognition of the right to combine long after trades unions had become general in England, and long after labour organisations had become a strong power in this country, and were being recognised by employers, by the Government, and by other constituted authorities as the medium of arrangement with large bodies of workmen. The Social Democrats of Germany were stirring up the workmen of the country to undertake agitation for higher wages. In this latter endeavour the Social Democratic party were only too successful. Since the year 1878, when their efforts were being prosecuted with a considerable degree of vigour, there have been more strikes in Germany than there had been in any previous period. Most of the strikes were undertaken for the purpose of securing a higher rate of wages. Some, and one so recently as 1889, were occasioned by the introduction of labour saving machinery. Other strikes, again, were designed to bring about a reduction of the hours of labour. In the first and the third of these aims, the German workmen have certainly been highly successful; but this does not necessarily mean that wages would not have been advanced, or that the hours of labour would not have been reduced, without the lamentable strikes that have been resorted to in order to bring these results about.

The *grand seigneur* system of handling large bodies of workmen that still obtains in some parts of Germany is well illustrated by the following address which was issued to his workmen by the Fried Krupp, in 1872 :-

(Translation from the Royal (privileged) Berlin Gazette of June 27.)

" ESSEN, *June* 24.

"TO THE WORKMEN OF THE CAST-STEEL WORKS.

" Forty-five years ago I was one of the few workmen in the original ruins of these works my patrimony. The daily wages of smiths and puddlers had then been raised from 18 stuber to 7½ silver groschen (about 9d.), the entire weekly wages being 1 thaler 15 silver groschen (about 4s. 5½d.). For fifteen years I gained no more than enabled me to pay to the workmen their wages: for my own cares and labour I acquired nothing more than the consciousness of having done my duty. With the change of affairs in general, and the progressive success of these works, I gradually raised the wages, as an invariable rule, of my own will, never waiting to be asked for it. That rule shall always remain in force. One useful institution after another has been added, and many more are yet in abeyance. The utmost exertions have been made to forward the interest of the workmen, and their dwellings in progress may be counted by thousands. When all branches of industry were lying low, when orders were not forthcoming, I still worked on, and never dismissed one faithful servant. Many of an advanced age are here now who can prove this. Ask them what had been done for them in the year 1848. The recent sacrifices during the years of war are well known to you all. Who can count the loss caused by the present want of coal? Mutual confidence has made these works great. I know that I deserve and possess your confidence, and therefore I address these words to you.

"Before I have occasion to complain of infidelity and resistance, I warn you of the fate which periodicals and strolling agitators are endeavouring to prepare for the large working-class, making, under the mask of benevolence, use of religious and moral sentences. Their harvest begins after having irrevocably undermined the existence of your class. They work with all their influence for your entire destruction, so that they may then cast their nets in troubled waters. Ask after the antecedents of these apostles, ask after their domestic and moral life. To them the contributions of the workmen for disseminating verbal and written scandal are an easier and more pleasant method of gain than honest labour offers. The *Essen News*, amongst others, by inventions of all kinds, endeavours to throw discredit upon the character of the management of my works, and stated yesterday, as a means to disturbance, that the conference had been coerced to agree to a considerable advance of wages for one class of furnacemen. To these and similar broad lies of evil-disposed opponents I add the following warning. Nothing — no succession of events – will ever induce me to concede anything to force. The management, with the benevolence which has always been as law to them, will continue to conduct these works in the spirit of my principles, and so long on my part as by their enduring fidelity I shall consider the workmen as part of this establishment. There is certainly no doubt that any day I may transfer my position to others, and I am equally certain that no company of capitalists would excel me in benevolence or willingness to make sacrifices. Nobody will believe that thirst after gain induces me to undergo the trouble and labour with which the management of such a business on my own account is connected. Everybody knows how I have always valued labour and the labourer; but may everybody be also assured, that a misconception of my sentiments would be sure to root up this implanted love for both.

"May you all be convinced that I never waver in my resolves, and that, as I have always done, I do not promise without fulfilling what I say! I therefore again warn you against the inducements to disturbances of rest and peace. To every brave and orderly workman within the circle of my undertakings there is, after a moderate time of service, offered the opportunity to spend his service pension in his own house, in a manner not surpassed in any part of the world. I expect and demand full confidence; I refuse to enter upon any unjust demands; I will, as heretofore, anticipate all just ones: and I ask, therefore, all those who are not content with this to give in their notice; and the sooner the better, so that they may not receive notice from me. Let them leave this establishment in a lawful manner and make room for others, with the assurance that in my house and on my ground, I am, and will ever remain, master. ALFRED KRUPP."

In the history of German trade disputes, one of the most interesting was the general strike of German coal-miners which took place in 1889. The miners on that occasion demanded an advance of 15 per cent. in wages, an eight-hours shift from bank to bank, the filling of the waggons up to a certain line, and the rejection of not more than ten waggons in all for the whole number of men in each shift on the score of insufficient weight. The miners demanded further that the timber wanted should be delivered in the pit; that wages should be paid twice a month regularly on the 1st and 15th; that the fines imposed by the foreman should be limited to 25 pfennige (3d.), and that a record should be kept of all fines imposed. They also stipulated that no delegates or strikers should be victimised; that the workmen who had received their discharge-papers should be immediately reinstated ; that overtime shifts should be abolished ; that work should not begin on Sundays before 11 P.M.; that house coal should be supplied at cost price; and that oil, powder, and other necessaries should be supplied at cost price. On the 3rd of May, 5,000 miners went on strike ; by the 6th there were 30,000 more ; and on 11th May the total number of strikers in Westphalia alone exceeded 100,000. In Silesia, the strikers numbered 26,000 ; in Saxony, 5,000 ; and in the Saar district, over 13,000. Even collieries which had offered a liberal increase of wages were included, and very few of the pitmen in any district withstood the pressure brought to bear upon them to abandon work.*

Probably the most remarkable episode of this strike was the fact that it was brought to an end by the direct personal mediation of the Emperor, who took occasion to advise the adoption of some permanent method of arriving at a mutual understanding on disputed matters.

Germany appears to have been well advanced among the nations of Europe in making provision for the settlement of trade disputes at an early date. According to testimony collected for the Royal Commission on Labour,† it appears that special courts for the settlement of industrial disputes have in some form or other been provided for by the German law since the beginning of the century.

Councils for this purpose, on the French system known as the *Conseil des Prud'hommes*, were established on the left bank of the Rhine, under the Napoleonic Code, as far back as 1808, and the system was afterwards largely extended, even after the Rhine provinces had reverted to Prussia. These councils continue to carry on their useful functions until the present time.

Information communicated to the Royal Commission on Labour ‡ states that, in the amendment to the Industrial Code

---

* *Royal Commission on Labour: Foreign Report.*, vol. v., p. 32.
† *Ibid.*, vol. v., Germany.
‡ *Ibid.*, vol. v., Germany.

of 1881 concerning the guilds, provision was made for the establishment of courts of arbitration, for the settlement of disputes between members of the guild and their journeymen or apprentices; and a further amendment of 1887 extended the jurisdiction of these courts in some cases to non members. Further, the Insurance Laws of 1883 and 1884 provided for arbitration in disputes between employers and their workpeople with regard to the amount which the employers should contribute to the sick funds, or the compensation due under the Accident Insurance Law. On the whole, however, the State provision for arbitration and conciliation in Germany has proved ineffective, and the advocates of this method of settling industrial disputes have, ever since 1873, made repeated efforts to secure additional powers. Bills on the subject were introduced into the Reichstag in 1873, 1874, and 1878, but without success. In 1886 a resolution was passed "To request the Chancellor of the Empire to introduce a bill for the compulsory establishment of industrial courts, with the condition that the assessors in such courts shall be elected in equal numbers by employers and employed, separately, and by ballot." The insertion of the word "compulsory" was due in a great measure to the influence of the Socialist members, and it was omitted in the further resolution passed in 1889.*

The law, finally passed on 29th July 1890, which came into effect on 1st April 1891, holds to the old principle of leaving the institution of industrial courts in the main to the communal authorities. It differs from the sections of the Industrial Code, which it supplants, by including a series of provisions for the formation, under certain circumstances, of a board of conciliation. The preamble states, that "in many recent strikes it has been felt that, although both sides were ready to treat, negotiations could not be initiated without long

---

* Lexis, *Handwörterbuch der Staatswissenschaften*, vol. iii., p. 950, Art., "Gewerbegericht," Stieda. Stieda, *Das Gewerbegericht*, 1890, pp. 50-69. *Das Reichsgesetz betr. die Gewerbegerichte*, 1890, pp. 5-10.

delay, because no regular and authoritative body existed which could undertake the conduct of such negotiations. The present law attempts to establish a body of this kind, which may be able to facilitate the amicable settlement of differences between employers and employed on points concerning the labour contract, and so to obviate the heavy losses entailed on both parties by strikes, or to bring the latter to a speedy conclusion where they have actually broken out. It is hoped that the constitution of the industrial courts, which ensures special knowledge and unbiassed judgment, may command the confidence of both employers and employed."

The authorities of a commune, or of a number of communes combined, may establish such a court; should they prove remiss, the employers and workmen concerned may appeal to the Central Government to order the establishment of a court. All expenses not covered by fees, costs, and fines, must be met by the commune. The court consists of a president nominated by the communal authorities and approved by the Government, and at least two assessors; but whatever be the number, half must represent the employers and half the employed. They are elected by ballot, and must be over thirty years of age; neither paupers nor persons under any legal disability are eligible, and all persons elected must have resided or been employed for two years in the district. Women may neither vote nor be elected. The electorate includes all persons over twenty-five years of age, who possess the qualifications required for assessors. The assessors, who cannot refuse election, except for special reasons, are compensated for travelling expenses and for loss of time. The contending parties may not be represented by lawyers, or by persons who are professionally engaged in legal proceedings. The courts may take the evidence on oath both of the parties concerned and of witnesses or experts, if the matter in dispute exceeds the value of 100 marks (£5); and appeal may be made against the decision of the court to the regular courts of the district.

Any industrial court may convert itself into a board of conciliation when appealed to by both parties. In this case the president nominates four assessors, two from each side, and the parties are represented by a limited number of delegates, as a rule three from each side; each party may also elect further assessors, provided that equality of representation is preserved.

The decisions of the court, when acting as a board of conciliation, are not legally binding, and cannot be enforced; in other cases, the court notifies its decision to the parties concerned, who must declare within a given time whether they accept it or not. If the assessors cannot come to an agreement, the president may withhold his vote, and simply declare that no judgment can be given. In any case, the result of the negotiations must be public. The court must give its opinion on industrial questions when required to do so by the Government or the communal authorities, and it is empowered to make suggestions to these authorities on matters relating to the persons or establishments under its jurisdiction. The law recognises the existing rights of the guilds and their courts, but calls upon all other industrial courts to revise their constitution before 1st April 1892, and to remodel it in accordance with the existing law.*

So far, 179 courts have been formed in the six largest German States,—or 133 in Prussia, 13 in Bavaria, 13 in Saxony, 9 in Würtemberg, 7 in Baden, and 4 in Hesse. Alsace and Lorraine, in spite of their great industrial development, have as yet taken no advantage of the Act; and the fact that Saxony has no more courts than Bavaria, seems to show that there is no definite relation between the provision for arbitration and the probable need of it. East of the Elbe there are 81 courts, but excluding the Potsdam and Schleswig districts only 52. The official statistics for Würtemberg state that up to the end of 1892 one court, that at Geisslingen, had not yet taken any action. During 1892, the remaining eight courts considered 160 complaints brought by employers against their workpeople, and 1,320 complaints brought by workmen against their em-

---

* Lexis, *Handwörterbuch der Staatswissenschaften*, vol. iii., p. 950, Art., "Gewerbegericht," Stieda. *Das Reichsgesetz betr. die Gewerbegerichte*, 1890.

ployers. A judgment was given in 410 of the 1,480 cases, 711 were settled by compromise, 291 were withdrawn, and 68 were pending at the end of the year. Thus the cases settled by compromise amounted to about 50 per cent. of the whole, whilst those in which a judgment was given were only 25 per cent. A very large proportion of the cases were settled within a week.

In Berlin, the election of assessors only took place on 20th February 1893, although the law came into force on 1st February 1891. The Berlin court consists of 420 assessors, 210 from each side; and the statutes provide that the president, nominated by the magistrate, and confirmed by the lord-lieutenant (*Oberpräsident*), must summon two assessors to each meeting. These assessors should, as far as possible, according to the statutes, be persons of the same trade as the disputants, or of a cognate trade; but this agreement seems likely to lead to confusion and delay, since the number of cases considered in one day would involve either the summoning of a number of assessors, or the postponement of cases until there was enough in a given trade to occupy the court for one day. The method of electing assessors adopted in Berlin appears open to objection, and contrasts unfavourably with the simpler method in use at Frankfurt. Here each voter must merely prove his right to vote on the election day itself; whilst in Berlin, voters are required to register their names on lists in the various electoral districts before a given date.

In the mining districts, the expense of organising the industrial courts is borne by the State instead of by the communal authorities, in accordance with the section of the law which provides that "any division of the administrative districts for a special purpose must be carried out after a uniform plan by the central authorities (*Landesbehörden*) in place of the local authorities." On 1st April 1893, five courts were instituted for the mining districts, two of which were for Silesia, and one each for Westphalia, the Aix la Chapelle, and Saarbrück districts.*

* *Socialpolitisches Centralblatt*, vol. ii., 1892-93, pp. 207, 241, 288, 404.

The Industrial Code of 1869, which regulated the industries of the Empire, contained a section, since repealed by the Act of 1890, which enacted that "disputes between independent industrial employers and their workmen respecting the commencement, continuation, or termination of the labour contract, their mutual obligations under it, and the granting or contents of certificates, must be submitted to specially appointed authorities in so far as such exist. Where such authorities do not exist, the matter must come before the regular communal authorities, against whose decision an appeal can be made at law. By local statutory regulations, courts of arbitration may be instituted by the communal authorities for the settlement of such disputes, the members of these courts being chosen from among the employers and the employed in equal numbers."

In 1870, the Prussian Minister of Commerce addressed a circular letter to the provincial authorities, recommending them to give effect to this section by establishing courts of arbitration. In 1869 one court was established, in 1870 four; but whilst the numbers rose in 1871 and 1872 to 19 and 21, they fell again to 7 and 4 in 1873 and 1874. At the end of 1889 only 74 in all had been created, and of these only 14 were formed between 1880 and 1889. Even amongst those nominally created some were never definitely organised owing to lack of business; "and it is worthy of note, that whilst several cities of small importance instituted courts of arbitration, great cities in many cases did nothing in consequence of the difficulties which they experienced in electing members." Although the authors of section 108 of the Industrial Code had had in view the formation of courts, which should intervene in collective disputes, the statutes of most of the tribunals actually established only empowered them to deal with individual matters. Leipzig, Frankfurt, and Berlin were exceptions to the general rule; the statutes of these courts directed the tribunal "to intervene as a board of conciliation whenever a strike was threatened or had already been declared, or whenever difficulties arose with regard to proposed wages or other conditions of labour."

In Leipzig and Frankfurt this intervention could only take place on the request of both parties to the dispute; in Berlin, it was sufficient that one should request the services of the court. It does not, however, appear that any use was made of these powers, and no instance can be found of any strike which was settled by the arbitration of any State court.

It would appear that, alike in Germany and in Austria, the inspectors of factories are often called upon to act as mediators, and to offer judgment on disputed points. In one case an inspector reported that in the year 1889 he had given 635 written opinions on points connected with factory labour.

CHAPTER XX.

LABOUR DISPUTES IN FRANCE.

THE country that originated and carried into successful daily practice the admirable system of *Conseils des Prud'hommes*, may fairly claim to have taken an early and a prominent part in the establishment of the system of industrial conciliation. Nevertheless, France has not escaped the difficulties and dangers that accompany and result from industrial disputes on a large scale. As we have elsewhere shown, industrial questions of a general character, and affecting large areas of productive operations, are not affected by, nor meant to come within the cognizance of the *Prud'hommes* system; and that system, therefore, leaves the more serious phases of the industrial problem as far as ever from settlement.

This fact was realised at an early stage of the history of the councils of experts, and hence it came about that steps were taken to supplement their functions and complete their work by syndical chambers, which, however, are of comparatively recent date, and do not quite cover the same ground as a board of arbitration of the ordinarily industrial type

The syndical chambers are of two different classes—those established among employers as such, and those founded by workmen as such. In 1891, there were 1,212 of the former and 648 of the latter throughout France.

The employers' syndicates are generally of a commercial character, and are mainly concerned with the settlement of disputes between employers only. Some of the workmen's syndicates, however, do provide for conciliation in disputes of an industrial character, and others specify in their rules that no strike shall be declared before all means of conciliation have been exhausted, and that "every strike declared without the authority of the central committee shall be at the cost of the sectional committee." Some of the mixed syndicates have formed joint-committees for conciliation; and in other cases, the separate syndicates of employers and employed have come together, and have made the necessary arrangements for the conciliation of labour disputes.

This system was, however, at the best only partial and intermittent, and hence it was felt that a more comprehensive and complete system was required to deal with industrial disputes as they arose. Long *pourparlers* between employers and employed, and numerous discussions in the Chamber, ultimately evolved the new law of arbitration of 27th December 1892.

This law has been defined as attempting "a compromise between a purely voluntary or permissive measure and a measure worked by State initiative. It does not in the meantime at least organise permanent boards, but seeks to prevent industrial crises. It offers help, but does not impose it." *

The new law provides for both conciliation and arbitration. If when a dispute is threatened, or has actually taken place, the disputants do not attempt to settle it by conciliation, the local justice of the peace is required to "take every possible or prudent step to induce the parties to submit the case to the machinery offered by the law." That machinery is fully provided for "at the least possible effort and cost to the disputants." † The arbitration is organised by the magistrate after consultation has failed, but no provision is made for cases where arbitration is refused by one or both parties, or when either party repudiates an award. The *raison d'être* of the system and its intent is set forth in an official document, from which the following paragraphs are taken :—

"Attentive observers have not failed to recognise that the best means of avoiding and overcoming the irritation arising from these differences, which in many cases spring from the

---

* *Royal Commission on Labour, Foreign Report*, vol. vi., p. 51.
† *De la Conciliation et de l'Arbitrage*, p. 602.

most trivial causes, is to bring about more frequent meetings and wider exchanges of views between the men, who usually only fight because they lack the means of appreciating and rendering justice to their respective intentions.

"Experience has everywhere justified this view, under the inspiration of which private initiative has established in England, Belgium, and America, admirable institutions of conciliation and arbitration, which, putting the masters and workmen in the same factory or the same industry in permanent relations, permit them to look into and to quietly decide, as soon as they appear, their trade disputes, and finally unite the representatives of capital and labour in perfect agreement.

"The law of the 27th December 1892 has the same objects in view, and for the future it points out clearly the way by which they may be obtained. This hope will not appear chimerical, if it be observed that, far from manifesting any desire to artificially create a current of opinion, the new law is in direct harmony with old aspirations, which were clearly evidenced during the strikes of recent years

"The tendency to substitute argument and peaceful discussion for the abrupt cessation of labour, for strikes, in fact, has been observed several times in France ; on the other hand, several remarkable strikes have been fortunately terminated by conciliation and arbitration ; finally, nearly half of the workmen's unions, constituted in accordance with the law of 1884, have spontaneously imposed upon themselves, by their statutes, the obligation to only resort to a strike after having exhausted all the means of conciliation.

"The law of 27th December 1892 can only be put into motion by three classes of persons—masters, workmen, or, failing them, the justices of the peace ; but you will be able to contribute very materially to make it popular.

"Certainly, the arbitration organised by the law of 1892 is only optional ; it can be protested against or rejected quite independently ; the liberty of joint action or of resorting to strikes remains entirely without any restriction. But the free procedure instituted by the law is so simple, it is so adapted to receive an almost instantaneous application in all cases, in all places, and with the least possible disarrangement; it is so considerate of all susceptibilities and interests, that you should not hesitate to recommend it on every occasion.

"This procedure is suited, in fact, to the conflicts which extend to all the various branches of an industry which may be spread over several communes or confined to one district, as also to those persons who are only interested in a single workshop, a single factory, or a section of a factory; it applies equally to the differences which occur in temporary works with a temporary staff, such as certain agricultural works, and road-making; it may be offered to workmen who have already ceased labour, as well as to those who are resolved only to resort to strike after having exhausted all means of conciliation. The infringement, also, of the liberty of labour, of which certain strikers may be guilty, should not deter you from making every effort to bring the opposing parties to the consideration of the advantages of the law of the 27th December 1892."*

It is clear from these citations that the new law of arbitration in France is purely permissive and voluntary. The prefect has only to see that the method or system of mediation provided for is applied or put in the way of application. He presents, in point of fact, the neutral ground on which the parties interested may meet.† He is not called upon to give decisions on the conflicting claims before him; "and far from having a preponderant voice in the discussion, he has not even a deliberative voice. He can only preside if the interested parties express a desire for it."

Here, again, the influence of public opinion is relied upon to deal with "a strike without motive or an unjustifiable resistance to these councils for reconciliation and pacification."‡

The question of the prevention and settlement of strikes

---

* Circular addressed by the Minister for Commerce and Industry to the Prefects of France on the application of the new law of Conciliation and Arbitration.

† *Royal Commission on Labour: Foreign Report*, vol. vi., p. 52.

‡ *De la Conciliation et de l'Arbitrage*, p. 601.

has assumed much greater importance in France within the last few years than it had in any former period. The tendency has been for labour disputes to increase year by year; and the number that has occurred during the last five years is probably larger, at any rate from the point of view of their duration and extent, than in the previous twenty years, so that the means of dealing satisfactorily with such disputes became an increasingly urgent problem. Most of the recent strikes in France have been due either to demands for an increase of wages or to proposals for a reduction of wages. In the mining industry, eighty eight strikes are stated to have occurred since 1852, of which forty-six were caused by a demand for an increase of wages, and only five were against a reduction of wages.

In France, as in other countries, with or without resort to arbitration, the wages of operatives engaged in productive industry have advanced considerably within recent years. Ample statistics illustrative of the fact are to be found in my own papers, read before the Royal Statistical Society,* and in the Royal Commission (on Labour) Reports on France.†

* "On the Comparative Earnings and Efficiency of Labour in Different Countries," 1884; and "On the Recent Movement of Labour in Different Countries in Reference to Earnings," &c. 1892.

† *Foreign Reports*, vol. vi.

CHAPTER XXI.

LABOUR DISPUTES IN OTHER COUNTRIES.

THE great strike movements which have of late years been equally characteristic of Continental and English industries are of comparatively recent origin, mainly because of the labour laws that prevailed until recently. The report of the Trades Union Commission, which was published in 1869, showed that at that time there were no trade unions in Belgium, the law having prohibited coalitions between workmen with a view to increase wages under a penalty of one to three months' imprisonment, until a few years previously, and even up to a later date the law imposed penalties against attempts to fetter or control the liberty of others. In France, combinations to influence the rate of wages were also illegal up to a recent date, and even in 1869 meetings could not be held without the sanction of the Prefecture of Police. In the States of the Zollverein, trades unions were unknown until 1869, being against the law until 1867, when several clauses of the Industrial Code of 1845 were repealed, giving greater liberty to workmen to combine for certain purposes. As regards other European countries, the Trades Union Commission reported in 1869 that in Russia no combinations of workmen exist for the purpose of regulating the price of labour employed for mining or manufacturing purposes, and the same may be said with regard to the Netherlands. In Denmark, associations of workmen are formed, the sole object of which is to raise funds for the relief of sick and infirm members, and for the payment of the burial expenses of those who die, but strikes for higher wages are of very unusual occurrence. Strikes are contrary to law in Austria, and are immediately put a stop to by the police, the ringleaders being liable to imprisonment for a term of eight days to three months. The penal code of Italy enacted that any combination among employers to compel their workmen to accept a reduction of wages, or to receive commodities in whole or part payment, if such should be followed by some overt act in execution of it, shall be punished by imprisonment not exceeding one month, and a fine of not less than 100 or more than 3000 francs. Every combination amongst workmen for the purpose of suspending or impeding work, or increasing its costs without reasonable cause, shall be punished with three months' imprisonment whenever it has begun to be carried into effect. In both instances promoters are liable to six months' imprisonment.

In view of the several laws against combinations, it is clear that it was a dangerous thing in most Continental countries to attempt to force up the rate of wages by pressure of a physical kind. In some cases where strikes were attempted, as at Brunn in 1867, the ringleaders were arrested. The workmen of Italy were probably as free as any, and several strikes were carried out, which generally ended in a compromise. In France, workmen's societies became active about 1865-66, and in the five following years a number of minor strikes were engaged in, and usually to the advantage of the workmen, who had, however, a very low rate of wages, which would probably have been improved in any case by the course of economic events. In some cases, indeed, the workmen who came out on strike ran grave risks; and even so recently as October 1869, a number of workmen at the coal mines of Aubin, who had come out for a rise of wages, were killed in encounters with the authorities.

Belgium.—In the active and industrious little kingdom of Belgium we have an example of a condition of industrial life which is in some respects of a very low type. The workmen have, until lately, had but little education, they have been accustomed to work very long hours, to live in a penurious style, to earn exceptionally low wages, and to have but imperfect resources of organisation. The employers, on the other hand, have had to contend with great difficulties in building up their national industries. The mining resources of the country are really poor and meagre, although developed on a considerable scale. The coal deposits are difficult and expensive to work ; the iron ore deposits adapted for utilisation are almost exhausted, so that most of the ores used have to be imported from Germany, France, or Luxembourg ; and the country can hardly be said to be endowed with any compensating advantages in the shape of commanding shipping resources, great wealth, cheap money, or highly efficient skilled labour, such as England has long enjoyed. Belgium, indeed, has made such progress as it has succeeded in achieving, mainly in consequence of its cheap labour ; and the levelling up of the general conditions of that labour to the English standard, would be likely to mean the loss, more or less partial at any rate, of the manufacturing prestige of the country.

For this reason, although the general rate of wages has greatly improved within recent years, it is still relatively low ; and measured in terms of the product of mining and metallurgical industry *per capita*, is relatively less efficient than the labour of neighbouring countries. But of late years the workmen of Belgium have put forward claims to share in the general amelioration of the conditions of work and wages that were taking place in other countries. They have not been so successful as the workmen of either France or Germany, much less the working men of Great Britain. Recent official statistics show that only in the province of Liége have the hours of mining labour been brought anywhere near the level of the hours worked in the principal mining districts of the two adjoining countries. In all the other provinces the miners work ten hours a day from bank to bank, and they work these ten hours for less money than is paid for a shorter day in competing countries.*

Nevertheless, the working men of Belgium appear to have made very little effort to secure an improvement in their circumstances until a comparatively recent period, and it is only

---

* *Report of the Royal Labour Commission.*

within the last ten or twelve years that strikes have become specially numerous or important. Mainly in consequence of the increase of trade disputes, a Labour Commission was constituted by royal decree of 15th April 1886 The report of that commission is a storehouse of valuable information as to the history and conditions of Belgian industry. Since the commission reported, labour legislation has received a considerable impetus, mainly as a result of its recommendations. In 1887, a law was passed instituting councils of industry and labour; in 1889, another measure was legalised revising the law under which councils of experts were previously appointed on the lines of the *Prud'hommes* of France; and in 1889, legislation was adopted to regulate the labour of women, young persons, and children in factories, &c.

It will be seen, then, that even in Belgium the working classes appear to be realising a higher ideal of labour. But this has not been attained without a good deal of friction and conflict. Many causes have operated to increase these relations, in spite of ameliorative legislation. One cause is said to be the abolition of the old guilds, the members of which respected the rights of others, while themselves striving for the recognition of their own.* Other causes are perhaps more common to all industrial countries alike, such as the more general introduction of labour-saving machinery, the establishment of large factories and workshops which has done much to separate the individual employer from the individual workmen, and the necessities of economical production entailed by foreign competition.

Trade unionism is not so general among the industrial population of Belgium as it is in some other countries, and hence they are not, as a rule, so well organised for purposes of mutual action with or against employers as in some other countries. Even among miners, who have probably in Belgium, as in France and Germany, proved the most troublesome class of workmen to deal with, the general union or

---

* M. Prins' *Report on Trade Associations*.

federation has less than one-half the total number on its books.*

Although there are no official returns of the total number or the objects of strikes in Belgium of late years, the information collected for the Royal Commission on Labour † shows that the strikes were generally organised for the purposes of an increase of wages, a reduction of the hours of labour, the establishment of a minimum wage, or for the reinstatement of dismissed members of trade unions. One variety of the genus strike appears to be frequent in Belgium that is less known in other countries. It is stated that in May 1887, 30,000 miners went out on strike for purely political purposes, and that such strikes are now of frequent occurrence, although unknown previous to 1886.‡

Since the earlier part of the century, the French system of *Conseils des Prud'hommes* has been carried on more or less successfully in Belgium, and has apparently found plenty of work to do. During the last twenty years the lowest number of cases disposed of by these councils in any one year has been 2,761, and the highest number has been 5,078. Of late years the number of cases dealt with has shown a tendency to increase considerably. By far the largest number of these cases have been arranged by conciliation. Of the 5,078 cases dealt with in 1891, 3,250 were settled in this way, while 838 cases had to be referred to arbitration, 967 cases were left undecided by the action of the parties concerned, and 23 cases were left pending. Of the same grand total, 4,782 cases were disputes between employers and workmen, and 215 cases were differences between the workmen themselves. According to the special law of July 1889, following the recommendations of the Labour Commission already referred to, special councils for certain industries, or groups of industries, can be established

---

* The official statistics show that there were 110,000 men employed in and about coal mines in 1891, and that only about 50,000 were members of the miners' federation.

† *Royal Labour Commission: Foreign Reports*, vol. iv., p. 15.

‡ *Ibid.*, vol. iv., p. 15.

in the same district, provided that the industries are of sufficient importance, or special chambers can be established in one and the same council. The employers and the workmen each meet to elect their several representatives, and vote by ballot. Half of the representatives retire every three years, but may be re-elected. The president and vice president, one of whom must be an employer and the other a workman, are appointed by Royal decree from the members of the council, or from a double list of candidates chosen by employers and employed. Where several chambers are included in a council, they elect their own presidents and vice-presidents. Each council appoints from among its members a board of conciliation (*Bureau de conciliation*), composed of one employer and one workman. An election is held quarterly, when the same members can be re-elected. The board meets at least once a week, and considers all matters in dispute before they are brought before the council, to which they must be referred if the board fails to arrange them.

The council meets at least twice a month, and can only sit when an equal number of employers' and of workmen's representatives are present, two of each forming a quorum. These cannot include the president and vice-president, unless they were appointed from among the members of the council. If the council is unable to hold a session, owing to the absence of any member from two consecutive meetings, such member is summoned before the court of appeal in the district, and sentenced to a fine of from 26 to 200 francs, and from three to eight days' imprisonment, or to one only of these penalties. The councils deal with disputes between workpeople, or between employers and workpeople, arising in connection with labour and wages. Without prejudice to the proceedings before the ordinary tribunals, they may also punish breaches of contract, and conduct tending to a breach of the peace. The punishment in such cases may not exceed a fine of 25 francs, and an appeal may be made within eight days to the civil court of first instance in the district. Matters outside the jurisdiction of the councils, such as disputes between employers, may, with the consent of both parties, be brought before them. The *prud'hommes* pronounce judgment without appeal for sums not exceeding 200 francs; above that sum, appeal may be made to the tribunal of commerce, or, in matters relating to mines, to the civil tribunal of first instance. The clerk of the council gives one day's notice to the parties of the place, date, and hour, when they are bound to appear, together with their witnesses. Should either party fail to appear, judgment is given by default, but in certain cases the parties may be represented by proxy. No lawyers are employed.

The expenditure incurred is provided for by all the communes comprised in the council and districts, in proportion to the number of workmen employed in each commune.

An important strike of miners occurred at the Mariemont Collieries in 1875, which led M. Julien Weiler, the engineer, to take steps to establish chambers of explanations, which were really committees of conciliation, and which, after a considerable period, marked by great distrust on the part of the workmen, came to be established on a firm basis.

In January 1888 a council of conciliation and arbitration was instituted at both Mariemont and Bascoup for all classes of workmen employed there. The rules of the two councils are almost identical; each is composed of six representatives from among the staff (*agents gradés*), including the general manager, and six other members are appointed to act as deputies. The workmen's representatives are nominated by an electoral body of thirty-six delegates, appointed by a majority of the votes of the workmen employed at the various pits, which are classed in six groups for the election of delegates. Only those workmen can vote who are over twenty-one years of age, and have been employed for at least six months at the colliery. The delegates and the company's representatives must be over thirty years of age, and have been engaged at the colliery for at least five years. A board, consisting of the workmen's president and secretary, and an assessor chosen by the meeting, conducts the election of the workmen's representatives, who are elected from among the delegates by a majority of votes. The members of the council serve for two years; half retire annually, but may be re-elected. A president and vice-president are appointed annually, one president and one secretary being chosen from the workmen. Chambers of explanations, to elucidate technicalities, may, if necessary, be established in any branch of the industry. Where these chambers exist, all questions must be submitted to them before being referred to the council. If necessary, boards of conciliation (*Bureaux de conciliation*) are instituted to examine questions which concern one group only, and matters which they cannot decide are referred to the council.

The president convokes meetings of the council, at which two-thirds of the representatives of each side can form a quorum. Questions of general interest must be discussed by the whole of the representatives. The president has one vote only; in case of an equality of votes the question is referred to the management of the company. Prior to the examination of a disputed point, and during its discussion, work must be continued under the conditions which existed when the difficulty arose. Both parties agree to accept the council's decisions, which are valid for at least three months, and the same question cannot be revived within that period. All the expenses of the council are defrayed by the company. Each representative and delegate is allowed two francs for each meeting that he attends, and is indemnified for all time thus lost; the secretaries receive in addition an annual salary determined by the council.

In consequence of the riots which occurred in the spring of 1886, it was considered necessary to establish some institution by which differences arising between employers and employed might be amicably settled. On 29th October 1886 two schemes were submitted to the Labour Commission by MM. Brantz and Denis, the former for the establishment of councils of conciliation, the latter for the institution of elective bodies which should concern themselves both theoretically and practically with all labour interests, and which should establish councils of conciliation wherever and whenever necessary. On 5th May of the same year M. Frère-Orban had brought before the Chamber a Bill for the establishment of councils of industry and labour, which became law on 16th August 1887.

These councils are instituted to be "primarily administrative bodies, charged with the collection of statistical data bearing on the state of industry, price of food, rate of wages, averages of rents, both at home and abroad, and on all matters connected with trade and labour; and secondarily, consultative institutions, bringing masters and men together, in the absence of any industrial struggle, and before any contest should break out, to deliberate and pronounce an opinion on all matters affecting their common interests." In certain cases the Government is obliged to consult these councils. Thus they differ both from the councils of conciliation and arbitration, and from the councils of *prud'hommes*. The former are voluntary tribunals due to private initiative, and their action is restricted to the amicable arrangements of industrial disputes. No general rules exist as to their electorate or mode of procedure. The main differences between the councils of industry and labour and the councils of *prud'hommes* are, that the latter consider questions arising out of a violation of contracts, and their deliberations and decisions are based on these contracts. They cannot compel an employer to pay a higher wage than that which he had undertaken to pay, or to decrease the hours of labour, if a given number of hours were explicitly or tacitly agreed to beforehand. The councils of industry and labour, on the other hand, deal with questions in which no contract is presupposed; their object is to induce the formation of new contracts on the best possible terms. To this end, it is necessary for them to be able to form an estimate of the state of the industry, the intensity of competition, the customs of the locality, and all other matters affecting industrial production. Again, the decisions of the *prud'hommes* are binding; whereas the opinions expressed by the councils of industry and labour may be accepted or not, at the discretion of the parties concerned.

The law of 16th August 1887, instituting the councils of industry and labour, was largely based on the law of 1859, reconstructing the councils of *prud'hommes*. Considerable difficulties arose as to the interpretation of articles 4 and 5, respecting the election of candidates, which referred to the analogous clauses in the law of 1859. The Royal decree of 31st July 1888, explaining the means of enforcing the law of 1887, was also necessarily based on the law respecting *prud'hommes*, the revision of which was already under discussion. On the publication of the law of 31st July 1889 concerning councils of *prud'hommes*, it was found necessary to make important modifications in the law constituting the councils of industry and labour; and a Royal decree was published on 15th August of the same year, by which the education test, and residence in the district of the council, are no longer required from electors.

The councils are established by Royal decree, either spontaneously, or at the request of the communal council, or of employers or employed residing in the district. The extent of the councils, and the number and nature of their sections, are determined by the decree. Each council is divided into sections corresponding in number to that of the industries in the locality of sufficient importance for representation. From six to twelve representatives of employers and men are comprised in each section.

Switzerland.—According to the Foreign Reports of the Royal Labour Commission, in the case of trade disputes occurring in Switzerland, mediation, especially when undertaken by State officials (*Staatsmänner* and *Beamten*), or other persons of recognised standing, has proved increasingly successful of late years, and may probably be expected to extend its beneficial influences.

The association of employers and employed for the promotion of a common object is suggested by Herr Krebs as an excellent means of encouraging good relations and closer communications between capital and labour. Such objects may be found in the institution of technical schools, the examination of apprentices, the organisation of sick funds, and similar associations. The formation of courts of arbitration and conciliation on the English model is an idea which finds favour with both parties, and has been carried into effect in some instances, though in general neither employers nor employed are sufficiently well organised to make such boards a complete success.

Boards of conciliation and arbitration have already been instituted in connection with twenty-five trades unions, and in some cantons they have been established and supported by the cantonal governments.

The principal object of these boards is to draw up wages lists and workshops rules, which employers and employed both agree to observe. The unions in which they have been established have found them both active and efficient. The board of the Embroiderers' Federation considered 665 cases of disputes between October 1885 and March 1889, 554 of which it brought to a satisfactory conclusion. The cantons where they have been established are Geneva, Neuchatel, Vaud, and Urban Bâle.

The *Tribunaux d'Arbitrage Industriel*, which were instituted at Geneva in 1874, consisted of a justice of the peace as president, and two arbitrators, elected respectively by the employers and employed. These arbitrators acted from political motives, and hence the board proved a failure. They were consequently abolished in 1883 to make room for *Conseils de prud'hommes* on the French pattern. Disputes referred to these courts are first brought before the conciliation board, then before the board of arbitration, while a court of appeal gives the final decision as to all cases in which the damages are estimated at more than 500 francs. The judge and clerks are paid by the State, and the whole process is free both to employers and employed. Besides their judicial functions, the *prud'hommes* are authorised to superintend the training of apprentices, the sanitary condition of workshops, and to make recommendations to the Government for the advancement of trade and industry in the canton. They thus form a kind of chamber of commerce (*Gewerbekammer*).

A peculiar feature in the constitution of these boards is that counsel are not allowed to either side (*Advokaten sind ausgesch-*

lessen), but plaintiff and defendant are represented by members of the trade to which they belong. To facilitate this representation the *prud'hommes* are divided into ten trade groups, comprising (1) the watch industry, (2) jewellers, (3) building trades; (4) wood-workers; (5) metal workers; (6) clothing trades, (7) food and chemicals, (8) paper and printing, (9) transport, (10) banking and commerce.

In 1888, 753 cases were brought before the board of conciliation, 21 of which were withdrawn and 522 were settled; the remaining 210 were passed on to the board of arbitration, 203 of which were settled by it and 6 by the court of appeal. The total number of cases for the first three years amounted to 2,182; of which 1,995 concerned questions of wages and compensation, 113 were cases of dismissal, 12 were connected with men who had left work without warning, 55 with breach of apprentice rules, 5 with certificates (*Forderung eines zeugnisses*), and 2 with breach of contract. The disputes on wages questions thus form 91.3 per cent. of the total number; and the percentage of disputes settled by conciliation, which in 1885 amounted to 53.6, had risen in 1888 to 69.3. The beneficial results of the board are stated to meet with general recognition, and it is proposed to extend its competence to agriculture also.*

An Act conferring similar powers was passed at Neuchâtel in 1885, with this difference, that whereas the Geneva boards are compulsory, in the canton of Neuchâtel they are optional, and are only formed in places which obtain the necessary powers from the cantonal government. Each board consists of from sixteen to thirty sworn members, and the president, who is elected for six months, is alternately an employer and a workman. Each board has a court of conciliation and a court of arbitration. The officials of the board are elected and paid by the cantonal government. These boards possess the same administrative powers as those of Geneva. Chaux-de-Fonds is the only place which has hitherto availed itself of the powers conferred under this Act, but the court established there has

---

* *Royal Commission on Labour: Foreign Reports.*

become a fixed institution, and is now regarded as indispensable.

A law authorising voluntary boards of arbitration and conciliation was passed for Canton Vaud in 1888; and in the following year boards were established at Lausanne, Vivis, Yverdon, and Ste. Croix.

A compulsory board of conciliation and arbitration for Urban Bâle was established in 1889.

A voluntary board of conciliation and arbitration was instituted by the board of Zürich in 1889. A federation was first formed, consisting of the employers' associations and trades unions of Zürich and the neighbourhood. Its object was the prompt and gratuitous settlement of all disputes between employer and employed with regard to the hire of labour (*louage de service*); and secondly, the prevention or settlement by conciliation of all disputes as to the payment of wages, labour contracts, and questions of apprenticeship. The federation was joined by six trades unions and by the master builders' association. Each association on joining the federation undertakes to refer all its disputes to the federation board and to it only, and to recognise the binding character of its decisions. The federation is managed by a committee consisting of two delegates and two substitutes (*Stellvertretern*) from each trade belonging to the federation, and by a president and vice-president, who may not be either employer or employed. The committee has also a paid secretary, who has a consultative vote at its sittings.

The arbitration board is appointed by the employers and employed; it consists of two presidents, one elected by the masters and the other by the men, and of at least three arbitrators besides. Substitutes must also be appointed to take the place of the presidents in case of their unavoidable absence. The presidents exercise their functions alternately, and one arbitrator from each side is summoned for each sitting. The proceedings are public, and the parties appear before the board in person. As a rule each case is decided in one sitting. The board does not consider cases in which the damages amount to more than 380 francs, or any claims under the Employers' Liability Act. The parties pay no costs, except a fee to the secretary in case they require a certificated copy of the award.

The board of conciliation is formed of the entire committee of the federation. Disputes are laid before the committee by three delegates from each side. When the delegates have been heard the committee suggests an arrangement, which the president must recommend to their acceptance. If he fails, the board can send a deputation to the meetings of the associations of both parties to try and effect a settlement. If this second attempt fails, the president must at once call the board together and invite it to issue a sentence, to which both parties must absolutely commit themselves. While this award is being made, the delegates interested in the case must withdraw from the committee.

APPENDIX I.

Scale under Clause 10 of the Agreement of 1st January 1892, as approved and adopted by the Sliding-Scale Joint-Committee in the Coal Trade of South Wales, 6th February 1892.

When the average net selling price of Coal per ton, F.O.B., is	and under	Wages to be at the following percentage above the Standard.	When the average net selling price of Coal per Ton, F.O.B., is	and under	Wages to be at the following percentage above the Standard.
s. d.	s. d.		s. d.	s. d.	
7 10.25	8 0.00	Standard.	10 10.29	11 0.00	26¼
8 0.00	8 1.71	1¼	11 0.00	11 1.71	27½
8 1.71	8 3.43	2½	11 1.71	11 3.43	28¾
8 3.43	8 5.14	3¾	11 3.43	11 5.14	30
8 5.14	8 6.86	5	11 5.14	11 6.86	31¼
8 6.86	8 8.57	6¼	11 6.86	11 8.57	32½
8 8.57	8 10.29	7½	11 8.57	11 10.29	33¾
8 10.29	9 0.00	8¾	11 10.29	12 0.00	35
9 0.00	9 1.71	10	12 0.00	12 1.71	36¼
9 1.71	9 3.43	11¼	12 1.71	12 3.43	37½
9 3.43	9 5.14	12½	12 3.43	12 5.14	38¾
9 5.14	9 6.86	13¾	12 5.14	12 6.86	40
9 6.86	9 8.57	15	12 6.86	12 8.57	41¼
9 8.57	9 10.29	16¼	12 8.57	12 10.29	42½
9 10.29	10 0.00	17½	12 10.29	13 0.00	43¾
10 0.00	10 1.71	18¾	13 0.00	13 1.71	45
10 1.71	10 3.43	20	13 1.71	13 3.43	46¼
10 3.43	10 5.14	21¼	13 3.43	13 5.14	47½
10 5.14	10 6.86	22½	13 5.14	13 6.86	48¾
10 6.86	10 8.57	23¾	13 6.86	13 8.57	50
10 8.57	10 10.29	25	13 8.57	13 10.29	51¼
			13 10.29	14 0.00	52½

APPENDIX II.

AN ACT *to provide for the* AMICABLE ADJUSTMENT OF GRIEVANCES AND DISPUTES *that may arise between* EMPLOYERS AND EMPLOYÉS, *and to authorise the creation of a* STATE BOARD OF MEDIATION AND ARBITRATION.

(NEW YORK, LAWS OF 1887, CHAP. 63.)

THE People of the State of New York, represented in Senate and Assembly, do enact as follows:

SECTION 1. Whenever any grievance or dispute of any nature shall arise between any employer and his employés, it shall be lawful to submit the same in writing to a board of arbitrators for hearing and settlement. Said board shall consist of three persons. When the employés concerned are members in good standing of any labour organisation which is represented by one or more delegates in a central body, the said body shall have power to designate one of said arbitrators, and the employer shall have power to designate one other of said arbitrators, and the said two arbitrators shall designate a third person, as arbitrator, who shall be chairman of the board. In case the employés concerned in any grievance or dispute are members in good standing of a labour organisation which is not represented in a central body, then the organisation of which they are members shall have the power to select and designate one arbitrator for said board, and said board shall be organised as hereinbefore provided. And in case the employés concerned in any grievance or dispute are not members of any labour organisation, then a majority of said employés, at a meeting duly held for that purpose, shall designate one arbitrator for said board, and the said board shall be organised as hereinbefore provided. In all cases of arbitration the grievance or matter of dispute shall be succinctly and clearly stated in writing, signed by the parties to the arbitration or some duly authorised person on their behalf, and submitted to such board of arbitration.

SECTION 2. Each arbitrator so selected shall sign a consent to act as such, and shall take and subscribe an oath before an officer duly authorised to administer oaths, to faithfully and impartially discharge his duties as such arbitrator, which consent and oath may be filed in the office of the clerk of the county where such dispute arises. When the said board is ready for the transaction of business it shall select one of its number to act as secretary, and the parties to the dispute shall receive notice of a time and place of hearing. The chairman shall have power to administer oaths, and to issue subpœnas for the production of books and papers, and for the attendance of witnesses, to the same extent that such power is possessed by the court of record or the judges thereof in this State. The board may make and enforce the rules for its government and the transaction of the business before it, and fix its sessions and adjournment, and shall hear and examine such witnesses as may be brought before the board, and such other proof as may be given relative to the matter in dispute.

SECTION 3. After the matter has been fully heard, the said board, or a majority of its members, shall, within ten days, render a decision thereon, in writing, signed by them, giving such details as will clearly show the nature of the decision and the points disposed of. Such decision shall be a settlement of the matter referred to said arbitrators, unless an appeal is taken therefrom as is hereinafter provided. The decision shall be in duplicate, one copy of which shall be filed in the office of the clerk of the county, and the other transmitted to the secretary of the State Board of Mediation and Arbitration, hereinafter mentioned, together with the testimony taken before said board.

Section 4. When the said board shall have rendered its decision its power shall cease, unless there may be in existence at the time other similar grievances or disputes between the same classes of persons, and in such case such persons may submit their differences to the said board, which shall have power to act, and arbitrate and decide upon the same as fully as if said board was originally created for the settlement of such other difference or differences.

Section 5. Within three days after the passage of this Act, the governor shall, with the advice and consent of the Senate, appoint a State Board of Mediation and Arbitration, to consist of three competent persons, each of whom shall hold his office for the term of three years, to commence immediately upon the expiration of the term of office of the members of the present State Board of Arbitration, created under chapter four hundred and ten of the laws of eighteen hundred and eighty-six. One of said persons shall be selected from the party which at the last general election cast the greatest number of votes for governor of this State, and one of said persons shall be selected from the party which at the last general election cast the next greatest number of votes for governor of this State, and the other of said persons shall be selected from a *bona fide* labour organisation of this State. If any vacancy happens by resignation or otherwise, he shall in the same manner appoint an arbitrator for the residue of the term. If the Senate shall not be in session at the time any vacancy shall occur or exist, the governor shall appoint an arbitrator to fill the vacancy, subject to the approval of the Senate when convened. Said board shall have a clerk or secretary, who shall be appointed by the board, to serve three years, whose duty it shall be to keep a full and faithful record of the proceedings of the board, and also all documents and testimony forwarded by the local boards of arbitration, and perform such other duties as the said board may prescribe. He shall have power, under the direction of the board, to issue subpœnas, to administer oaths in all cases before said board, to call for and examine books, papers, and documents of any parties to the controversy, with the same authority to enforce their production as is possessed by the courts of record or the judges thereof in this State. Such arbitrators and clerk shall take and subscribe the constitutional oath of office, and be sworn to the due and faithful performance of the duties of their respective offices before entering upon the discharge of the same. An office shall be set apart in the Capitol by the person or persons having charge thereof, for the proper and convenient transaction of the business of said board.

SECTION 6. An appeal may be taken from the decision of any local board of arbitration, within ten days after the rendition and filing of such decision. It shall be the duty of said State Board of Mediation and Arbitration to hear and consider appeals from the decisions of local boards, and promptly to proceed to the investigation of such cases, and the decision of said board thereon shall be final and conclusive in the premises, upon both parties to the arbitration. Such decision shall be in writing, and a copy thereof shall be furnished to each party. Any two of the arbitrators shall constitute a quorum for the transaction of business, and may hold meetings at any time or place within the State. Examinations or investigations ordered by the board may be held and taken by and before any one of their number, if so directed. But the proceedings and decision of any single arbitrator shall not be deemed conclusive until approved by the board or a majority thereof. Each arbitrator shall have power to administer oaths.

SECTION 7. Whenever any grievance or dispute of any nature shall arise between any employer and his employés, it shall be lawful for the parties to submit the same directly to said State board in the first instance, in case such parties elect to do so, and shall jointly notify said board or its clerk, in writing, of such election. Whenever such notification to said board or its clerk is given, it shall be the duty of said board to proceed, with as little delay as possible, to the locality of such grievance or dispute, and inquire into the cause or causes of grievance or dispute. The parties to the grievance or dispute shall thereupon submit to said board, in writing, succinctly, clearly, and in detail, their grievances and complaints, and the cause or causes thereof, and severally agree, in writing, to submit to the decision of said board as to matters so submitted, and a promise or agreement to continue on in business or at work, without a lockout or strike, until the decision of said board, provided it shall be rendered within ten days after the completion of the investigation. The board shall thereupon proceed to fully investigate and inquire into the matters in controversy, and to take testimony, under oath, in relation thereto, and shall have power, by its chairman or clerk, to administer oaths, to issue subpœnas for the attendance of witnesses, the production of books and papers, to the same extent as such power is possessed by courts of record or the judges thereof in this State.

SECTION 8. After the matter has been fully heard, the said board, or a majority of its members, shall within ten days render a decision thereon in writing, signed by them or a majority of them, stating such details as will clearly show the nature of the decision and the points disposed of by them. The decision shall be in triplicate, one copy of which shall be filed by the clerk of the board in the clerk's office of the county where the controversy arose, and one copy shall be served on each of the parties to the controversy.

SECTION 9. Whenever a strike or lockout shall occur, or is seriously threatened in any part of the State, and shall come to the knowledge of the board, it shall be its duty, and it is hereby directed to proceed, as soon as practicable, to the locality of such strike or lockout, and put themselves in communication with the parties to the controversy, and endeavour by mediation to effect an amicable settlement of such controversy; and, if in their judgment it is deemed best, to inquire into the cause or causes of the controversy, and to that end the board is hereby authorised to subpœna witnesses, compel their attendance, and send for persons and papers, in like manner and with the same powers as it is authorised to do by section seven of this Act.

SECTION 10. The fees of witnesses shall be fifty cents for

each day's attendance, and four cents per mile travelled by the nearest route in getting to or returning from the place where attendance is required by the board. All subpœnas shall be signed by the secretary of the board, and may be served by any person of full age authorised by the board to serve the same.

SECTION 11. Said board shall make a yearly report to the legislature, and shall include therein such statements, facts, and explanations as will disclose the actual working of the board, and such suggestions as to legislation as may seem to them conducive to harmonising the relations of, and disputes between, employers and the wage-earning masses, and the improvement of the present system of production.

SECTION 12. Each arbitrator shall be entitled to an annual salary of three thousand dollars, payable in quarterly instalments from the treasury of the State. The clerk or secretary shall receive an annual salary of two thousand dollars, payable in like manner.

SECTION 13. Whenever the term "employer" or "employers" is used in this Act, it shall be held to include "firm," "joint-stock association," "company," or "corporation," as fully as if each of the last-named terms was expressed in each place.

SECTION 14. This Act shall take effect immediately.

APPENDIX III.

FRENCH LAW *providing for* CONCILIATION AND ARBITRATION *in cases of* COLLECTIVE DISPUTES *between* EMPLOYERS AND EMPLOYED (*27th December* 1892).

THE Senate and the Chamber of Deputies have adopted, the President of the Republic promulgates, the following law:

ARTICLE 1. Employers, workmen or employés, between whom a dispute of a collective character relating to conditions of employment has arisen, may submit the questions which divide them to a committee of conciliation, or, in default of an agreement of this committee, to a council of arbitration, and these shall be constituted in the following manner.

ARTICLE 2. The employers, workmen or employés, may, together or separately, in person or by proxy, address a declaration in writing to the justice of the peace (*juge de paix*) of the canton or one of the cantons in which the dispute has arisen, and shall contain—

1. The names, capacities, and domiciles of the applicants or their proxies.

2. The matter of dispute, with a succinct account of the motives pleaded by the other side (*partie*).

3. The names, capacities, and domiciles of the persons to whom the proposal of conciliation or arbitration should be notified.

4. The names, capacities, and domiciles of the delegates chosen from amongst those concerned by the applicants, in order to assist or represent them; the number of these delegates not exceeding five.

ARTICLE 3. The justice of the peace delivers acknowledgment of the receipt of this declaration, with indication of the date and hour of the deposit, within twenty-four hours, to the opposing party or its representatives, by letter, or, if need be, by notices posted on the gates of the courts of justice of the canton, and on those of the mayoralty of the commune in which the dispute has arisen.

ARTICLE 4. On receipt of this notification, or within three days, those concerned must send their reply to the justice of the peace. The period having passed, their silence is taken as a refusal.

If they accept, they give in their reply the names, capacities, and domiciles of the delegates chosen to assist or represent them, the number of these latter not exceeding five.

If the departure or absence of the persons to whom the proposal is notified, or the necessity of consulting the principals (*mandants*), partners, or an administrative council, does not permit of a reply within three days, the representatives of the said persons should within the three days declare what is the delay necessary for arrangement of a reply. This declaration is transmitted by the justice of the peace to the applicants within twenty-four hours.

ARTICLE 5. If the proposal is accepted, the justice of the peace urges (*invite d'urgence*) the parties or their delegates to form among them a committee of conciliation. The meetings take place in the presence of the justice of the peace, who may be appointed by the committee to preside at the debates.

ARTICLE 6. If an agreement is arrived at as to the conditions of conciliation, the conditions are set down in a report drawn up by the justice of the peace, and signed by the parties or their delegates.

ARTICLE 7. If an agreement is not arrived at, the justice of the peace invites the parties to appoint either one or more arbitrators each, or a common arbitrator.

If the arbitrators do not agree as to the solution of the dispute, they may choose a new arbitrator to act as umpire.

ARTICLE 8. If the arbitrators can neither decide on the

solution of the dispute, nor agree as to the new arbitrator, they must declare the fact in the report, and this arbitrator will be named by the president of the civil tribunal after inspection of the report, which shall be sent to him forthwith by the justice of the peace.

ARTICLE 9. The decision on the points at issue (*fond*) which has been arrived at, revised, and attested by the arbitrators, is sent to the justice of the peace.

ARTICLE 10. When a strike occurs in default of initiative on the part of those concerned in it, the justice of the peace, *ex officio*, and by the means indicated in Article 3, invites the employers, workmen, or employed, or their representatives, to make known to him within three days —

1. The matter of dispute with a succinct account of the alleged motives.

2. The acceptance or refusal of conciliation and arbitration.

3. The names, capacities, and domiciles of the delegates chosen, where the case occurs (*le cas échéant*), by the parties, the number of the persons chosen by each side not exceeding five.

The delay of three days may be increased for the reasons and under the conditions indicated in Article 4. If the proposal is accepted, it shall proceed conformably to Articles 5 and following.

ARTICLE 11. The reports and decisions mentioned in Articles 6, 8, and 9 above, are preserved in the minutes at the office of the justice of the peace, who sends a copy free of charge to each of the parties, and addresses another to the Minister of Commerce and Industry through the prefect.

ARTICLE 12. The demand for conciliation and arbitration, the refusal or failure to reply of the opposing party, the decision of the committee of conciliation or of the arbitrators notified by the justice of the peace to the mayor of each of the communes over which the dispute is spread, are made public by each of these mayors, who post them up in the place assigned to official notices.

The posting up of these decisions may be done by the

parties concerned. The notices are exempted from stamp duty.

ARTICLE 13. The premises necessary for the meetings of the committees of conciliation or councils of arbitration are provided, heated, and lighted by the communes in which they meet.

The expenses arising therefrom are included among the compulsory expenses of the communes.

The outlay of the committees of conciliation and arbitration shall be fixed by a notice of the prefect of the department, entered among the compulsory departmental expenses.

ARTICLE 14. All deeds executed in carrying out the present law are exempt from stamps, and registered gratis.

ARTICLE 15. The arbitrators and the delegates nominated under the present law must be French citizens.

In professions or trades where women are employed, they may be chosen as delegates on the condition that they are of French nationality.

ARTICLE 16. The present law applies to the colonies of Guadaloupe, Martinique, and the Réunion.

The present law deliberated and adopted by the Senate and the Chamber of Deputies, shall be carried out as a law of the State.

Executed at Paris, 27th December 1892.

CARNOT.

By the President of the Republic: the Minister of Commerce, of Industry, and the Colonies.

JULES SIEGFRIED.

Appendix IV.

Rules of the Board of Conciliation and Arbitration in the Staffordshire Potteries.

1. That this board be styled the " Board of Conciliation and Arbitration" for the Staffordshire china and earthenware manufacturers.

2. That the leading principle shall be the continuance of work at existing prices pending any dispute. The decision of the board or umpire to date backward to the time of the appeal being made.

3. The object of the board shall be to arbitrate on wages or any other matters affecting their respective interests that may be referred to it from time to time by the employers or operatives, and by conciliatory means to interpose its influence to prevent disputes and put an end to any that may arise. It is, however, understood and agreed that under these rules neither employers or operatives shall arbitrate on the following questions:—(1) Good from oven; (2) limitation of apprentices, except in the oven branch, and then only when a change is proposed to be made during the year at a manufactory in the proportion of apprentices to journeymen working together in a set; (3) alteration of trade rules.

4. That the board consist of ten employers and ten operatives, four of each to form a quorum; and first board shall hold their first meeting as soon as practicable after their appointment; the operatives to be elected by their own body, and the employers by their own body; the members of the board to

serve for one year, and to be eligible for re-election; the new board to be elected in the month of July in each year.

5. That the board shall, at its first meeting in each year, elect an umpire, president, and vice-president; also two secretaries, one for the employers and one for the operatives, who shall continue in office one year, and be eligible for re-election.

6. That the board shall meet for the transaction of business once a quarter, namely, the first Monday in the months of October, January, April, and July; but, on a requisition to the president, signed by three members of the board, specifying the nature of the business to be transacted, he, or in case of his absence the vice-president, shall, within seven days, convene a meeting of the board. The circular calling such meeting shall specify the nature of the business for consideration.

7. A reference to the board may be made by either party to any dispute, but the primary obligation to appeal to the board shall rest upon the party who wishes to alter existing arrangements, subject however to Rules 15 and 21.

8. That no employer or operative shall be entitled to appeal to the board (except with the consent of the board), unless he has been a subscriber from the commencement of the current year of subscription.

9. The parties to any dispute intended to be submitted to the board shall, if possible, agree to a joint written statement of their case; but if they cannot agree, a statement in writing on behalf of each party shall be made, and every such statement shall be sent to the secretaries at least two days prior to the board meeting. Each party shall have power to adduce oral evidence before the board.

10. The umpire shall preside at the sittings of the board when cases are referred to it for arbitration which concern the whole trade or affect the interest of a whole branch. The question in dispute shall be decided by the umpire, whose award shall be final and binding on each party.

11. That the president shall preside over such meetings of the board as are not convened for the purposes of arbitration, and in his absence the vice president. In the absence of both

president and vice president a chairman shall be elected by the majority present.

12. That when at any meeting of the board the number of employers and operatives is unequal, all shall have the right of fully entering into the discussion of any matter brought before them, but only an equal number of each shall vote. The withdrawal of the members of whichever body may be in excess to be by lot.

13. That the parties to any dispute which has been submitted to the board shall be bound by its decision.

14. That each party shall pay their own secretary and separate expenses, but the joint expenses of the board shall be borne equally by the employers and operatives.

15. A committee consisting of four, that is to say, two employers and two operatives, shall inquire into any dispute that may arise at any individual manufactory and that does not affect the interest of a whole branch, and such committee shall use its influence in the settlement of disputes, and have power to make an award. Before such committee shall commence to inquire into any dispute it shall appoint a referee, before whom the case shall be laid by such committee in the event of its being unable to adjust the business referred to it. The decision of the referee shall be accepted by both parties to the dispute. If such committee shall not be able to agree upon a referee the umpire of the board shall make the appointment, and the case shall proceed. Such committee, however, shall not deal with any question which cannot be dealt with under these rules.

16. That if any one or more of the board shall be immediately affected by the dispute, they shall not be appointed upon the committee referred to in Rule 15.

17. That the board shall recognise the trade rules set forth in the schedule as binding upon the parties to any dispute, and for the regulation of the trade.

18. That no alteration or addition be made to these rules, except at a quarterly meeting, or special meeting convened for the purpose. Notice of any proposed alteration shall be given in writing to the secretaries one month previous to such meet-

ing, and the secretaries shall give one week's notice thereof to each member of the board.

19. That it be an understanding, in connection with the proceedings of the board, that while the general wages question, as it relates to the condition of the markets, shall be arbitrated upon (at Martinmas) as one case for all the trade, except ovenmen, each branch shall have a right at such arbitration to make special reference to any question or subject that especially concerns its interests or modes of working.

20. That when a general arbitration shall take place involving a reduction or increase of wages, the case in respect of all branches, except ovenmen, shall be dealt with as one ; and when the umpire has finished the hearing of such case, he shall then consider the case of the ovenmen, and give to them a separate award.

21. When there is no general arbitration at Martinmas affecting the interests of the whole trade, any two branches, but not more, may make a separate and special appeal to the board for change in prices on any special ground that may seem to them to justify such a change, and in like manner the employers shall be at liberty to claim an arbitration in case of there being a dispute with any two branches. Any dispute affecting more than two branches shall be dealt with as a subject for general arbitration.

22. That the umpire shall have full opportunity to verify any figures or statements made in evidence, providing that such verification be not allowed to interfere with, or expose, the private business of any firm ; such verification shall be made through a sworn accountant, appointed by and responsible to the umpire, and shall be disclosed to no other person.

APPENDIX V.

A Scheme *for the* Establishment *of a* System of Boards of Arbitration, *submitted by* Mr W. J. Parry (*Chairman of the Joint Standing Committee of the Carnarvonshire County Council, and largely interested in the Welsh Slate Industry*), *advocating the establishment of* State Boards of Arbitration (*submitted to the Royal Commission on Labour*).

I. That this country should be divided into six trade arbitration courts:—
    (*a.*) Middlesex, Surrey, Sussex, and Kent.
    (*b.*) Shropshire, Staffordshire, Leicestershire, Rutlandshire, Northamptonshire, Cambridgeshire, Norfolk, and the remaining counties in the South of England.
    (*c.*) The English counties to the north of those named in (*b*).
    (*d.*) Scotland.
    (*e.*) Ireland.
    (*f.*) Wales and Monmouthshire.

II. That a court should be established in each of these divisions, consisting of two judges or arbitrators, one to be appointed from a class representing the employers of labour, and the other from a class representing the wage-earners. Both were to be permanent officials, and paid by the Government.

III. That in every case of dispute, after the demands of the aggrieved party had been rejected by the other side, and within a stated number of days, either party could give notice to the court to investigate the causes of the dispute, with full powers to decide the same.

IV. That the court should consist of such two judges, and that the judge of the county court within whose jurisdiction the dispute arose, or the judge of any other county court, or of the High Court, selected by the Home Secretary, should act as umpire.

V. That the costs of the investigation should be borne by the rates of the county in which the disputes arose, except in cases where one of the parties declined to abide by the decision of the court, when that court should have power to charge such party with all the costs.

Mr Parry added that the men in the North Wales slate quarries had repeatedly passed resolutions in favour of the Government establishing boards of arbitration. These boards should be constituted by the State rather than by a mutual agreement, both because it seemed impossible for employers and employed to agree upon their composition, and also because State boards could be invested with stronger powers. Their decisions might carry equal authority with judicial Orders of Court.

APPENDIX VI.

Mr Mundella's BILL TO MAKE BETTER PROVISION FOR THE SETTLEMENT OF LABOUR DISPUTES (*29th March 1894*).

BE it enacted by the Queen's most Excellent Majesty, by and with the advice and consent of the Lords Spiritual and Temporal, and Commons, in this present Parliament assembled, and by the authority of the same, as follows :—

I. Where a difference exists or is apprehended between an employer, or any class of employers, and workmen, or between different classes of workmen, the Board of Trade may, if they think fit, exercise all or any of the following powers, namely,—

(*a*.) Inquire into the causes and circumstances of the difference, and make such report, if any, thereon as appears to the Board expedient ; and

(*b*.) Invite the parties to the difference to meet together, by themselves or their representatives, under the presidency of a chairman mutually agreed upon or nominated by the Board of Trade or by some other person or body, with a view to the amicable settlement of the difference.

II. (1.) In the case of any difference to which the foregoing section applies, the Board of Trade may, on the application of any of the employers or workmen interested, and if the Board, after taking into consideration the circumstances of the case and the means available for conciliation in the district or the trade, are of opinion that the circumstances are such as to justify them in proceeding under this section, appoint a person or persons to act as conciliator or as a board of conciliation, and the person or persons so appointed shall inquire into the causes and circumstances of the difference by communication with the parties and otherwise, and shall endeavour to bring about a settlement of the difference.

(2.) If it is agreed or arranged to refer any question arising out of or incidental to any such difference to a person appointed by the Board of Trade or to two or more persons, of whom one is to be appointed by the Board of Trade, the Board of Trade may, if they think fit, make an appointment accordingly.

III. If it appears to the Board of Trade that in any district or trade where disputes are of frequent occurrence adequate means do not exist for having disputes submitted to a board of conciliation for the district or trade, they may appoint any person or persons to inquire into the conditions of the district or trade, and to confer with employers and employed with the view of establishing a local board of conciliation or arbitration composed of representatives of employers and employed.

IV. The Board of Trade shall keep a register of boards of conciliation and arbitration, and shall enter therein such particulars with respect thereto as to the Board may seem expedient.

V. The Board of Trade shall present to Parliament annually a report of their proceedings under this Act.

VI. This Act may be cited as the Conciliation Act, 1894.

INDEX.

Acts of Parliament, 5 Geo. III., 23rd May 1775, 56; of 7th June 1842, 56; of 1843, 57; Coal Mines Regulation Act of 1872, 60.
Appendices: Sliding scale in South Wales Coal Industry, 173; Act creating State Board for New York, 174; French Law of 1892, 180; Rules of Board of Conciliation in Potteries, 184; W. J. Parry's Proposals, 188; Mr Mundella's Conciliation (Labour Disputes) Bill, 190.
Arbitration, definition of, 31.
Attempts at solution of labour problem, 19.
Attitude of employers, 109; of workmen, 115.
Arbitration boards, effect of, on rate of wages, 37.
Arbitration v. sliding-scales, 41.
— law of 1892, in France, 155. See under heads of Germany, France, &c.
— required to determine a fair day's wage, 43.
— cannot always determine the rate of wages, 47.
— in Staffordshire industries, 81; in North of England industries, 87, 90.
Association of coal-owners in South Wales, 73.
Awards, Sir R. Kettle on the legal execution of, 37; in finished iron trade, 93; of Thos. Hughes, 94; acceptance of, 97.

Basis of sliding-scales, 78.
Blast furnacemen, wages of, 77; labour, conditions of, 80.
Bedworth collieries scale, 66.
Belgium, condition of workmen in, 160; rate of wages paid, 161; hours of work, 161; trade unionism in, 162; strikes, 163; *Conseils des Prud'hommes*, 163; council of conciliation, 165; riots, 166; councils of industry, 167. See Conciliation and Arbitration.

Bessemer converters, 14.
Board of arbitration in North of England iron trade, 96.
Board of conciliation in Belgium, 164.
Brassey, Lord, on co-operative production, 4.
Briggs, Messrs, industrial partnership scheme of, 7.
British iron smelters, 105.
Burnett, John, xii.
Building trade of Wolverhampton, conciliation in, 24.
Burt, Thomas, xii.

Carpet trade of Durham, conciliation in, 22.
Cannock Chase collieries, sliding-scales in the, 66.
Capital, protection of, 17.
Chain, nail, bolt, and lock makers, conciliation, 103.
Chamberlain, J., on sliding-scales, 83.
Charter of working-classes, 1, 9.
Cleveland iron industry, 79.
Coal industry, sliding-scales in the, 62, 84.
Coal-mines Regulation Act of 1892, effects of, 60.
Coal-owners, control of national destinies by, 9.
Coal-mining industry as it was, 55.
Collectivism, 12.
Commercial supremacy, backbone of, v.
Colliers, social condition of, in 1775, 56.
Condition of England question, v.
Committees, standing, 97.
Compulsory arbitration, 124.
Co-operative production, 4, 5.
Conciliation (Trade Disputes) Bill, Mr Mundella's, 126.
Conciliation in Durham carpet trade, 22; in Macclesfield silk trade, 23; in printing trade, 23; in Nottingham hosiery and lace trades, 24; in Wolverhampton building trades, 24; in North of England iron trade, 24; in other industries, 103.

Conciliation distinguished from arbitration, 27, 28.
Conseils des Prud'hommes, viii.; in Germany, 147; in France, 154; in Belgium, 162.
Cotton factories, development of, 14.
Council of conciliation in Belgian mining industry, 165.
Crompton on conciliation in Macclesfield silk trade, 23.
Cumberland collieries, sliding-scale in the, 68.
Cutlery trade of Sheffield, 105.

Dale, David, xii.; recommendation of conciliation by, 88; presentation to, 120.
Demarcation differences, 108.
Difficulties attending early boards of arbitration, 38.
Durham coal industry, sliding-scales in, 63.

Employers of old school, 10; attitude of, 109.
Engineering trades, conciliation in, 30, 106.
Examination of employers' books, 40.
Extraneous circumstances affecting wages, 39.

Fair day's wage, Sir R. Kettle on, 44.
Fox, Head, & Co., industrial partnership scheme of, 7.
France, co-operative production in, 5.
French system of Conseils des Prud'hommes, viii.
France, labour disputes in, 154; Conseils de Prud'hommes, 154; arbitration law of 1892, 8, 155; advance of wages in, 158.
Frankenstein, a modern, 17.

Germany, labour disputes and their settlement in, 142: mediæval guilds, 142; social democrats, 143; Krupp's manifesto, 144; coal-miners' strike of 1889; special courts, 147; Conseils des Prud'hommes, 147; insurance laws of 1883-84, 148; industrial code, 148; Berlin court, 151; organisation of courts by the State, 151; progress of courts of arbitration, 152; inspectors of factories as mediators, 153.

Hartland's, Sir F. Dixon, Bill, 124
Henderson, William, conciliation introduced by, in carpet trade of Durham, 21.
Higgling of the market, 20.
History of arbitration, sliding-scales, &c. See under their headings Hosiery, and Lace Trades of Nottingham, conciliation in, 24.

Ignorance of workmen as affecting strikes, vii.
Industrial conciliation, 25; arbitration, 31; sliding-scales, 50.
Industrial partnership, 6.
Iron trade of North of England, conciliation in, 24, 87; of South Staffordshire, 80.

Kettle, Sir Rupert, xii., on functions of boards of arbitration, 31; on a fair day's wage, 44; awards in finished iron industry, 93.

Labour Commission, recommendations of, 126.
Laws against combination, 1; on Continent, 160.
Legal execution of awards, Sir R. Kettle on, 37.
Legislation and pending proposals, 123.
Limitation of number of unions, 37.
Lord St Leonards' Act, 123.
Lubbock's, Sir John, Bill, 123.

Macclesfield, conciliation in silk trade of, 23.
Martineau, Sir Thomas, and Midland sliding-scales, 82.
Matters proper for arbitration, 43.
M'Cosh, A. K., evidence of, cited, viii.
Migration of labour, 47.
Mill, John Stuart, on wages and labour, 2.
Miners, early grievances of, 58.
Mining industry of Belgium, conciliation in, 164. See Colliers, Pitmen.

Mundella, A. J., his plan of a "long jaw," 9; testimony of, 29; Bill to promote conciliation, 125.

Nail trade, conciliation in, 108.
Nihilism, 12.
"Nothing to arbitrate," 47.
Nottingham hosiery and lace trades, conciliation in, 24.
Northumberland coal industry, sliding-scales in the, 65.

Ocean collieries scale, 66.
Origin of *Conseils des Prud'hommes*, 20, 21.
Ouseburn engine works, industrial partnership at, 8.
Overtime, 45; pending proposals and legislation, 123.

Pig-Iron industry, sliding-scales in the, 77.
Pitmen's union, the first, 58.
Prices as affecting wages, 39.
Printing trades, conciliation in, 23.
Problem of to-day, the, 13.
Public opinion, force of, 49.

Qualifications of an umpire or arbitrator, 34.

Rates paid for overtime, 45.
Realised selling prices, ascertainment of, 78.
Refusal to accept arbitration, 47.
Rules of Coal-owners' Association in South Wales, 73; of arbitration board in the finished iron industry of the North of England, 91.

Scotland, rapid fluctuations in miners' wages, viii.
— sliding-scale in coal industry, 66.
Shand, Lord, and the Midland miners, x.
Shipbuilding trade, 106.
Shorland collieries, co-operative partnership at, 8.
Sliding-scales, industrial, 50; definition of, 50; applied to puddlers and millmen, 51; to Scotch miners, 53; to pig-iron industry, 77; to Staffordshire coal and iron industries, 81; to North of England iron industry, 100.
— objections to, by workmen, 52, 54; functions of, 53.

Smith, Adam, on wages and labour, 2.
Socialism, 12.
Somerset collieries scale, 66.
South Wales coal trade, sliding-scales in the, 69, 71.
State boards of arbitration, 107, 188.
Strikes, first, in Durham coal industry, 58, 59; in South Wales coal industry, 70; remedy proposed for, 120; at Thornmount collieries, 165.
Standing committees, 97.
Steel Smelters' Amalgamated Association, 104.
Switzerland, mediation in trade disputes, 168; boards of conciliation, 169; *Tribunaux d'arbitrage industriel*, 169; trade groups, 170; cases dealt with, 170; cantonal boards, 171; arbitration board, 171; conciliation board, 172.

Tyndall, Professor, on national destinies, 9.
Trade union rules as to conciliation, 107; growth of, 1; in France and Zollverein States, 159; in Belgium, 162.

Umpire, choice of a, 33.
United States, co-operative production in, 5; conciliation and arbitration in, 131; strikes in, 132; losses by, 134; State boards, 135; Homestead strike, 139; sliding-scales, 140.
Unions, trade, required for arbitration purposes, 36.

Variations in wages and prices, 11.

Wages paid in different centres of engineering trade, 46; in Welsh coal trade, 74; in Durham, 60.
Watson, R. S., as an umpire, 35.
Wear shipbuilding trade, conciliation boards in, x.
West Cumberland pig-iron industry, sliding-scale in, 79.
Whitwell, William, xii.: on iron trade board, 96.
Wicks, J. D., on conciliation, xi.
Wright, Carroll D., on conciliation, xi.
Workmen, attitude of, 115.

7, STATIONERS' HALL COURT, LONDON, E.C.
May, 1894

A CATALOGUE OF BOOKS

INCLUDING NEW AND STANDARD WORKS IN
ENGINEERING: CIVIL, MECHANICAL, AND MARINE;
ELECTRICITY AND ELECTRICAL ENGINEERING;
MINING, METALLURGY; ARCHITECTURE,
BUILDING, INDUSTRIAL AND DECORATIVE ARTS;
SCIENCE, TRADE AND MANUFACTURES;
AGRICULTURE, FARMING, GARDENING;
AUCTIONEERING, VALUING AND ESTATE AGENCY;
LAW AND MISCELLANEOUS.

PUBLISHED BY

CROSBY LOCKWOOD & SON.

MECHANICAL ENGINEERING, etc.

D. K. Clark's Pocket-Book for Mechanical Engineers.
THE MECHANICAL ENGINEER'S POCKET-BOOK OF TABLES, FORMULÆ, RULES AND DATA. A Handy Book of References for Daily Use in Engineering Practice. By D. KINNEAR CLARK, M Inst.C.E., Author of "Railway Machinery," "Tramways," &c. Second Edition, Revised and Enlarged. Small 8vo, 700 pages, 9s. bound in flexible leather covers, with rounded corners and gilt edges.

SUMMARY OF CONTENTS.

MATHEMATICAL TABLES.—MEASUREMENT OF SURFACES AND SOLIDS.—ENGLISH WEIGHTS AND MEASURES.—FRENCH METRIC WEIGHTS AND MEASURES.—FOREIGN WEIGHTS AND MEASURES.—MONEYS.—SPECIFIC GRAVITY, WEIGHT AND VOLUME.—MANUFACTURED METALS.—STEEL PIPES.—BOLTS AND NUTS.—SUNDRY ARTICLES IN WROUGHT AND CAST IRON, COPPER, BRASS, LEAD, TIN, ZINC.—STRENGTH OF MATERIALS.—STRENGTH OF TIMBER.—STRENGTH OF CAST IRON.—STRENGTH OF WROUGHT IRON—STRENGTH OF STEEL.—TENSILE STRENGTH OF COPPER, LEAD, ETC.—RESISTANCE OF STONES AND OTHER BUILDING MATERIALS.—RIVETED JOINTS IN BOILER PLATES.—BOILER SHELLS.—WIRE ROPES AND HEMP ROPES.—CHAINS AND CHAIN CABLES.—FRAMING.—HARDNESS OF METALS, ALLOYS AND STONES.—LABOUR OF ANIMALS.—MECHANICAL PRINCIPLES.—GRAVITY AND FALL OF BODIES—ACCELERATING AND RETARDING FORCES.—MILL GEARING, SHAFTING, ETC.—TRANSMISSION OF MOTIVE POWER—HEAT.—COMBUSTION: FUELS.—WARMING, VENTILATION, COOKING STOVES.—STEAM.—STEAM ENGINES AND BOILERS.—RAILWAYS—TRAMWAYS - STEAM SHIPS.—PUMPING STEAM ENGINES AND PUMPS.—COAL GAS, GAS ENGINES ETC.—AIR IN MOTION.—COMPRESSED AIR.—HOT AIR ENGINES.—WATER POWER.—SPEED OF CUTTING TOOLS.—COLOURS.—ELECTRICAL ENGINEERING.

⁂ OPINIONS OF THE PRESS.

"Mr. Clark manifests what is an innate perception of what is likely to be useful in a pocket book, and he is really unrivalled in the art of condensation. Very frequently we halt at some treatment of the results obtained. There is a very restless effort visible, occupying five an last page, and there are tables given to meet late needs, where rules cannot be found other work, as, for example, that on page 4, for getting at the quantity of water in steam proceeding in any known weight of steam. It is very difficult to hit upon any mechanical process or anything concerning which the workshops have been informed on, and there are entirely absent from a title to its utility. In one word, it is an exceedingly handy and efficient help-meet for which the engineer will be well to buy a work to calculate, or at more wear, me but through the various text books and treatises at hand, as such, we can heartily recommend it to our readers who must often run away with the idea that Mr. Clark's Pocket-book is only the work in another form. On the contrary, each contains what is not to be found in the rest. Mr. Clark takes more room than ideal at more length with many subjects than Molesworth does." — *Lockwood*.

[faded text lines]

"In the back lof which the case seems to have nearly reached" — *Which We Know*

MR. HUTTON'S PRACTICAL HANDBOOKS.

Handbook for Works' Managers.

THE WORKS' MANAGER'S HANDBOOK OF MODERN RULES, TABLES, AND DATA For Engineers, Millwrights, and Boiler Makers; Tool Makers, Machinists, and Metal Workers; Iron and Brass Founders, &c. By W. S. HUTTON, Civil and Mechanical Engineer, Author of "The Practical Engineer's Handbook." Fourth Edition, carefully Revised and partly Re-written. In One handsome Volume, medium 8vo, price 15s. strongly bound.

☞ *The Author having compiled Rules and Data for his own use in a great variety of modern engineering work, and having found his notes extremely useful, decided to publish them—revised to date—believing that a practical work, suited to the* DAILY REQUIREMENTS OF MODERN ENGINEERS, *would be favourably received.*

In the Fourth Edition the First Section has been re-written and improved by the addition of numerous Illustrations and new matter relating to STEAM ENGINES *and* GAS ENGINES. *The Second Section has been enlarged and Illustrated, and throughout the book a great number of emendations and alterations have been made, with the object of rendering the book more generally useful.*

⁎⁎⁎ OPINIONS OF THE PRESS.

"The author treats every subject from the point of view of one who has collected workshop-notes for application in workshop practice, rather than from the theoretical or literary a'pe t. The volume contains a great deal of that kind of information which is gained only by practical experience, and is seldom written in books."—*Engineer.*

"The volume is an exceedingly useful one, brimful with engineers' notes, memoranda, and rules, and well worthy of being on every mechanical engineer's bookshelf."—*Mechanical World.*

"The information is precisely that likely to be required in practice. . . . The work for a desirable addition to the library not only of the works manager, but of anyone connected with general engineering."—*Mining Journal.*

"A formidable mass of facts and figures, readily accessible through an elaborate index . . . . Such a volume will be found absolutely necessary as a book of reference in all sorts of 'works' connected with the metal trades."—*Ryland's Iron Trades Circular.*

"Brimful of useful information, stated in a concise form, Mr. Hutton's books have met a pressing want among engineers. The book must prove extremely useful to every practical man possessing a copy."—*Practical Engineer.*

New Manual for Practical Engineers.

THE PRACTICAL ENGINEER'S HAND-BOOK. Comprising a Treatise on Modern Engines and Boilers: Marine, Locomotive and Stationary. And containing a large collection of Rules and Practical Data relating to recent Practice in Designing and Constructing all kinds of Engines, Boilers, and other Engineering work. The whole constituting a comprehensive Key to the Board of Trade and other Examinations for Certificates of Competency in Modern Mechanical Engineering. By WALTER S. HUTTON, Civil and Mechanical Engineer, Author of "The Works' Manager's Handbook for Engineers," &c. With upwards of 370 Illustrations. Fourth Edition, Revised, with Additions. Medium 8vo, nearly 500 pp., price 18s. Strongly bound.

☞ *This work is designed as a companion to the Author's* "WORKS' MANAGER'S HAND-BOOK." *It possesses many new and original features, and contains, like its predecessor, a quantity of matter not originally intended for publication, but collected by the author for his own use in the construction of a great variety of* MODERN ENGINEERING WORK.

The information is given in a condensed and concise form, and is illustrated by upwards of 370 Woodcuts; and comprises a quantity of tabulated matter of great value to all engaged in designing, constructing, or estimating for ENGINES, BOILERS, *and* OTHER ENGINEERING WORK.

⁎⁎⁎ OPINIONS OF THE PRESS.

"We have kept it at hand for several weeks, referring to it as occasion arose and we have not on a single occasion consulted its pages without finding the information of which we were in quest."—*Athenæum.*

"A thoroughly good practical handbook, which no engineer can go through without learning something that will be of service to him."—*Marine Engineer.*

"An excellent book of reference for engineers, and a valuable textbook for students of engineering."—*Scotsman.*

"This valuable manual embodies the results and experience of the leading authorities on mechanical engineering."—*Building News.*

"The author has collected together a surprising quantity of rules and practical data, and has shown much judgment in the selections he has made. . . . There is no doubt that this book is one of the most useful of its kind published, and will be a very popular compendium."—*Engineer.*

"A mass of information, set down in simple language, and in such a form that it can be easily referred to at any time. The matter is uniformly good and well chosen and is greatly elucidated by the illustrations. The book will find its way on to most engineers' shelves, where it will rank as one of the most useful books of reference."—*Practical Engineer.*

"Full of useful information and should be found on the office shelf of all practical engineers."—*English Mechanic.*

MR. HUTTON'S PRACTICAL HANDBOOKS—*continued.*

Practical Treatise on Modern Steam-Boilers.

STEAM-BOILER CONSTRUCTION. A Practical Handbook for Engineers, Boiler-Makers, and Steam Users. Containing a large Collection of Rules and Data relating to Recent Practice in the Design, Construction, and Working of all Kinds of Stationary, Locomotive, and Marine Steam-Boilers. By WALTER S. HUTTON, Civil and Mechanical Engineer, Author of "The Works' Manager's Handbook," "The Practical Engineer's Handbook," &c. With upwards of 300 Illustrations. Second Edition. Medium 8vo, 18s. cloth.

☞ *This work is issued in continuation of the Series of Handbooks written by the Author, viz:—"* THE WORKS' MANAGER'S HANDBOOK *' and "* THE PRACTICAL ENGINEER'S HANDBOOK," *which are so highly appreciated by Engineers for the practical nature of their information; and is consequently written in the same style as those works.*

The Author believes that the concentration, in a convenient form for easy reference, of such a large amount of thoroughly practical information on Steam-Boilers, will be of considerable service to those for whom it is intended, and he trusts the book may be deemed worthy of as favourable a reception as has been accorded to its predecessors.

*** OPINIONS OF THE PRESS.

"Every detail, both in boiler design and management, is clearly laid before the reader. The volume shows that boiler construction has been reduced to the condition of a science not established; and such a book is of the utmost value to the Architect Engineer and Works Manager."—*Marine Engineer.*

"There has long been room for a modern handbook on steam boilers; there is not that room now, because Mr. Hutton has filled it. It is a thoroughly practical work for those who are occupied in the construction, design, selection, or use of boilers."—*Engineer.*

"The book is of so important and complehensive a character that it is on its way into the libraries of every one interested in or having or holding men in his trust; they wish to be thoroughly informed. We strongly recommend the book for the intrinsic value of its contents.—*Machinery Market.*

"The value of this book can hardly be over-estimated. The other rise of firmly, &c., are all very fresh, and it is up to date to turn the work and not find what you want. No practical engineer should be without it."—*Colliery Guardian.*

Hutton's "Modernised Templeton."

THE PRACTICAL MECHANICS' WORKSHOP COMPANION. Comprising a great variety of the most useful Rules and Formulæ in Mechanical Science, with numerous Tables of Practical Data and Calculated Results for Facilitating Mechanical Operations. By WILLIAM TEMPLETON, Author of "The Engineer's Practical Assistant," &c. &c. Sixteenth Edition, Revised, Modernised, and considerably Enlarged by WALTER S. HUTTON, C.E., Author of "The Works' Manager's Handbook," "The Practical Engineer's Handbook," &c. Fcap. 8vo, nearly 500 pp., with 8 Plates and upwards of 250 Illustrative Diagrams, 6s., strongly bound for workshop or pocket wear and tear.

*** OPINIONS OF THE PRESS.

"In its modernised form Hutton's 'Templeton' should have a wide sale, for it contains much valuable information which the mechanic will often find of use, and in a few cases and notes which he might look for in vain in other works. This modernised edition will be appreciated by all who have learned to value the original editions of 'Templeton.'—*English Mechanic.*

"It has met with great success in the engineering workshop, as we can testify; and there are a great many men who, in a great measure, owe their rise in life to this little book."—*Building News.*

"This familiar text-book—well known to all the hands and engineers—is of essential service to the every-day requirements of engineers, millwrights, and the various trades connected with engineering and building. The new modernised edition is worth its weight in gold."—*Building News.* (Second Notice.)

"This well-known and largely used book contains information, brought up to date, of the sort so useful to the foreman and draughtsmen. So much fresh information has been introduced as to constitute it practically a new book. It will be largely used in the office and workshop."—*Mechanical World.*

"The publishers have issued in the task fresh in their hands the best possible editor in Mr. Hutton, than whom a more competent man they could hardly had."

Templeton's Engineer's and Machinist's Assistant.

THE ENGINEER'S, MILLWRIGHT'S, and MACHINIST'S PRACTICAL ASSISTANT. A collection of Useful Tables, Rules and Data. By WILLIAM TEMPLETON. 7th Edition, with Additions. 18mo, 2s. 6d. cloth.

*** OPINIONS OF THE PRESS.

"Occupies a foremost place among books of this kind. A more suitable present to an apprentice to any of the mechanical trades could not possibly be made."—*Building News.*

"A deservedly popular work. It should be in the drawer of every mechanic."—*English Mechanic.*

Foley's Office Reference Book for Mechanical Engineers.

THE MECHANICAL ENGINEER'S REFERENCE BOOK, for Machine and Boiler Construction. In Two Parts. Part I. GENERAL ENGINEERING DATA. Part II. BOILER CONSTRUCTION. With 51 Plates and numerous Illustrations. By NELSON FOLEY, M.I.N.A. Folio, £3 3s. half-bound.

SUMMARY OF CONTENTS.

PART I.

MEASURES.—CIRCUMFERENCES AND AREAS, &c., SQUARES, CUBES, FOURTH POWERS.—SQUARE AND CUBE ROOTS.—SURFACE OF TUBES—RECIPROCALS.—LOGARITHMS. — MENSURATION. — SPECIFIC GRAVITIES AND WEIGHTS.—WORK AND POWER.—HEAT.—COMBUSTION.—EXPANSION AND CONTRACTION.—EXPANSION OF GASES.—STEAM.—STATIC FORCES.—GRAVITATION AND ATTRACTION.—MOTION AND COMPUTATION OF RESULTING FORCES.—ACCUMULATED WORK.—CENTRE AND RADIUS OF GYRATION.—MOMENT OF INERTIA.—CENTRE OF OSCILLATION.—ELECTRICITY.—STRENGTH OF MATERIALS.—ELASTICITY. — TEST SHEETS OF METALS.—FRICTION. — TRANSMISSION OF POWER.—FLOW OF LIQUIDS.—FLOW OF GASES.—AIR PUMPS, SURFACE CONDENSERS, &c.—SPEED OF STEAMSHIPS—PROPELLERS — CUTTING TOOLS.—FLANGES. — COPPER SHEETS AND TUBES.—SCREWS, NUTS, BOLT HEADS, &c.—VARIOUS RECIPES AND MISCELLANEOUS MATTER.

WITH DIAGRAMS FOR VALVE-GEAR, BELTING AND ROPES, DISCHARGE AND SUCTION PIPES, SCREW PROPELLERS, AND COPPER PIPES.

PART II.

TREATING OF, POWER OF BOILERS.—USEFUL RATIOS.—NOTES ON CONSTRUCTION. — CYLINDRICAL BOILER SHELLS. — CIRCULAR FURNACES. — FLAT PLATES.—STAYS.—GIRDERS.—SCREWS. — HYDRAULIC TESTS. — RIVETING.—BOILER SETTING, CHIMNEYS, AND MOUNTINGS.—FUELS, &c.—EXAMPLES OF BOILERS AND SPEEDS OF STEAMSHIPS.—NOMINAL AND NORMAL HORSE POWER.

WITH DIAGRAMS FOR ALL BOILER CALCULATIONS AND DRAWINGS OF MANY VARIETIES OF BOILERS.

, OPINIONS OF THE PRESS.

"This appears to be a work for which there should be a large demand on the part of mechanical engineers. It is no easy matter to compile a book of this class, and the labour involved is enormous, particularly when—as the author informs us—the majority of the tables and diagrams have been specially prepared for the work. The diagrams are exceptionally well executed, and generally constructed on the method adopted in a previous work by the same author. . . . The tables are very numerous, and deal with a greater variety of subjects than will generally be found in a work of this kind; they have evidently been compiled with great care and are unusually complete. All the information given appears to be well up to date. . . . It would be quite impossible within the limits at our disposal to even enumerate all the subjects treated: it should, however, be mentioned that the author does not confine himself to a mere bald statement of formulæ and laws, but in very many instances shows succinctly how these are derived. . . . The latter part of the book is devoted to diagrams relating to Boiler Construction, and to nineteen beautifully-executed plates of working drawings of boilers and their details. As samples of how such drawings should be got out, they may be cordially recommended to the attention of all young, and even some elderly, engineers. . . . Altogether the book is one which every mechanical engineer may, with advantage to himself add to his library."—*Industries*.

"Mr. Foley is well fitted to compile such a work. . . . The diagrams are a great feat of the work. . . . Regarding the whole work, it may be very fairly stated that Mr. Foley has produced a volume which will undoubtedly fulfil the desire of the author and become indispensable to all mechanical engineers."—*Marine Engineer*.

"We have carefully examined this work, and pronounce it a most excellent reference book for the use of marine engineers."—*Journal of American Society of Naval Engineers*.

"A veritable monument of industry on the part of Mr. Foley, who has succeeded in producing what is simply invaluable to the engineering profession."—*Steamship*.

Coal and Speed Tables.

A POCKET BOOK OF COAL AND SPEED TABLES, for Engineers and Steam-users. By NELSON FOLEY, Author of "The Mechanical Engineer's Reference Book." Pocket-size, 3s. 6d. cloth.

"These tables are designed to meet the requirements of every-day use; they are of sufficient scope for most practical purposes, and may be commended to engineers and users of steam."—*Iron*.

"This pocket-book well merits the attention of the practical engineer. Mr. Foley has compiled a very useful set of tables, the information contained in which is frequently required by engineers, coal consumers and users of steam."—*Iron and Coal Trades Review*.

Steam Engine.

TEXT-BOOK ON THE STEAM ENGINE. With a Supplement on Gas Engines, and PART II. ON HEAT ENGINES. By T. M. GOODEVE, M.A., Barrister-at-Law, Professor of Mechanics at the Royal College of Science, London; Author of "The Principles of Mechanics," "The Elements of Mechanism," &c. Twelfth Edition, Enlarged. With numerous Illustrations. Crown 8vo, 6s. cloth.

"Professor Goodeve has given us a treatise on the steam engine which will bear comparison with anything written by Huxley or Maxwell, and we can award it no higher praise." — *Engineer.*
"Mr. Goodeve's text-book is a work of which every young engineer should possess himself." — *Mining Journal.*

Gas Engines.

ON GAS-ENGINES. With Appendix describing a Recent Engine with Tube Igniter. By T. M. GOODEVE M.A. Crown 8vo, 2s. 6d. cloth. [*Just published.*

"Like all Mr. Goodeve's writings, the present is no exception in point of general excellence. It is a valuable little volume." — *Mechanical World.*

Steam Engine Design.

A HANDBOOK ON THE STEAM ENGINE, with especial Reference to Small and Medium-sized Engines. For the Use of Engine-Makers, Mechanical Draughtmen, Engineering Students and Users of Steam Power. By HERMAN HAEDER, C.E. English Edition, Re-edited by the Author from the Second German Edition, and Translated, with considerable Additions and Alterations, by H. H. P. POWLES, A.M.I.C.E., M.I.M.L. With nearly 1,100 Illustrations. Crown 8vo, 9s. cloth.

"A perfect encyclopædia of the steam engine and its details, a book which no one keeps open that plans in English drawing-offices at work here." — *American Patentee.*
"This is an excellent book, and when I beg in the hands of all who are interested in the construction and design of medium size rotary engines... A careful study of this text and the arrangement of the sections leads to the conclusion that there is probably no other like it in this country. The volume aims at showing the results of practical experience and certainly may claim a complete achievement of this idea." — *Nature.*
"There can be no question as to its value. We today commend it to general notice design and construction of the steam engine." — *Mechanical World.*

Steam Boilers.

A TREATISE ON STEAM BOILERS: *Their Strength, Construction, and Economical Working.* By ROBERT WILSON, C.E. Fifth Edition. 12mo, 6s. cloth.

"The best treatise that has ever been published on steam boilers." — *Engineer.*
"The author shows himself perfect master of his subject, and we heartily recommend all employing steam power to possess themselves of the work." — *Ryland's Iron Trade Circular.*

Boiler Chimneys.

BOILER AND FACTORY CHIMNEYS; *Their Draught-Power and Stability.* With a Chapter on *Lightning Conductors.* By ROBERT WILSON, A.I.C.E., Author of "A Treatise on Steam Boilers," &c. Second Edition. Crown 8vo, 3s. 6d. cloth.

"A valuable contribution to the literature of scientific building." — *The Builder.*

Boiler Making.

THE BOILER-MAKER'S READY RECKONER & ASSISTANT. With Examples of Practical Geometry and Templating, for the Use of Platers, Smiths and Riveters. By JOHN COURTNEY, Edited by D. K. CLARK, M.I.C.E. Third Edition, 480 pp., with 140 Illusts. Fcap. 8vo, 7s. half-bound.

"No workman or apprentice should be without this book." — *Iron Trade Circular.*

Locomotive Engine Development.

THE LOCOMOTIVE ENGINE AND ITS DEVELOPMENT. A Popular Treatise on the Gradual Improvements made in Railway Engines between 1803 and 1893. By CLEMENT E. STRETTON, C.E., Author of "Safe Railway Working," &c. Second Edition, Revised and much Enlarged. With 95 Illustrations. Crown 8vo, 3s. 6d. cloth. [*Just published.*

"Students of railway history and all who are interested in the evolution of the modern locomotive will find much to attract and entertain in this volume." — *The Times.*
"The author of this work is well known to the railway world and no one is more thoroughly to a better knowledge of the history and development of the locomotive. The volume will be of value to all connected with the railway system of the country." — *Nature.*

Fire Engineering.

FIRES, FIRE-ENGINES, AND FIRE-BRIGADES. With a History of Fire Engines, their Construction, Use, and Management; Remarks on Fire-Proof Buildings, and the Preservation of Life from Fire; Statistics of the Fire Appliances in English Towns; Foreign Fire Systems Hints on Fire Brigades, &c. &c. By CHARLES F. T. YOUNG, C.E. With numerous Illustrations. 544 pp., demy 8vo, £1 4s. cloth.

"To the whole interested in the subject of fires and fire apparatus we most heartily commend the book. It is the only English work we now have upon the subject."—*Engineering.*
"It displays much evidence of careful research; and Mr. Young has put his facts neatly together. He has put together with the practical details of the construction of steam fire engines, old and new, all the common sense hints on the property they should possess, in a separate and full."—*Engineer.*

Estimating for Engineering Work, &c.

ENGINEERING ESTIMATES, COSTS AND ACCOUNTS: A Guide to Commercial Engineering. With numerous Examples of Estimates and Costs of Millwright Work, Miscellaneous Productions, Steam Engines and Steam Boilers; and a Section on the Preparation of Costs Accounts. By A GENERAL MANAGER. Demy 8vo, 12s. cloth.

"This is an excellent and very useful book, covering a subject matter on constant requisition in every factory and workshop. . . . The book is valuable, not only to the young engineer, but also to the estimate department of every works."—*Builder.*
"We accord the work unqualified praise. The information given in a plain, straightforward manner and the first rough evidence of it is the practical acquaintance of the author with every phase of commercial engineering."—*Mechanical World.*

Engineering Construction.

PATTERN-MAKING: A Practical Treatise, embracing the Main Types of Engineering Construction, and including Gearing, both Hand and Machine made, Engine Work, Sheaves and Pulleys, Pipes and Columns, Screws, Machine Parts, Pumps and Cocks, the Moulding of Patterns in Loam and Greensand, &c., together with the methods of Estimating the weight of Castings; to which is added an Appendix of Tables for Workshop Reference. By A FOREMAN PATTERN MAKER. Second Edition, thoroughly Revised and much Enlarged. With upwards of 450 Illustrations. Crown 8vo, 7s. 6d. cloth. [*Just published.*

"A well-written technical guide, evidently written by a man who understands and has practised what he has written about. . . . We confidently recommend it to engineering students, young journeymen, and others desirous of being initiated into the mysteries of pattern-making."—*Builder.*
"More than 470 illustrations help to explain the text, which is, however, always clear and explicit, thus rendering the work an excellent *vade mecum* for the apprentice who desires to become master of his trade."—*English Mechanic.*

Dictionary of Mechanical Engineering Terms.

LOCKWOOD'S DICTIONARY OF TERMS USED IN THE PRACTICE OF MECHANICAL ENGINEERING, embracing those current in the Drawing Office, Pattern Shop, Foundry, Fitting, Turning, Smith's and Boiler Shops, &c. &c. Comprising upwards of 6,000 Definitions. Edited by A FOREMAN PATTERN-MAKER, Author of "Pattern Making." Second Edition, Revised, with Additions. Crown 8vo, 7s. 6d. cloth.

"Just the sort of handy dictionary required by the various trades engaged in mechanical engineering. The practical engineering pupil will find the book of great value in his studies, and every foreman engineer and mechanic should have a copy."—*Building News.*
"Not merely a dictionary, but, to a certain extent, also a most valuable guide. It strikes us as a happy idea to combine with a definition of the phrase useful information on the subject of which it treats."—*Machinery Market.*

Mill Gearing.

TOOTHED GEARING: A Practical Handbook for Offices and Workshops. By A FOREMAN PATTERN MAKER, Author of "Pattern Making," "Lockwood's Dictionary of Mechanical Engineering Terms," &c. With 184 Illustrations. Crown 8vo, 6s. cloth. [*Just published.*

SUMMARY OF CONTENTS.

CHAP. I. PRINCIPLES.—II. FORMATION OF TOOTH PROFILES.—III. PROPORTIONS OF TEETH.—IV. METHODS OF MAKING TOOTH FORMS.—V. INVOLUTE TEETH.—VI. SOME SPECIAL TOOTH FORMS.—VII. BEVEL WHEELS. —VIII. SCREW GEARS.—IX. WORM GEARS.—X. HELICAL WHEELS.—XI. SKEW BEVELS.—XII. VARIABLE AND OTHER GEARS.—XIII. DIAMETRICAL PITCH.—XIV. THE ODONTOGRAPH.—XV. PATTERN GEARS.—XVI. MACHINE MOULDING GEARS.—XVII. MACHINE CUT GEARS.—XVIII. PROPORTION OF WHEELS.

"We must give the book our unqualified praise for its thoroughness of treatment, and we can heartily recommend it to all interested as the most practical book on the subject yet written.—*Mechanical World.*

Stone-working Machinery.

STONE-WORKING MACHINERY, and the Rapid and Economical Conversion of Stone. With Hints on the Arrangement and Management of Stone Works. By M. POWIS BALE, M.I.M.E. With Illusts. Crown 8vo, 9s.

"The book should be in the hands of every mason or student of stone-work."—*Colliery Guardian.*

"A capital handbook for all who manipulate stone for building or ornamental purposes."—*Machinery Market.*

Pump Construction and Management.

PUMPS AND PUMPING: A Handbook for Pump Users. Being Notes on Selection, Construction and Management. By M. POWIS BALE, M.I.M.E., Author of "Woodworking Machinery," "Saw Mills,' &c. Second Edition, Revised. Crown 8vo, 2s. 6d. cloth.

"The matter is set forth as concisely as possible. In fact, condensation rather than looseness has been the author's aim throughout; yet he does not seem to have omitted anything likely to be of use."—*Journal of Gas Lighting.*

"Thoroughly practical and clearly written."—*Glasgow Herald.*

Milling Machinery, etc.

MILLING MACHINES AND PROCESSES: A Practical Treatise on Shaping Metals by Rotary Cutters, including Information on Making and Grinding the Cutters. By PAUL N. HASLUCK, Author of "Lathework," "Handybooks for Handicrafts," &c. With upwards of 300 Engravings, including numerous Drawings by the Author. Large crown 8vo, 352 pages, 12s. 6d. cloth.

"A new departure in engineering literature.... We can recommend this work to all interested in milling..."—*Engineer.*

"A modern treatise... those who are already acquainted with the process..."

Turning.

LATHE-WORK: A Practical Treatise on the Tools, Appliances, and Processes employed in the Art of Turning. By PAUL N. HASLUCK. Fourth Edition, Revised and Enlarged. Cr. 8vo, 5s cloth.

"Written by a man who knows not only how work ought to be done, but who also knows how to do it, and how to convey his knowledge to others. To all turners this book would be valuable."—*Engineering.*

"We can safely recommend the work to young engineers. To the amateur it will simply be invaluable. To the student it will convey a great deal of useful information."—*Engineer.*

Screw-Cutting.

SCREW THREADS: And Methods of Producing Them. With Numerous Tables, and complete directions for using Screw-Cutting Lathes. By PAUL N. HASLUCK, Author of "Lathe-Work," &c. With Seventy four Illustrations. Third Edition, Revised and Enlarged. Waistcoat-pocket size, 1s. 6d. cloth.

"Full of useful information. Hints and practical criticism. Taps, dies and screwing tools generally are illustrated and their application defined."—*Mechanical World.*

"It is a complete compendium of all the latest of the screw cutting lathe; in fact a multum in parvo on all the subjects it treats of."—*Carpenter and Builder.*

Smith's Tables for Mechanics, etc.

TABLES, MEMORANDA, AND CALCULATED RESULTS, FOR MECHANICS, ENGINEERS, ARCHITECTS, BUILDERS, etc. Selected and Arranged by FRANCIS SMITH. Fifth Edition, thoroughly Revised and Enlarged, with a New Section of ELECTRICAL TABLES, FORMULÆ, and MEMORANDA. Waistcoat-pocket size, 1s. 6d. limp leather.

"It would, perhaps, be as difficult to make a small pocket-book selection of notes and formulæ to suit ALL engineers as it would be to make a universal medicine; but Mr. Smith's waistcoat-pocket collection may be looked upon as a successful attempt."—*Engineer.*

"The best example I have ever seen of 27 pages of useful matter packed into the dimensions of a card-case."—*Building News.* "A veritable pocket treasury of knowledge."—*Iron.*

French-English Glossary for Engineers, etc.

A POCKET GLOSSARY of TECHNICAL TERMS: ENGLISH-FRENCH, FRENCH-ENGLISH; with Tables suitable for the Architectural, Engineering, Manufacturing and Nautical Professions. By JOHN JAMES FLETCHER, Engineer and Surveyor. Second Edition, Revised and Enlarged, 200 pp. Waistcoat-pocket size, 1s. 6d. limp leather.

"It is a very great advantage for readers and correspondents in France and England to have so large a number of the words relating to engineering and manufactures collected in a lilliputian volume. The little book will be useful to the students and travellers."—*Architect.*

"The glossary of terms is very complete, and many of the tables are new and well arranged. We cordially commend the book."—*Mechanical World.*

Year Book of Engineering Formulæ, &c.

THE ENGINEER'S YEAR-BOOK FOR 1897. Comprising Formulæ, Rules, Tables, Data and Memoranda in Civil, Mechanical, Electrical, Marine and Mine Engineering. By H. R. KEMPE, A.M. Inst. C.E., M.I.E.E., Technical Officer of the Engineer-In-Chief's Office, General Post Office, London, Author of "A Handbook of Electrical Testing," "The Electrical Engineer's Pocket Book," &c. With 700 Illustrations, specially Engraved for the work. Crown 8vo, 600 pages, 8s. leather. *Just published.*

"Represent an enormous amount of work... indeed a kind of *cyclopædia.*"—*Engineer.*

"The book is distinctly in advance of most similar publications in this country."—*Engineering.*

"This valuable and well-designed book of reference merits the demand which it assuredly meets with amongst engineers."—*Saturday Review.*

"Teems with up-to-date information in every branch of engineering in a concise form."—*Building News.*

"The needs of the engineering profession could hardly be supplied in a more admirably complete and convenient form. To say that it meets in every respect parallel with predecessors of the highest sort, and that it may justly be said of it..."—*Mining Journal.*

"There is certainly room for the new comer, which supplies explanations and references as well as formulæ and tables. It deserves to become one of the most successful of the ever-multiplying annuals."—*Architect.*

"Brings together with great skill all the technical information which an engineer is at any time to refer to day by day. It is in every way admirably equipped, and sure to prove most useful."—*Ironmonger.*

"The up-to-dateness of Mr. Kempe's compilation is a quality that will not escape the notice of any people for whom the work is intended."—*Civil and Military Herald.*

Portable Engines.

THE PORTABLE ENGINE; ITS CONSTRUCTION AND MANAGEMENT. A Practical Manual for Owners and Users of Steam Engines generally. By WILLIAM DYSON WANSBROUGH. With 90 Illustrations. Crown 8vo, 3s. 6d. cloth.

"This is a work of value to those who use steam machinery. . . . Should be read by every one who has a steam engine, on a farm or elsewhere."—*Mark Lane Express.*

"We cordially commend this work to buyers and owners of steam engines, and to those who have to do with their construction or use."—*Timber Trades Journal.*

"Such a general knowledge of the steam engine as Mr. Wansbrough furnishes to the reader should be acquired by all intelligent owners and others who use the steam engine."—*Building News.*

"An excellent text-book of this useful form of engine. The Hints to Purchasers contain a good deal of commonsense and practical wisdom."—*English Mechanic.*

Iron and Steel.

"IRON AND STEEL": A Work for the Forge, Foundry, Factory, and Office. Containing ready, useful, and trustworthy Information for Ironmasters and their Stock-takers; Managers of Bar, Rail, Plate, and Sheet Rolling Mills; Iron and Metal Founders; Iron Ship and Bridge Builders; Mechanical, Mining, and Consulting Engineers; Architects, Contractors, Builders, and Professional Draughtsmen. By CHARLES HOARE, Author of "The Slide Rule," &c. Eighth Edition, Revised throughout and considerably Enlarged. 32mo, 6s. leather.

"For comprehensiveness the book has not its equal."—*Iron.*

"One of the best of the pocket books."—*English Mechanic.*

"We cordially recommend this book to those engaged in considering the details of all kinds of iron and steel works."—*Naval Science.*

Elementary Mechanics.

CONDENSED MECHANICS. A Selection of Formulæ, Rules, Tables, and Data for the Use of Engineering Students, Science Classes, &c. In Accordance with the Requirements of the Science and Art Department. By W. G. CRAWFORD HUGHES, A.M.I.C.E. Crown 8vo, 2s. 6d. cloth.

"The book is well fitted for those who are either confronted with practical problems in their work, or are preparing for examination and wish to refresh their knowledge by going through their formulæ again."—*Marine Engineer.*

"It is well arranged, and meets the wants of those for whom it is intended."—*Railway News.*

Steam.

THE SAFE USE OF STEAM. Containing Rules for Unprofessional Steam-users. By an ENGINEER. Sixth Edition. Sewed, 6d.

"If steam-users would but learn this little book by heart, boiler explosions would become sensations by their rarity."—*English Mechanic.*

Warming.

HEATING BY HOT WATER; with Information and Suggestions on the best Methods of Heating Public, Private and Horticultural Buildings. By WALTER JONES. Second Edition. With 96 Illustrations. Crown 8vo, 2s. 6d. net.

"We confidently recommend all interested in heating by hot water to secure a copy of this valuable little treatise."—*The Plumber and Decorator.*

THE POPULAR WORKS OF MICHAEL REYNOLDS
("THE ENGINE DRIVER'S FRIEND").

Locomotive-Engine Driving.

LOCOMOTIVE-ENGINE DRIVING: A Practical Manual for Engineers in charge of Locomotive Engines. By MICHAEL REYNOLDS, Member of the Society of Engineers, formerly Locomotive Inspector L. B. and S. C. R. Ninth Edition. Including a KEY TO THE LOCOMOTIVE ENGINE. With Illustrations and Portrait of Author. Crown 8vo, 4s. 6d. cloth.

"Mr. Reynolds has supplied a want, and has supplied it well. We can confidently recommend the book, not only to the practical driver, but to everyone who takes an interest in the performance of locomotive engines."—*The Engineer.*

"Mr. Reynolds has opened a new chapter in the literature of the day. This admirable practical treatise, of the practical utility of which we have to speak in terms of warm commendation."—*Athenæum.*

"Evidently the work of one who knows his subject thoroughly."—*Railway Service Gazette.*

"Were the cautions and rules given in the book to become part of the every-day working of our engine-drivers, we might have fewer distressing accidents to deplore."—*Scotsman.*

Stationary Engine Driving.

STATIONARY ENGINE DRIVING: A Practical Manual for Engineers in charge of Stationary Engines. By MICHAEL REYNOLDS. Fifth Edition, Enlarged. With Plates and Woodcuts. Crown 8vo, 4s. 6d. cloth.

"The author is thoroughly acquainted with his subjects, and his advice on the various points treated is clear and practical. . . . He has produced a manual which is an exceedingly useful one for the class for whom it is specially intended."—*Engineering.*

"Our author leaves no stone unturned. He is determined that his readers shall not only know something about the stationary engine, but all about it."—*Engineer.*

"An engineman who has mastered the contents of Mr. Reynolds's book will require but little actual experience with boilers and engines before he can be trusted to look after them."—*English Mechanic.*

The Engineer, Fireman, and Engine-Boy.

THE MODEL LOCOMOTIVE ENGINEER, FIREMAN, and ENGINE-BOY. Comprising a Historical Notice of the Pioneer Locomotive Engines and their Inventors. By MICHAEL REYNOLDS. With numerous Illustrations and a fine Portrait of George Stephenson. Crown 8vo, 4s. 6d. cloth.

"From the technical knowledge of the author it will appeal to the railway man of to-day more forcibly than anything written by Dr. Smiles. . . . The volume contains information of a technical kind, and facts that every driver should be familiar with."—*English Mechanic.*

"We should be glad to see this book in the possession of every one in the kingdom who has ever laid, or is to lay, hands on a locomotive engine."—*Iron.*

Continuous Railway Brakes.

CONTINUOUS RAILWAY BRAKES: A Practical Treatise on the several Systems in Use in the United Kingdom; their Construction and Performance. With copious Illustrations and numerous Tables. By MICHAEL REYNOLDS. Large crown 8vo, 9s. cloth.

"A popular explanation of the different brakes. It will be of great assistance in forming public opinion, and will be studied with benefit by those who take an interest in the brake."—*Engineer Mechanic.*

"Written with sufficient technical detail to enable the principle and relative connection of the various parts of each particular brake to be readily grasped."—*Mechanical World.*

Engine-Driving Life.

ENGINE-DRIVING LIFE: Stirring Adventures and Incidents in the Lives of Locomotive-Engine Drivers. By MICHAEL REYNOLDS. Third and Cheaper Edition. Crown 8vo, 1s. 6d. cloth. [*Just published.*

"From first to last perfectly fascinating. Wilkie Collins's most thrilling conceptions are thrown into the shade by true incidents, endless in their variety, related in every page."—*North British Mail.*

"Anyone who wishes to get a real insight into railway life cannot do better than read 'Engine-Driving Life' for himself; and if he once take it up he will find that the author's enthusiasm and real love of the engine-driving profession will carry him on till he has read every page."—*Saturday Review.*

Pocket Companion for Enginemen.

THE ENGINEMAN'S POCKET COMPANION AND PRACTICAL EDUCATOR FOR ENGINEMEN, BOILER ATTENDANTS, AND MECHANICS. By MICHAEL REYNOLDS. With Forty-five Illustrations and numerous Diagrams. Third Edition, Revised. Royal 18mo, 3s. 6d., strongly bound for pocket wear.

"This admirable work is well calculated to accomplish its object, being the honest workmanship of a competent engineer."—*Glasgow Herald.*

"A most meritorious work, giving in a succinct and practical form all the information an engine-minder desirous of mastering the scientific principles of his daily calling would require."—*The Miller.*

"A boon to those who are striving to become efficient mechanics."—*Daily Chronicle.*

CIVIL ENGINEERING, SURVEYING, etc.

MR. HUMBER'S VALUABLE ENGINEERING BOOKS.

The Water Supply of Cities and Towns.
A COMPREHENSIVE TREATISE on the WATER-SUPPLY OF CITIES AND TOWNS. By WILLIAM HUMBER, A.M.Inst.C.E., and M. Inst. M.E., Author of "Cast and Wrought Iron Bridge Construction," &c. &c. Illustrated with 50 Double Plates, 1 Single Plate, Coloured Frontispiece, and upwards of 250 Woodcuts, and containing 400 pages of Text. Imp. 4to, £6 6s. elegantly and substantially half-bound in morocco.

List of Contents.

I. Historical Sketch of some of the means that have been adopted for the Supply of Water to Cities and Towns. II. Water and the Foreign Matter usually associated with it. III. Rainfall and Evaporation.—IV. Springs and the water-bearing formations of various districts.—V. Measurement and Estimation of the flow of Water.—VI. On the Selection of the Source of Supply.—VII. Wells.—VIII. Reservoirs.—IX. The Purification of Water. X. Pumps.—XI. Pumping Machinery.—XII. Conduits.—XIII. Distribution of Water.—XIV. Meters, Service Pipes, and House Fittings.—XV. The Law and Economy of Water Works. XVI. Constant and Intermittent Supply.—XVII. Description of Plates.—Appendices, giving Tables of Rates of Supply, Velocities, &c., together with Specifications of several Works illustrated, among which will be found: Aberdeen, Hull, Ipswich, Canterbury, Dundee, Halifax, Lambeth, Rotherham, Dublin, and others.

"The most systematic and valuable work upon water supply hitherto produced in English, or any other language. . . . Mr. Humber's work is a painstaking and almost thorough-going one, and it is conscientiousness much more distinctive of French and German than of English technical treatises."—*Engineer.*

"We can congratulate Mr. Humber on having been able to give so large an amount of information on a subject so important as the water supply of cities and towns. The plates, fifty in number, are mostly drawings of executed works, and alone would have commanded the attention of every engineer whose practice may lie in this branch of the profession."—*Builder.*

Cast and Wrought Iron Bridge Construction.
A COMPLETE AND PRACTICAL TREATISE ON CAST AND WROUGHT IRON BRIDGE CONSTRUCTION, including Iron Foundations. In Three Parts—Theoretical, Practical, and Descriptive. By WILLIAM HUMBER, A.M.Inst.C.E., and M.Inst.M.E. Third Edition, Revised and much improved, with 115 Double Plates (20 of which now first appear in this edition), and numerous Additions to the Text. In Two Vols., imp. 4to, £6 16s. 6d. half-bound in morocco.

"A very valuable contribution to the standard literature of civil engineering. In addition to elevations, plans and I sections, large scale details are given which very much enhance the instructive worth of those illustrations."—*Civil Engineer and Architect's Journal.*

"Mr. Humber's stately volumes, lately issued—in which the most important bridges erected during the last five years, under the direction of the late Mr. Brunel, Sir W. Cubitt, Mr. Hawkshaw, Mr. Page, Mr. Fowler, Mr. Hemans, and others among our most eminent engineers, are drawn and specified in great detail."—*Engineer.*

Strains, Calculation of.
A HANDY BOOK FOR THE CALCULATION OF STRAINS IN GIRDERS AND SIMILAR STRUCTURES, AND THEIR STRENGTH. Consisting of Formulæ and Corresponding Diagrams, with numerous details for Practical Application, &c. By WILLIAM HUMBER, A.M.Inst.C.E., &c. Fifth Edition. Crown 8vo, nearly 100 Woodcuts and 3 Plates, 7s. 6d. cloth.

"The formulæ are neatly expressed, and the diagrams good."—*Athenæum.*

"We heartily commend this really handy book to our engineer and architect readers."—*English Mechanic.*

Barlow's Strength of Materials, enlarged by Humber.
A TREATISE ON THE STRENGTH OF MATERIALS; with Rules for Application in Architecture, the Construction of Suspension Bridges, Railways, &c. By PETER BARLOW, F.R.S. A New Edition, Revised by his Sons, P. W. BARLOW, F.R.S., and W. H. BARLOW, F.R.S.; to which are added, Experiments by HODGKINSON, FAIRBAIRN, and KIRKALDY; and Formulæ for Calculating Girders, &c. Arranged and Edited by WM. HUMBER, A.M.Inst.C.E. Demy 8vo, 400 pp., with 19 large Plates and numerous Woodcuts, 18s. cloth.

"Valuable alike to the student, tyro, and the experienced practitioner, it will always rank in future, as it has hitherto done, as the standard treatise on that particular subject."—*Engineer.*

"There is no greater authority than Barlow."—*Building News.*

"As a scientific work of the first class, it deserves a foremost place on the bookshelves of every civil engineer and practical mechanic."—*English Mechanic.*

CIVIL ENGINEERING, SURVEYING, etc.

MR. HUMBER'S GREAT WORK ON MODERN ENGINEERING.

Complete in Four Volumes, imperial 4to, price £12 12s., half-morocco. Each Volume sold separately as follows:—

A RECORD OF THE PROGRESS OF MODERN ENGINEERING. First Series. Comprising Civil, Mechanical, Marine, Hydraulic, Railway, Bridge, and other Engineering Works, &c. By WILLIAM HUMBER, A-M.Inst.C.E., &c. Imp. 4to, with 36 Double Plates, drawn to a large scale, Photographic Portrait of John Hawkshaw, C.E., F.R.S., &c., and copious descriptive Letterpress, Specifications, &c., £3 3s. half-morocco.

List of the Plates and Diagrams.

Victoria Station and Roof, L. B. & S. C. R. (8 plates); Southport Pier (2 plates); Victoria Station and Roof, L. C. & D. and G. W. R. (6 plates); Roof of Cremorne Music Hall; Bridge over G. N. Railway; Roof of Station, Dutch Rhenish Rail (2 plates); Bridge over the Thames, West London Extension Railway (5 plates); Armour Plates; Suspension Bridge, Thames (4 plates); The Avon Empire Suspension Bridge, Avon (3 plates); Underground Railway (3 plates).

"Handsomely lithographed and printed. It will be a favour with many who desire to preserve in a permanent form copies of the plans and specifications prepared for the guidance of the contractors for many important engineering works."—*Engineer.*

HUMBER'S PROGRESS OF MODERN ENGINEERING. Second Series. Imp. 4to, with 36 Double Plates, Photographic Portrait of Robert Stephenson, C.E., M.P., F.R.S., &c., and copious descriptive Letterpress, Specifications, &c., £3 3s. half-morocco.

List of the Plates and Diagrams.

Birkenhead Docks, Low Water Basin (15 plates); Charing Cross Station Roof, C. C. Railway (3 plates); Digswell Viaduct, Great Northern Railway; Robery Wood Viaduct, Great Northern Railway; Iron Permanent Way; Clydach Viaduct, Merthyr, Tredegar, and Abergavenny Railway; Ebbw Viaduct, Merthyr, Tredegar, and Abergavenny Railway; College Wood Viaduct, Cornwall Railway; Dublin Winter Palace Roof (3 plates); Bridge over the Thames, L. C. & D. Railway (6 plates); Albert Harbour, Greenock (4 plates).

"Mr. Humber has done the profession good and true service, by the fine selection of examples he has here brought before the profession and the public."—*Practical Mechanic's Journal.*

HUMBER'S PROGRESS OF MODERN ENGINEERING. Third Series. Imp. 4to, with 40 Double Plates, Photographic Portrait of J. R. M'Clean, late Pres. Inst. C.E., and copious descriptive Letterpress, Specifications, &c., £3 3s. half-morocco.

List of the Plates and Diagrams.

MAIN DRAINAGE, METROPOLIS.—*North Side.*—Map showing Interception of Sewers; Middle Level Sewer (2 plates); Outfall Sewer, Bridge over River Lea (3 plates); Outfall Sewer, Bridge over Marsh Lane, North Woolwich Railway, and Bow and Barking Railway Junction; Outfall Sewer, Bridge over Bow and Barking Railway (3 plates); Outfall Sewer, Bridge over East London Waterworks' Feeder (2 plates); Outfall Sewer, Reservoir (2 plates); Outfall Sewer, Tumbling Bay and Outlet; Outfall Sewer, Penstocks. *South Side.*—Outfall Sewer, Bermondsey Branch (2 plates); Outfall Sewer, Reservoir and Outlet (4 plates); Outfall Sewer, Filth Hoist, Sections of Sewers Shown at 15 with Scale.

THAMES EMBANKMENT.—Section of River Wall; Steamboat Pier, Westminster (2 plates); Landing Stairs between Charing Cross and Waterloo Bridges; York Gate (2 plates); Overflow and Outlet at Savoy Street Sewer (3 plates); Steamboat Pier, Waterloo Bridge (3 plates); Junction of Sewers, Plans and Sections; Gullies, Plans and Sections; Rolling Stock, Granite and Iron Forts.

"The drawings have a constantly increasing value, and whoever desires to possess clear representations of the two great works carried out by our Metropolitan Board will obtain Mr. Humber's volume."—*Engineer.*

HUMBER'S PROGRESS OF MODERN ENGINEERING. Fourth Series. Imp. 4to, with 36 Double Plates, Photographic Portrait of John Fowler, late Pres. Inst. C.E., and copious descriptive Letterpress, Specifications, &c., £3 3s. half-morocco.

List of the Plates and Diagrams.

Abbey Mills Pumping Station, Main Drainage, Metropolis (4 plates); Barrow Docks (5 plates); Manquis Viaduct, Santiago and Valparaiso Railway (2 plates); Adam's Locomotive, St. Helen's Canal Railway (2 plates); Cannon Street Station Roof, Charing Cross Railway (3 plates); Road Bridge over the River Moka (2 plates); Telegraphic Apparatus for Mesopotamia; Viaduct over the River Wye, Midland Railway (3 plates); St. Germans Viaduct, Cornwall Railway (2 plates); Wrought Iron Cylinder for Diving Bell; Millwall Docks (6 plates); Milroy's Patent Excavator; Metropolitan District Railway (6 plates); Harbours, Forts, and Breakwaters (3 plates).

"We gladly welcome another year's issue of this valuable publication from the able pen of Mr. Humber. The advantages and general excellence of this work are well known, while its usefulness in giving the measurements and details of some of the latest examples of engineering as carried out by the most eminent men in the profession, cannot be too highly prized."—*Engineer.*

Statics, Graphic and Analytic.

GRAPHIC AND ANALYTIC STATICS, in their Practical Application to the Treatment of Stresses in Roofs, Solid Girders, Lattice, Bowstring and Suspension Bridges, Braced Iron Arches and Piers, and other Frameworks. By R. HUDSON GRAHAM, C.E. Containing Diagrams and Plates to Scale. With numerous Examples, many taken from existing Structures. Specially arranged for Class work in Colleges and Universities. Second Edition, Revised and Enlarged. 8vo, 16s. cloth.

"Mr. Graham's book will find a place wherever graphic and analytic statics are used or studied." —*Engineer.*

"The work is excellent from a practical point of view, and has evidently been prepared with much care. The directions for working are ample, and are illustrated by an abundance of well-selected examples. It is an excellent text book for the practical draughtsman." —*Athenæum.*

Practical Mathematics.

MATHEMATICS FOR PRACTICAL MEN: Being a Commonplace Book of Pure and Mixed Mathematics. Designed chiefly for the use of Civil Engineers, Architects and Surveyors. By OLINTHUS GREGORY, LL.D., F.R.A.S., Enlarged by HENRY LAW, C.E. 4th Edition, carefully Revised by J. R. YOUNG, formerly Professor of Mathematics, Belfast College. With 13 Plates. 8vo, £1 1s. cloth.

"The engineer or architect will here find ready to his hand rules for solving nearly every mathematical difficulty that may arise in his practice. The rules are in all cases explained by means of examples, in which every step of the process is clearly worked out." —*Builder.*

"One of the most serviceable books for practical mechanics. . . . It is an instructive book for the student, and a text-book for him who, having once mastered the subjects it treats of, needs occasionally to refresh his memory upon them." —*Building News.*

Hydraulic Tables.

HYDRAULIC TABLES, CO-EFFICIENTS, and FORMULÆ for finding the Discharge of Water from Orifices, Notches, Weirs, Pipes, and Rivers. With New Formulæ, Tables, and General Information on Rainfall, Catchment-Basins, Drainage, Sewerage, Water Supply for Towns and Mill Power. By JOHN NEVILLE, Civil Engineer, M.R.I.A. Third Ed., carefully Revised, with considerable Additions. Numerous Illusts. Cr. 8vo, 14s. cloth.

"Alike valuable to students and engineers in practice; its study will prevent the annoyance of avoidable failures, and assist them to select the readiest means of successfully carrying out any given work connected with hydraulic engineering." —*Mining Journal.*

"It is, of all English books on the subject, the one nearest to completeness. . . . From the good arrangement of the matter, the clear explanations, and abundance of formulæ, the carefully calculated tables, and, above all, the thorough acquaintance with both theory and construction, which is displayed from first to last, the book will be found to be an acquisition." —*Architect.*

Hydraulics.

HYDRAULIC MANUAL. Consisting of Working Tables and Explanatory Text. Intended as a Guide in Hydraulic Calculations and Field Operations. By LOWIS D'A. JACKSON, Author of "Aid to Survey Practice," "Modern Metrology," &c. Fourth Edition, Enlarged. Large cr. 8vo, 16s. cl.

"The author has had a wide experience in hydraulic engineering and has been a careful observer of the facts which have come under his notice, and from the great mass of material at his command he has constructed a manual which may be accepted as a trustworthy guide to this branch of the engineer's profession. We can heartily recommend this volume to all who desire to be acquainted with the latest development of this important subject." —*Engineering.*

"The standard-work in this department of mechanics." —*Scotsman.*

"The most useful feature of this work is its freedom from what is superannuated, and its thorough adoption of recent experiments: the text is, in fact, in great part a short account of the great modern experiments." —*Nature.*

Drainage.

ON THE DRAINAGE OF LANDS, TOWNS, AND BUILDINGS. By G. D. DEMPSEY, C.E., Author of "The Practical Railway Engineer," &c. Revised, with large Additions on RECENT PRACTICE IN DRAINAGE ENGINEERING, by D. KINNEAR CLARK, M.Inst.C.E. Author of "Tramways: Their Construction and Working," "A Manual of Rules, Tables, and Data for Mechanical Engineers," &c. Second Edition, Corrected. Fcap. 8vo, 5s. cloth.

"The new matter added to Mr. Dempsey's excellent work is characterised by the comprehensive grasp and accuracy of detail for which the name of Mr. D. K. Clark is a sufficient voucher." —*Athenæum.*

"As a work on recent practice in drainage engineering, the book is to be commended to all who are making that branch of engineering science their special study." —*Iron.*

"A comprehensive manual on drainage engineering, and a useful introduction to the student." —*Building News.*

Water Storage, Conveyance, and Utilisation.

WATER ENGINEERING: A Practical Treatise on the Measurement, Storage, Conveyance, and Utilisation of Water for the Supply of Towns, for Mill Power, and for other Purposes. By CHARLES SLAGG, Water and Drainage Engineer, A M Inst.C E., Author of "Sanitary Work in the Smaller Towns, and in Villages," &c. With numerous Illusts. Cr. 8vo, 7s. 6d. cloth.

"As a small practical treatise on the water supply of towns and on some applications of water power, the work is in many respects excellent."—*Engineering*.

"The author has collated the results deduced from the experiments of the most eminent authorities, and has presented them in a compact and practical form, a ... ... very clear and detailed explanations. ... The application of water as a motive power is treated very carefully and exhaustively."—*Builder*.

"For anyone who desires to begin the study of hydraulics with a consideration of the practical applications of the science there is no better guide."—*Architect*.

River Engineering.

RIVER BARS: The Causes of their Formation, and their Treatment by "Induced Tidal Scour;" with a Description of the Successful Reduction by this Method of the Bar at Dublin. By I. J. MANN, Assist. Eng. to the Dublin Port and Docks Board. Royal 8vo, 7s. 6d. cloth.

"We recommend all interested in dock works and harbour ... ... erected in the improvements of rivers generally to read Mr. Mann's interesting work on the treatment of river bars."—*Engineer*.

Trusses.

TRUSSES OF WOOD AND IRON. Practical Applications of Science in Determining the Stresses, Breaking Weights, Safe Loads, Scantlings, and Details of Construction, with Complete Working Drawings. By WILLIAM GRIFFITHS, Surveyor, Assistant Master, Tranmere School of Science and Art. Oblong 8vo, 4s. 6d. cloth.

"This handy little book enters so minutely into every detail connected with the construction of roof trusses, that no student need be ignorant of these matters."—*Practical Engineer*.

Railway Working.

SAFE RAILWAY WORKING. A Treatise on Railway Accidents: Their Cause and Prevention; with a Description of Modern Appliances and Systems. By CLEMENT E. STRETTON, C.E., Vice-President and Consulting Engineer, Amalgamated Society of Railway Servants. With Illustrations and Coloured Plates. Third Edition, Enlarged. Crown 8vo, 3s. 6d. cloth.

"A book for the engineer, the directors, the managers; and, in short, all who wish for information on railway matters will find a perfect encyclopædia in 'Safe Railway Working.'"—*Railway Review*.

"We commend the remarks on railway signalling to all railway managers, especially where a uniform code and practice is advocated."—*Herepath's Railway Journal*.

"The author may be congratulated on having collected, in a very convenient form, much valuable information on the principal questions affecting the safe working of railways."—*Railway Engineer*.

Oblique Bridges.

A PRACTICAL AND THEORETICAL ESSAY ON OBLIQUE BRIDGES. With 13 large Plates. By the late GEORGE WATSON BUCK, M.I.C.E. Third Edition, revised by his Son, J. H. WATSON BUCK, M.I.C.E.; and with the addition of Description to Diagrams for Facilitating the Construction of Oblique Bridges, by W. H. BARLOW, M.I.C.E. Royal 8vo, 12s. cloth.

"The standard text-book for all engineers regarding skew arches is Mr. Buck's treatise, and it would be impossible to consult a better."—*Engineer*.

"Mr. Buck's treatise is recognised as a standard text-book, and his treatment has divested the subject of many of the intricacies ... ... As a guide to the engineer and architect, on a confessedly difficult subject, Mr. Buck's work is unsurpassed."—*Building News*.

Tunnel Shafts.

THE CONSTRUCTION OF LARGE TUNNEL SHAFTS: A Practical and Theoretical Essay. By J. H. WATSON BUCK, M.Inst.C.E., Resident Engineer, London and North-Western Railway. Illustrated with Folding Plates. Royal 8vo, 12s. cloth.

"Many of the methods given are of extreme practical value to the mason; and the observations on the form of arch, the ... ... for order ... well ... ... as all the centre truss of the templates will be found of considerable use. We commend the book to the engineering profession."—*Building News*.

"Will be regarded by civil engineers as of the utmost value, and calculated to save much time and obviate many ... ..."

Student's Text-Book on Surveying.

PRACTICAL SURVEYING: A Text Book for Students preparing for Examination or for Survey-work in the Colonies. By GEORGE W. USILL, A.M.I.C.E., Author of "The Statistics of the Water Supply of Great Britain," With Four Lithographic Plates and upwards of 330 Illustrations. Third Edition, Revised and Enlarged. Including Tables of Natural Sines, Tangents, Secants, &c. Crown 8vo, 7s. 6d. cloth; or, ex. THIN PAPER, bound in limp leather, gilt edges, rounded corners, for pocket use, 12s. 6d.

"The best forms of instruments are described as to their construction, uses and modes of employment, and there are innumerable hints on work and apparatus such as it is believed no experience as surveyor, draughtsman, and teacher, has found necessary, and which the student in his inexperience will find most useful."—*Engineer.*

"The latest treatise in the English language on surveying, and we have no hesitation in saying that the student will find it a better guide than any of its predecessors. . . . Deserves to be recognised as the first book which has been put in to his hands for use of Civil Engineering, and every gentleman of education who sets out for the Colonies would do well to have a copy."—*Architect.*

Survey Practice.

AID TO SURVEY PRACTICE, for Reference in Surveying, Levelling, and Setting-out; and in Route Surveys of Travellers by Land and Sea. With Tables, Illustrations, and Records. By LOWIS D'A. JACKSON, A.M.I.C.E., Author of "Hydraulic Manual," "Modern Metrology," &c. Second Edition, Enlarged. Large crown 8vo, 12s. 6d. cloth.

"A valuable vade-mecum for the surveyor. We can recommend this book as containing an admirable supplement to the teaching of the accomplished surveyor."—*Athenæum.*

"As a text-book we should advise all surveyors to place it in their libraries, and study well the matured instructions afforded in its pages."—*Colliery Guardian.*

"The author brings to his work a fortunate union of theory and practical experience which, aided by a clear and lucid style of writing, renders the book a very useful one."—*Builder.*

Surveying, Land and Marine.

LAND AND MARINE SURVEYING, in Reference to the Preparation of Plans for Roads and Railways; Canals, Rivers, Towns' Water Supplies; Docks and Harbours. With Description and Use of Surveying Instruments. By W. D. HASKOLL, C.E., Author of "Bridge and Viaduct Construction," &c. Second Edition, Revised, with Additions. Large cr. 8vo, 9s. cl.

"This book must prove of great value to the student. We have no hesitation in recommending it, feeling assured that it will more than repay a careful study."—*Mechanical World.*

"A most useful and well arranged book. We can strongly recommend it as a carefully written and valuable text-book. It enjoys a well-deserved repute among surveyors."—*Builder.*

"This volume cannot fail to prove of the utmost practical utility. It may be safely recommended to all students who aspire to become clean and expert surveyors."—*Mining Journal.*

Field-Book for Engineers.

THE ENGINEER'S, MINING SURVEYOR'S, AND CONTRACTOR'S FIELD-BOOK. Consisting of a Series of Tables, with Rules, Explanations of Systems, and use of Theodolite for Traverse Surveying and Plotting the Work with minute accuracy by means of Straight Edge and Set Square only; Levelling with the Theodolite, Casting-out and Reducing Levels to Datum, and Plotting Sections in the ordinary manner; setting-out Curves with the Theodolite by Tangential Angles and Multiples, with Right and Left-hand Readings of the Instrument; Setting-out Curves without Theodolite, on the System of Tangential Angles by sets of Tangents and Offsets; and Earthwork Tables to 80 feet deep, calculated for every 6 inches in depth. By W. D. HASKOLL, C.E. Fourth Edition. Crown 8vo, 12s. cloth.

"The book is very handy; the separate tables of sines and tangents to every minute will make it useful for many other purposes, the genuine traverse tables existing all the same."—*Athenæum.*

"Every person engaged in engineering field operations will estimate the importance of such a work and the amount of valuable time which will be saved by reference to a set of reliable tables prepared with the accuracy and fulness of those given in this volume."—*Railway News.*

Levelling.

A TREATISE ON THE PRINCIPLES AND PRACTICE OF LEVELLING. Showing its Application to purposes of Railway and Civil Engineering, in the Construction of Roads; with Mr. TELFORD's Rules for the same. By FREDERICK W. SIMMS, F.G.S., M.Inst.C.E. Seventh Edition, with the addition of LAW's Practical Examples for Setting-out Railway Curves, and TRAUTWINE's Field Practice of Laying-out Circular Curves. With 7 Plates and numerous Woodcuts. 8vo, 8s. 6d. cloth. **** TRAUTWINE on Curves may be had separate, 5s.

"The text-book on levelling in most of our engineering schools and colleges."—*Engineer.*

"The publishers have rendered a substantial service to the profession, especially to the younger members, by bringing out the present edition of Mr. Simms's useful work."—*Engineering.*

Trigonometrical Surveying.

AN OUTLINE OF THE METHOD OF CONDUCTING A TRIGONOMETRICAL SURVEY, for the Formation of Geographical and Topographical Maps and Plans, Military Reconnaissance, Levelling, &c., with Useful Problems, Formulæ, and Tables. By Lieut.-General FROME, R.E. Fourth Edition, Revised and partly Re-written by Major General Sir CHARLES WARREN, G.C.M.G., R.E. With 19 Plates and 115 Woodcuts. Royal 8vo, 16s. cloth.

"The simple fact that a fourth edition has been called for is the best testimony to its merits. No words of praise from us can strengthen the position so well and so steadily maintained by this work. Sir Charles Warren has revised the entire work, and it is such had fitness as were necessary to bring every portion of the contents up to the present date. — *Broad Arrow.*"

Field Fortification.

A TREATISE ON FIELD FORTIFICATION, THE ATTACK OF FORTRESSES, MILITARY MINING, AND RECONNOITRING. By Colonel I. S. MACAULAY, late Professor of Fortification in the R.M.A., Woolwich. Sixth Edition. Crown 8vo, with separate Atlas of 12 Plates, 12s. cloth.

Tunnelling.

PRACTICAL TUNNELLING. Explaining in detail the Setting-out of the works, Shaft-sinking and Heading-driving, Ranging the Lines and Levelling underground, Sub-Excavating, Timbering, and the Construction of the Brickwork of Tunnels, with the amount of Labour required for, and the Cost of, the various portions of the work. By FREDERICK W. SIMMS, F.G.S., M.Inst.C.E. Third Edition, Revised and Extended by D. KINNEAR CLARK, M.Inst.C.E. Imperial 8vo, with 21 Folding Plates and numerous Wood Engravings, 30s. cloth.

"The estimation in which Mr Simms's book on tunnelling has been held for over thirty years cannot be more truly expressed than in the words of the late Prof. Rankine — 'The best source of information on the subject of tunnels is Mr. F. W. Simms's work on Practical Tunnelling.' — *Architect.*
"It has been regarded from the first as a text-book of the subject. . . . Mr. Clark has added immensely to the value of the book." — *Engineer.*"

Tramways and their Working.

TRAMWAYS: THEIR CONSTRUCTION AND WORKING. Embracing a Comprehensive History of the System; with an exhaustive Analysis of the various Modes of Traction, including Horse-Power, Steam, Cable Traction, Electric Traction, &c.; a Description of the Varieties of Rolling Stock; and ample Details of Cost and Working Expenses. New Edition, Thoroughly Revised, and Including the Progress recently made in Tramway Construction, &c. &c. By D. KINNEAR CLARK, M.Inst.C.E. With numerous Illustrations and Folding Plates. In One Volume, 8vo, 700 pages, price about 25s. *[Nearly ready.*

"All interested in tramways must refer to it, as all railway engineers have turned to the author's work 'Railway Machinery.'" — *Engineer.*
"An exhaustive and practical work on tramways, in which the history of this kind of locomotion, and a description and cost of the various modes of laying tramways, are to be found. — *Building News.*
"The best form of rails, the best mode of construction, and the best mechanical appliances are so fairly indicated in the work under review, that any engineer about to construct a tramway will be enabled at once to obtain the practical information which will be of most service to him. — *Athenæum.*"

Curves, Tables for Setting-out.

TABLES OF TANGENTIAL ANGLES AND MULTIPLES for Setting-out Curves from 5 to 200 Radius. By ALEXANDER BEAZELEY, M.Inst.C.E. Fourth Edition. Printed on 48 Cards, and sold in a cloth box, waistcoat-pocket size, 3s. 6d.

"Each table is printed on a small card, which, being placed on the theodolite, leaves the hands free to manipulate the instrument — no small advantage as regards the rapidity of work. — *Engineer.*
"Very handy; a man may know that all his day's work must fall on two of these cards, which he puts into his own card-case, and leaves the rest behind. — *Athenæum.*"

Earthwork.

EARTHWORK TABLES. Showing the Contents in Cubic Yards of Embankments, Cuttings, &c., of Heights or Depths up to an average of 80 feet. By JOSEPH BROADBENT, C.E., and FRANCIS CAMPIN, C.E. Crown 8vo, 5s. cloth.

"The way in which accuracy is attained, by a system of moderate subdivisions of three elements, two in which are constant and one variable, is ingenious..."

Heat, Expansion by.

EXPANSION OF STRUCTURES BY HEAT. By JOHN KEILY, C.E., late of the Indian Public Works and Victorian Railway Departments. Crown 8vo, 3s. 6d. cloth.

SUMMARY OF CONTENTS.

Section I. FORMULAS AND DATA.
Section II. METAL BARS.
Section III. SIMPLE FRAMES.
Section IV. COMPLEX FRAMES AND PLATES.
Section V. THERMAL CONDUCTIVITY.
Section VI. MECHANICAL FORCE OF HEAT.
Section VII. WORK OF EXPANSION AND CONTRACTION.
Section VIII. SUSPENSION BRIDGES.
Section IX. MASONRY STRUCTURES.

"The aim the author has set before him, viz., to show the effects of heat upon metallic and other structures, is a laudable one, for this is a branch of physics upon which the engineer or architect can find but little reliable and comprehensive data in books."—*Builder*.

"Whoever is concerned to know the effect of changes of temperature on such structures as suspension bridges and the like, could not do better than consult Mr. Keily's valuable and handy exposition of the geometrical principles involved in these changes."—*Scotsman*.

Earthwork, Measurement of.

A MANUAL ON EARTHWORK. By ALEX. J. S. GRAHAM, C.E. With numerous Diagrams. Second Edition. 18mo, 2s. 6d. cloth.

"A great amount of practical information, very admirably arranged, and available for rough estimates, as well as for the more exact calculations required in the engineer's and contractor's offices."—*Artizan*.

Strains in Ironwork.

THE STRAINS ON STRUCTURES OF IRONWORK; with Practical Remarks on Iron Construction. By F. W. SHEILDS, M.Inst.C.E. Second Edition, with 5 Plates. Royal 8vo, 5s. cloth.

The student cannot find a better little book on this subject.—*Engineer*.

Cast Iron and other Metals, Strength of.

A PRACTICAL ESSAY ON THE STRENGTH OF CAST IRON AND OTHER METALS. By THOMAS TREDGOLD, C.E. Fifth Edition, including HODGKINSON'S Experimental Researches. 8vo, 12s. cloth.

Oblique Arches.

A PRACTICAL TREATISE ON THE CONSTRUCTION OF OBLIQUE ARCHES. By JOHN HART. Third Edition, with Plates. Imperial 8vo, 8s. cloth.

Girders, Strength of.

GRAPHIC TABLE FOR FACILITATING THE COMPUTATION OF THE WEIGHTS OF WROUGHT IRON AND STEEL GIRDERS, etc., for Parliamentary and other Estimates. By J. H. WATSON BUCK, M.Inst.C.E. On a Sheet, 2s. 6d.

Water Supply and Water-Works.

A PRACTICAL TREATISE ON THE WATER SUPPLY OF TOWNS AND THE CONSTRUCTION OF WATER-WORKS. By W. K. BURTON, A.M.Inst C.E., Professor of Sanitary Engineering in the Imperial University, Tokyo, Japan, and Consulting Engineer to the Tokyo Water-Works. With an Appendix on Water-Works in Countries subject to Earthquakes, by JOHN MILNE, F.R.S., Professor of Mining in the Imperial University of Japan. With numerous Plates and Pluts. *In the press*.

MARINE ENGINEERING, SHIPBUILDING, NAVIGATION, etc.

Pocket-Book for Naval Architects and Shipbuilders.
THE NAVAL ARCHITECT'S AND SHIPBUILDER'S POCKET-BOOK of Formulæ, Rules, and Tables, and MARINE ENGINEER'S AND SURVEYOR'S Handy Book of Reference. By CLEMENT MACKROW, Member of the Institution of Naval Architects, Naval Draughtsman. Fifth Edition, Revised and Enlarged to 700 pages, with upwards of 300 Illustrations. Fcap., 12s. 6d. strongly bound in leather.

SUMMARY OF CONTENTS.

SIGNS AND SYMBOLS, DECIMAL FRACTIONS.—TRIGONOMETRY.—PRACTICAL GEOMETRY.—MENSURATION.—CENTRES AND MOMENTS OF FIGURES.—MOMENTS OF INERTIA AND RADII OF GYRATION.—ALGEBRAICAL EXPRESSIONS FOR SIMPSON'S RULES.—MECHANICAL PRINCIPLES.—CENTRE OF GRAVITY.—LAWS OF MOTION.—DISPLACEMENT, CENTRE OF BUOYANCY.—CENTRE OF GRAVITY OF SHIP'S HULL.—STABILITY CURVES AND METACENTRES.—SEA AND SHALLOW-WATER WAVES.—ROLLING OF SHIPS.—PROPULSION AND RESISTANCE OF VESSELS.—SPEED TRIALS, SAILING, CENTRE OF EFFORT.—DISTANCES DOWN RIVERS, COAST LINES.—STEERING AND RUDDERS OF VESSELS.—LAUNCHING CALCULATIONS AND VELOCITIES.—WEIGHT OF MATERIAL AND GEAR.—GUN PARTICULARS AND WEIGHT.—STANDARD GAUGES.—RIVETED JOINTS AND RIVETING.—STRENGTH AND TESTS OF MATERIALS.—BINDING AND SHEARING STRESSES, ETC.—STRENGTH OF SHAFTING, PILLARS, WHEELS, ETC.—HYDRAULIC DATA, ETC.—CONIC SECTIONS, CATENARIAN CURVES.—MECHANICAL POWERS, WORK.—BOARD OF TRADE REGULATIONS FOR BOILERS AND ENGINES.—BOARD OF TRADE REGULATIONS FOR SHIPS.—LLOYD'S RULES FOR BOILERS.—LLOYD'S WEIGHT OF CHAINS.—LLOYD'S SCANTLINGS FOR SHIPS.—DATA OF ENGINES AND VESSELS.—SHIPS' FITTINGS AND TESTS.—SEASONING PRESERVING TIMBER.—MEASUREMENT OF TIMBER.—ALLOYS, PAINTS, VARNISHES.—DATA FOR STOWAGE.—ADMIRALTY TRANSIENT REGULATIONS.—RULES FOR HORSE-POWER, SCREW PROPELLERS, ETC.—PERCENTAGES FOR BUILT STEAM, ETC.—PARTICULARS OF YACHTS.—MASTING AND RIGGING VESSELS.—DISTANCES OF FOREIGN PORTS.—TONNAGE TABLES.—VOCABULARY OF FRENCH AND ENGLISH TERMS.—ENGLISH WEIGHTS AND MEASURES.—FOREIGN WEIGHTS AND MEASURES.—DECIMAL EQUIVALENTS.—FOREIGN MONEY.—DISCOUNT AND WAGE TABLES.—USEFUL NUMBERS AND READY RECKONERS.—TABLES OF CIRCULAR MEASURES.—TABLES OF AREAS OF AND CIRCUMFERENCES OF CIRCLES.—TABLES OF AREAS OF SEGMENTS OF CIRCLES.—TABLES OF SQUARES AND CUBES AND ROOTS OF NUMBERS.—TABLES OF LOGARITHMS OF NUMBERS.—TABLES OF HYPERBOLIC LOGARITHMS.—TABLES OF NATURAL SINES, TANGENTS, ETC.—TABLES OF LOGARITHMIC SINES, TANGENTS, ETC.

"In these days of advanced knowledge a work like this is of the greatest value. It contains a vast amount of information. We unhesitatingly say that it is the most valuable of its kind for its specific purpose that has ever been printed. No naval architect, engineer, surveyor, or seaman, wood or iron shipbuilder, can afford to be without this work."—*Nautical Magazine.*

"Should be used by all who are engaged in the construction or designs of vessels. . . . Will be found to contain the most useful tables and formulæ required by shipbuilders, carefully collected from the best authorities, and put together in a popular and simple form."—*Engineer.*

"The professional shipbuilder has now, in a convenient and accessible form, reliable data for solving many of the numerous problems that present themselves in the course of his work." . . .

"There is no doubt that a pocket-book of this description must be of service to the shipbuilding trade. . . . The volume contains a vast amount of useful information, clearly expressed and presented in a handy form."—*Times.*

Marine Engineering.

MARINE ENGINES AND STEAM VESSELS (A Treatise on). By ROBERT MURRAY, C.E. Eighth Edition, thoroughly Revised, with considerable Additions by the Author and by GEORGE CARLISLE, C.E., Senior Surveyor to the Board of Trade at Liverpool. 12mo, 5s. cloth boards.

"Well adapted to give the young steamship engineer or marine engine and boiler maker a general introduction into his practical work."—*Mechanical World.*

"We feel sure that this thoroughly revised edition will continue to be as popular in the future as it has been in the past, as, for its size, it contains more useful information than any similar treatise."—*Industries.*

"As a compendious and useful guide to engineers of our mercantile and royal navy we think it cannot be too highly commended."—*Iron and Steel Trades Journal.*

"The information given is both sound and sensible, and well qualified to meet the requirements of sea-going hands on the straightforward route to extra chief's certificate. . . . May be strongly recommended to all engineers in port, dockyardsmen, and young engineers."—*Glasgow Herald.*

c

Pocket-Book for Marine Engineers.

A POCKET-BOOK OF USEFUL TABLES AND FORMULÆ FOR MARINE ENGINEERS. By FRANK PROCTOR, A.I.N.A. Third Edition. Royal 32mo, leather, gilt edges, with strap, 4s.

"We recommend it to our readers as giving for to sum y a book for want." — *Naval Science.*
"A most useful companion to all marine engineers." — *United Service Gazette.*

Introduction to Marine Engineering.

ELEMENTARY ENGINEERING: *A Manual for Young Marine Engineers and Apprentices.* In the Form of Questions and Answers on Metals, Alloys, Strength of Materials, Construction and Management of Marine Engines and Boilers, Geometry, &c. &c. With an Appendix of Useful Tables. By JOHN SHERREN BREWER, Government Marine Surveyor, Hongkong. Second Edition, Revised. Small crown 8vo, 2s. cloth.

"Contains much valuable information for the class for whom it is intended, especially in the chapters on the management of boilers in long voyages." — *Nautical Magazine.*
"A useful introduction to the more elaborate text-books." — *Steamship.*
"To a student who has the requisite desire and resolve to attain a thorough knowledge, Mr. Brewer offers decidedly useful help." — *Athenæum.*

Navigation.

PRACTICAL NAVIGATION. Consisting of THE SAILOR'S SEA-BOOK, by JAMES GREENWOOD and W. H. ROSSER; together with the requisite Mathematical and Nautical Tables for the Working of the Problems, by HENRY LAW, C.E., and Professor J. R. YOUNG. Illustrated. 12mo, 7s. strongly half-bound.

Drawing for Marine Engineers.

LOCKIE'S MARINE ENGINEER'S DRAWING-BOOK. Adapted to the Requirements of the Board of Trade Examinations. By JOHN LOCKIE, C.E. With 22 Plates, Drawn to Scale. Royal 8vo, 3s. 6d. cloth.

"The student who learns from these drawings will have nothing to unlearn." — *Engineer.*
"The examples chosen are entirely practical, and are such as will present themselves to engineers generally, while admirably fulfilling their specific purpose." — *Mechanical World.*

Sailmaking.

THE ART AND SCIENCE OF SAILMAKING. By SAMUEL B. SADLER, Practical Sailmaker, late in the employment of Messrs. Ratsey and Lapthorne, of Cowes and Gosport. With Plates and other Illustrations. Small 4to, 12s. 6d. cloth.

SUMMARY OF CONTENTS.

CHAP. I. THE MATERIALS USED AND THEIR RELATION TO SAILS.—II. ON THE CENTRE OF EFFORT.—III. ON MEASURING.—IV. ON DRAWING.—V. ON THE NUMBER OF CLOTHS REQUIRED.—VI. ON ALLOWANCES.—VII. CALCULATION OF GORES.—VIII. ON CUTTING OUT.—IX. ON ROPING.—X. ON DIAGONAL-CUT SAILS.—XI. CONCLUDING REMARKS.

"This work is very ably written, and is illustrated by diagrams and carefully worked calculations. The work should be in the hands of every sailmaker, whether employer or employed. It cannot fail to assist them in the pursuit of their important avocations." — *Isle of Wight Herald.*
"This extremely practical work gives a complete elucidation in all of the branches of the manufacture, cutting out, roping, seaming, and gearing. It is copiously illustrated, and will form a first-rate text-book and guide." — *Portsmouth Times.*
"The author of this work has rendered a distinct service to all interested in the art of sailmaking. The subject of which he treats is a congenial one. Mr. Sadler is a practical sailmaker, and has devoted years of careful observation and study to the subject; and the results of the experience thus gained he has set forth in the volume before us. — *Steamship.*

Chain Cables.

CHAIN CABLES AND CHAINS. Comprising Sizes and Curves of Links, Studs, &c., Iron for Cables and Chains, Chain Cable and Chain Making, Forming and Welding Links, Strength of Cables and Chains, Certificates for Cables, Marking Cables, Prices of Chain Cables and Chains, Historical Notes, Acts of Parliament, Statutory Tests, Charges for Testing, List of Manufacturers of Cables, &c. &c. By THOMAS W. TRAILL, F.E.R.N., M. Inst. C.E., Engineer Surveyor in Chief, Board of Trade, Inspector of Chain Cable and Anchor Proving Establishments, and General Superintendent, Lloyd's Committee on Proving Establishments. With numerous Tables, Illustrations and Lithographic Drawings. Folio, £2 2s. cloth, bevelled boards.

"It contains a vast amount of valuable information. Nothing seems to be wanting to make it a complete and standard work of reference on the subject." — *Nautical Magazine.*

MINING AND METALLURGY.

Mining Machinery.

MACHINERY FOR METALLIFEROUS MINES: A Practical Treatise for Mining Engineers, Metallurgists, and Managers of Mines. By E. HENRY DAVIES, M.E., F.G.S. Crown 8vo, 580 pp., with upwards of Illustrations, 12s. 6d. cloth. [*Just published*

"Mr. Davies, in this handsome volume, has done the above and the manager of mines good service. Almost every kind of machinery in actual use is carefully described, and 400 cuts and plates are good."—*Athenæum.*

"From cover to cover the work exhibits all the same characteristics which distinguish his reference and attract the attention of the student as he peruses these first pages. The work may safely be recommended. By its publication the literature connected with the industry will be enriched, and the reputation of its author enhanced.—*Mining Journal.*

"Mr. Davies has endeavoured to bring before his readers the best of everything in modern mining appliances. His work carries internal evidence of the author's impartiality, and this constitutes one of the great merits of the book. Throughout his work the critical remarks are based on his own or other reliable experience."—*Iron and Steel Trades Journal.*

"The work deals with nearly every kind of machinery that is likely to be met with or required in connection with metalliferous mining, and is one which we can every confidence in recommending.—*Practical Engineer.*

Metalliferous Minerals and Mining.

A TREATISE ON METALLIFEROUS MINERALS AND MINING. By D. C. DAVIES, F.G.S., Mining Engineer, &c., Author of "A Treatise on Slate and Slate Quarrying." Fifth Edition, thoroughly Revised and much Enlarged, by his Son, E. HENRY DAVIES, M.E., F.G.S. With about 150 Illustrations. Crown 8vo, 12s. 6d. cloth.

"Neither the practical miner nor the general reader interested in mines can have a better book for his companion and his guide."—*Mining Journal.* [*Mining World.*

"We are doing our readers a service in calling their attention to this valuable work.

"A book that will not only be useful to the geologist, the practical miner, and the metallurgist, but also very interesting to the general public."—*Iron.*

"As a history of the present state of mining throughout the world this book has a real value, and it supplies an actual want."—*Athenæum.*

Earthy Minerals and Mining.

A TREATISE ON EARTHY & OTHER MINERALS AND MINING. By D. C. DAVIES, F.G.S., Author of "Metalliferous Minerals," &c. Third Edition, revised and Enlarged, by his Son, E. HENRY DAVIES, M.E., F.G.S. With about 100 Illustrations. Crown 8vo, 12s. 6d. cloth.

"We do not remember to have met with any English work on mining matters that contains the same amount of information packed in equally convenient form."—*Academy.*

"We should be inclined to rank it as among the very best of the handy technical and trades manuals which have recently appeared.—*British Quarterly Review.*

Metalliferous Mining in the United Kingdom.

BRITISH MINING: A Treatise on the History, Discovery, Practical Development, and Future Prospects of Metalliferous Mines in the United Kingdom. By ROBERT HUNT, F.R.S., Editor of "Ure's Dictionary of Arts, Manufactures, and Mines," &c. Upwards of 950 pp., with 230 Illustrations. Second Edition, Revised. Super-royal 8vo, £3 3s. cloth.

"One of the most valuable works of reference of modern times. Mr. Hunt, as Keeper of Mining Records of the United Kingdom, has had opportunities for such a task not enjoyed by anyone else, and has evidently made the most of them. . . . The language and style adopted are good, and the treatment of the various subjects laborious, conscientious, and scientific."—*Engineering.*

"The book is, in fact, a treasure-house of statistical information on mining subjects, and we know of no other work embodying so great a mass of matter of this kind. Were this the only merit of Mr. Hunt's volume, it would be sufficient to render it indispensable in the library of everyone interested in the development of the mining and metallurgical industries of this country."—*Athenæum.*

"A mass of information not elsewhere available, and of the greatest value to those who may be interested in our great mineral industries.—*Engineer.*

Underground Pumping Machinery.

MINE DRAINAGE. Being a Complete and Practical Treatise on Direct-Acting Underground Steam Pumping Machinery, with a Description of a large number of the best known Engines, their General Utility and the Special Sphere of their Action, the Mode of their Application, and their merits compared with other forms of Pumping Machinery. By STEPHEN MICHELL. 8vo, 15s. cloth.

"Will be highly esteemed by colliery owners and lessees, mining engineers, and students generally who require to be acquainted with the best means of securing the drainage of mines. It is a most valuable work, and stands almost alone in the literature of steam pumping machinery."—*Colliery Guardian.*

"Much valuable information is given, so that the book is thoroughly worthy of an extensive circulation amongst practical men and purchasers of machinery.—*Mining Journal.*

Prospecting for Gold and other Metals.

THE PROSPECTOR'S HANDBOOK: A Guide for the Prospector and Traveller in Search of Metal-Bearing or other Valuable Minerals. By J. W. ANDERSON, M.A. (Camb.), F.R.G.S., Author of "Fiji and New Caledonia." Fifth Edition, thoroughly Revised and Enlarged. Small crown 8vo, 3s. 6d. cloth.

"Will supply a much felt want, especially among Colonists, in whose way are so often thrown many mineralogical specimens the value of which it is difficult to determine."—*Engineer.*

"How to find commercial minerals, and how to identify them when they are found, are the leading points to which attention is directed. The author has managed to pack as much practical detail into his pages as would supply material for a book three times its size."—*Mining Journal.*

Mining Notes and Formulæ.

NOTES AND FORMULÆ FOR MINING STUDENTS. By JOHN HERMAN MERIVALE, M.A., Certificated Colliery Manager, Professor of Mining in the Durham College of Science, Newcastle-upon-Tyne. Third Edition, Revised and Enlarged. Small crown 8vo, 2s. 6d. cloth.

"Invaluable to anyone who is working up for an examination on mining subjects."—*Iron and Coal Trades Review.*

"The author has done his work in an exceedingly creditable manner, and has produced a book that will be of service to students, and those who are practically engaged in mining operations."—*Engineer.*

Handybook for Miners.

THE MINER'S HANDBOOK: A Handybook of Reference on the Subjects of Mineral Deposits, Mining Operations, Ore Dressing, &c. For the Use of Students and others interested in Mining matters. Compiled by JOHN MILNE, F.R.S., Professor of Mining in the Imperial University of Japan. Square 18mo, 7s. 6d. cloth. [*Just published.*

"Professor Milne's handbook is sure to be received with favour by all connected with mining, and will be extremely popular among students."—*Athenæum.*

Miners' and Metallurgists' Pocket-Book.

A POCKET-BOOK FOR MINERS AND METALLURGISTS. Comprising Rules, Formulæ, Tables, and Notes, for Use in Field and Office Work. By F. DANVERS POWER, F.G.S., M.E. Fcap. 8vo, 9s. leather, gilt edges.

"This excellent book is an admirable example of its kind, and ought to find a large sale amongst English-speaking prospectors and mining engineers."—*Engineering.*

"Miners and metallurgists will find in this work a useful *vade mecum* containing a mass of rules, formulæ, tables, and various other information, the necessity for reference to which occurs in their daily duties."—*Iron.*

Mineral Surveying and Valuing.

THE MINERAL SURVEYOR AND VALUER'S COMPLETE GUIDE, comprising a Treatise on Improved Mining Surveying and the Valuation of Mining Properties, with New Traverse Tables. By WM. LINTERN. Third Edition, Enlarged. 12mo, 4s. cloth.

"Mr. Lintern's book forms a valuable and thoroughly trustworthy guide."—*Iron and Coal Trades Review.*

Asbestos and its Uses.

ASBESTOS: Its Properties, Occurrence, and Uses. With some Account of the Mines of Italy and Canada. By ROBERT H. JONES. With Eight Collotype Plates and other Illustrations. Crown 8vo, 12s. 6d. cloth.

"An interesting and invaluable work."—*Colliery Guardian.*

Explosives.

A HANDBOOK ON MODERN EXPLOSIVES. Being a Practical Treatise on the Manufacture and Application of Dynamite, Gun-Cotton, Nitro-Glycerine, and other Explosive Compounds. Including the Manufacture of Collodion-Cotton. By M. EISSLER, Mining Engineer and Metallurgical Chemist, Author of "The Metallurgy of Gold," "The Metallurgy of Silver," &c. With about 100 Illusts. Crown 8vo, 10s. 6d. cloth.

"Useful not only to the miner, but also to officers of both services to whom blasting and the use of explosives generally may at any time become a necessary auxiliary."—*Nature.*

"A veritable mine of information on the subject of explosives employed for military, mining, and blasting purposes."—*Army and Navy Gazette.*

Colliery Management.

THE COLLIERY MANAGER'S HANDBOOK: A Comprehensive Treatise on the Laying-out and Working of Collieries. Designed as a Book of Reference for Colliery Managers, and for the Use of Coal-Mining Students preparing for First-class Certificates. By CALEB PAMELY, Mining Engineer and Surveyor; Member of the North of England Institute of Mining and Mechanical Engineers; and Member of the South Wales Institute of Mining Engineers. With nearly 500 Plans, Diagrams, and other Illustrations. Second Edition, Revised, with Additions. Medium 8vo, about 700 pages. Price £1 5s. strongly bound.

SUMMARY OF CONTENTS.

GEOLOGY.—SEARCH FOR COAL.—MINERAL LEASES AND OTHER HOLDINGS.—SHAFT SINKING.—FITTING UP THE SHAFT AND SURFACE ARRANGEMENTS.—STEAM BOILERS AND THEIR FITTINGS.—TIMBERING AND WALLING.—NARROW WORK AND METHODS OF WORKING.—UNDERGROUND CONVEYANCE.—DRAINAGE.—THE GASES MET WITH IN MINES; VENTILATION.—ON THE FRICTION OF AIR IN MINES.—THE PRIESTMAN OIL ENGINE; PETROLEUM AND NATURAL GAS - SURVEYING AND PLANNING.—SAFETY LAMPS AND FIRE DAMP DETECTORS—SUNDRY AND INCIDENTAL OPERATIONS AND APPLIANCES.—COLLIERY EXPLOSIONS.—MISCELLANEOUS QUESTIONS & ANSWERS.

Appendix: SUMMARY OF REPORT OF H.M. COMMISSIONERS ON ACCIDENTS IN MINES.

_{*} OPINIONS OF THE PRESS.

"Mr. Pamely has not only given us a comprehensive reference book of a very high order, suitable to the requirements of mining engineers and colliery managers, but at the same time has provided mining students with a class-book that is as interesting as it is instructive.—*Colliery Manager*.

"Mr. Pamely's work is eminently suited to the purpose for which it is intended—being clear, interesting, exhaustive, rich in detail, and up to date, giving descriptions of the very latest machines in every department. . . . A mining engineer could scarcely go wrong who followed this work."—*Colliery Guardian*.

"This is the most complete 'all-round' work on coal-mining published in the English language. . . . No library of coal-mining books is complete without it."—*Colliery Engineer* (Scranton, Pa., U.S.A.).

"Mr. Pamely's work is in all respects worthy of our admiration. No person in any responsible position connected with mines should be without a copy."—*Westminster Review*.

Coal and Iron.

THE COAL AND IRON INDUSTRIES OF THE UNITED KINGDOM. Comprising a Description of the Coal Fields, and of the Principal Seams of Coal, with Returns of their Produce and its Distribution, and Analyses of Special Varieties. Also an Account of the occurrence of Iron Ores in Veins or Seams; Analyses of each Variety; and a History of the Rise and Progress of Pig Iron Manufacture. By RICHARD MEADE, Assistant Keeper of Mining Records. With Maps. 8vo, £1 5s. cloth.

"The book is one which must find a place on the shelves of all interested in coal and iron production, and in the iron, steel, and other metallurgical industries."—*Engineer*.

"Of this book we may unreservedly say that it is the best of its class which we have ever met. . . . A book of reference which no one engaged in the iron or coal trades should omit from his library."—*Iron and Coal Trades Review*.

Coal Mining.

COAL AND COAL MINING: A Rudimentary Treatise on. By the late Sir WARINGTON W. SMYTH, M.A., F.R.S., &c., Chief Inspector of the Mines of the Crown. Seventh Edition, Revised and Enlarged. With numerous Illustrations. 12mo, 4s. cloth boards.

"As an outline is given of every known coal-field in this and other countries, as well as of the principal methods of working, the book will doubtless interest a very large number of readers."—*Mining Journal*.

Subterraneous Surveying.

SUBTERRANEOUS SURVEYING, Elementary and Practical Treatise on, with and without the Magnetic Needle. By THOMAS FENWICK, Surveyor of Mines, and THOMAS BAKER, C.E. Illust. 12mo, 3s. cloth boards.

Granite Quarrying.

GRANITES AND OUR GRANITE INDUSTRIES. By GEORGE F. HARRIS, F.G.S., Membre de la Société Belge de Géologie, Lecturer on Economic Geology at the Birkbeck Institution, &c. With Illustrations. Crown 8vo, 2s. 6d. cloth.

"A clearly and well written manual on the granite industry."—*Scotsman*.

"An interesting work, which will be deservedly esteemed."—*Colliery Guardian*.

"An exceedingly interesting and valuable monograph on a subject which has hitherto received unaccountably little attention in the shape of systematic literary treatment."—*Scottish Leader*.

Gold, Metallurgy of.

THE METALLURGY OF GOLD: A Practical Treatise on the Metallurgical Treatment of Gold-bearing Ores. Including the Processes of Concentration and Chlorination, and the Assaying, Melting, and Refining of Gold. By M. EISSLER, Mining Engineer and Metallurgical Chemist, formerly Assistant Assayer of the U.S. Mint, San Francisco. Third Edition, Revised and greatly Enlarged. With 187 Illustrations. Crown 8vo, 12s. 6d. cloth.

"This book thoroughly deserves its title of a 'Practical Treatise.' The whole process of gold milling, from the breaking of the quartz to the assay of the bullion, is described in clear and orderly narrative and with much, but not too much, fulness of detail."—*Saturday Review.*

"The work is a storehouse of information and valuable data, and we strongly recommend it to all professional men engaged in the gold-mining industry."—*Mining Journal.*

Silver, Metallurgy of.

THE METALLURGY OF SILVER: A Practical Treatise on the Amalgamation, Roasting, and Lixiviation of Silver Ores. Including the Assaying, Melting and Refining, of Silver Bullion. By M. EISSLER, Author of "The Metallurgy of Gold," &c. Second Edition, Enlarged. With 150 Illustrations. Crown 8vo, 10s. 6d. cloth.

"A practical treatise, and a technical work which we are convinced will supply a long felt want amongst practical men, and at the same time be of value to students and others indirectly connected with the industries."—*Mining Journal.*

"From first to last the book is thoroughly sound and reliable."—*Colliery Guardian.*

"For chemists, practical miners, assayers, and investors alike, we do not know of any work on the subject so handy and yet so comprehensive."—*Glasgow Herald.*

Lead, Metallurgy of.

THE METALLURGY OF ARGENTIFEROUS LEAD: A Practical Treatise on the Smelting of Silver-Lead Ores and the Refining of Lead Bullion. Including Reports on various Smelting Establishments and Descriptions of Modern Smelting Furnaces and Plants in Europe and America. By M. EISSLER, M.E., Author of "The Metallurgy of Gold," &c. Crown 8vo, 400 pp., with 183 Illustrations, 12s. 6d. cloth.

"The numerous metallurgical processes, which are fully and extensively treated of, embrace all the stages experienced in the passage of the lead from the various natural states to its issue from the refinery as an article of commerce."—*Practical Engineer.*

"The present volume fully maintains the reputation of the author. Those who wish to obtain a thorough insight into the present state of this industry cannot do better than read this volume, and all mining engineers cannot fail to find many useful hints and suggestions in it."—*Industries.*

"It is most carefully written and illustrated with capital drawings and diagrams. In fact, it is the work of an expert for experts, by whom it will be prized as an indispensable text-book."—*Bristol Mercury.*

Iron, Metallurgy of.

METALLURGY OF IRON. Containing History of Iron Manufacture, Methods of Assay, and Analyses of Iron Ores, Processes of Manufacture of Iron and Steel, &c. By H. BAUERMAN, F.G.S., A.R.S.M. With numerous Illustrations. Sixth Edition, Revised and Enlarged. 12mo, 5s. 6d. cloth.

"Carefully written, it has the merit of brevity and clearness, as to less important points, while all material matters are very fully and thoroughly entered into."—*Standard.*

Iron Mining.

THE IRON ORES OF GREAT BRITAIN AND IRELAND: Their Mode of Occurrence, Age, and Origin, and the Methods of Searching for and Working them, with a Notice of some of the Iron Ores of Spain. By J. D. KENDALL, F.G.S., Mining Engineer. With Plates and Illustrations. Crown 8vo, 16s. cloth.

"The author has a thorough practical knowledge of his subject, and has supplemented a careful study of the available literature by unpublished information derived from his own observations. The result is a very useful volume which cannot fail to be of value to all interested in the iron industry of the country."—*Industries.*

"Constitutes a systematic and careful account of our present knowledge of the origin and occurrence of the iron ores of Great Britain, and embraces a description of the means employed in reaching and working these ores."—*Iron.*

"Mr. Kendall is a great authority on this subject and writes from personal observation."—*Colliery Guardian.*

"Mr. Kendall's book is thoroughly well done. In it there are the outlines of the history of ore mining in every centre and there is everything that we want to know as to the character of the ores of each district, their commercial value and the cost of working them."—*Iron and Steel Trades Journal.*

ELECTRICITY, ELECTRICAL ENGINEERING, etc.

Electrical Engineering.

THE ELECTRICAL ENGINEER'S POCKET-BOOK OF MODERN RULES, FORMULÆ, TABLES, AND DATA. By H. R. Kempe, M.Inst.E.E., A.M.Inst.C.E., Technical Officer, Postal Telegraphs. Author of "A Handbook of Electrical Testing," &c. Second Edition, thoroughly Revised, with Additions. With numerous Illustrations. Royal 32mo, oblong, 5s. leather.

"There is very little in the shape of formulæ or data which the electrician is likely to want in a hurry which cannot be found in its pages."—*Practical Engineer.*

"A very useful book of reference for daily use in practical electrical engineering and its various applications to the industries of the present day."—*Iron.*

"It is the best book of its kind."—*Electrical Engineer.*

"Well arranged and compact. The 'Electrical Engineer's Pocket-Book' is a good one."—*Electrician.*

"Strongly recommended to those engaged in the various electrical industries."—*Electrical Review.*

Electric Lighting.

ELECTRIC LIGHT FITTING: A Handbook for Working Electrical Engineers, embodying Practical Notes on Installation Management. By John W. Urquhart, Electrician, Author of "Electric Light," &c. With numerous Illustrations. Second Edition, Revised, with Additional Chapters. Crown 8vo, 5s. cloth.

"This volume deals with what may be termed the minutiæ of electric lighting, and is addressed to men who are already engaged in the work or are training for it. The work traverses a great deal of ground, and may be read as a sequel to the same author's useful work on 'Electric Light.'"—*Electrician.*

"This is an attempt to state in the simplest language the precautions which should be adopted in installing the electric light, and to give information for the guidance of those who have to run the plant when installed. The book is well worth the perusal of the workmen for whom it is written."—*Electrical Review.*

"We have read this book with a good deal of pleasure. We believe that the book will be of use to practical workmen, who would not be alarmed by finding matters of which they are unable to understand."—*Electrical Plant.*

"Eminently practical and useful. . . . Ought to be in the hands of everyone in charge of an electric light plant."—*Electrical Engineer.*

"Mr. Urquhart has succeeded in producing a really useful book, which we have no hesitation in recommending to the notice of working electricians and electrical engineers."—*Mechanical World.*

Electric Light.

ELECTRIC LIGHT: *Its Production and Use.* Embodying Plain Directions for the Treatment of Dynamo-Electric Machines, Batteries, Accumulators, and Electric Lamps. By J. W. Urquhart, C.E., Author of "Electric Light Fitting," "Electroplating," &c. Fifth Edition, carefully Revised, with Large Additions and 145 Illustrations. Crown 8vo, 7s. 6d. cloth.

"The whole ground of electric lighting is more or less covered and explained in a very clear and concise manner."—*Electrical Review.*

"Contains a good deal of very interesting information, especially in the parts where the author gives dimensions and workings."—*Electrical Engineer.*

"A miniature vade-mecum of the salient facts connected with the science of electric lighting."—*Electrician.*

"You cannot for your purpose have a better book than 'Electric Light, by Urquhart.'"—*Engineer.*

"The book is by far the best that we have yet met with on the subject."—*Athenæum.*

Construction of Dynamos.

DYNAMO CONSTRUCTION: *A Practical Handbook for the Use of Engineer Constructors and Electricians-in-Charge.* Embracing Framework Building, Field Magnet and Armature Winding and Grouping, Compounding, &c. With Examples of leading English, American, and Continental Dynamos and Motors. By J. W. Urquhart, Author of "Electric Light," "Electric Light Fitting," &c. With upwards of 100 Illustrations. Crown 8vo, 7s. 6d. cloth.

"Mr. Urquhart's book is the first one which deals with these matters in such a way that the engineering student can understand them. The book is very readable, and the author leads his readers up to difficult subjects by reasonably simple tests."—*Engineer's Review.*

"The author deals with his subject in a style so popular as to make his work a handbook of great practical value to engineer contractors and electricians in charge of existing installations."—*Scotsman.*

"'Dynamo Construction' more than sustains the high character of the author's previous publications. It is sure to be widely read by the large and increasing number of practical electricians."—*Glasgow Herald.*

"A book for which a demand has long existed."—*Electrical World.*

A New Dictionary of Electricity.

THE STANDARD ELECTRICAL DICTIONARY. A Popular Dictionary of Words and Terms Used in the Practice of Electrical Engineering. Containing upwards of 3,000 Definitions. By T. O'Connor Sloane, A.M., Ph.D., Author of "The Arithmetic of Electricity," &c. Crown 8vo, 610 pp., 350 Illustrations, 7s. 6d. cloth. [*Just published.*]

"The work has many attractive features in it, and is beyond all doubt, a well-put-together and useful publication. The amount of ground covered may be gathered from the fact that in the index about 5,000 references will be found. The inclusion of such comparatively modern words as 'Impedence,' 'reluctance,' &c., shows that the author has desired to be up to date, and in feel there are other indications of carefulness of computation. The work, if one which shews the author great credit and it should prove of great value, especially to students."—*Electrical Review.*

"We have found the book very complete and reliable, and can, therefore, commend it heartily."—*Mechanical World.*

"Very complete and contains a large amount of useful information."—*Electric.*

"An encyclopædia of electrical science in the compass of a dictionary. The information given is sound and clear. The book is well printed, well illustrated, and well up to date, and may be confidently recommended."—*Builder.*

"We hail the appearance of this little work as one which we did meet a want that has been keenly felt for some time . . . . The author is to be congratulated on the excellent manner in which he has accomplished his task."—*Practical Engineer.*

"The volume is excellently printed and illustrated, and should form part of the library of every one who is directly or indirectly connected with electrical matters."—*Hardware Trade Journal.*

Electric Lighting of Ships.

ELECTRIC SHIP-LIGHTING: A Handbook on the Practical Fitting and Running of Ship's Electrical Plant. For the Use of Shipowners and Builders, Marine Electricians, and Sea-going Engineers-in-Charge. By J. W. Urquhart, C.E., Author of "Electric Light," &c. With 88 Illustrations. Crown 8vo, 7s. 6d. cloth.

"The subject of ship electric lighting is one of vast Importance in these days, and Mr Urquhart is to be highly complimented for placing such a valuable work at the service of the practical marine electrician."—*The Steamship.*

"Distinctly a book which of its kind stands almost alone, and for which there should be a demand."—*Electrical Review.*

Electric Lighting.

THE ELEMENTARY PRINCIPLES OF ELECTRIC LIGHTING. By Alan A. Campbell Swinton, Associate I.E.E. Third Edition, Enlarged and Revised. With 16 Illustrations. Crown 8vo, 1s. 6d. cloth.

"Anyone who desires a short and thoroughly clear exposition of the elementary principles of electric lighting cannot do better than read this little work."—*Bradford Observer.*

Dynamic Electricity.

THE ELEMENTS OF DYNAMIC ELECTRICITY AND MAGNETISM. By Philip Atkinson, A.M., Ph.D., Author of "Elements of Static Electricity," "The Elements of Electric Lighting," &c. &c. Crown 8vo, 417 pp., with 120 Illustrations, 10s. 6d. cloth.

Electric Motors, &c.

THE ELECTRIC TRANSFORMATION OF POWER and its Application by the Electric Motor, including Electric Railway Construction. By P. Atkinson, A.M., Ph.D, Author of "The Elements of Electric Lighting," &c. With 96 Illustrations. Crown 8vo, 7s. 6d. cloth.

Dynamo Construction.

HOW TO MAKE A DYNAMO: *A Practical Treatise for Amateurs.* Containing numerous Illustrations and Detailed Instructions for Constructing a Small Dynamo, to Produce the Electric Light. By Alfred Crofts. Fourth Edition, Revised and Enlarged. Crown 8vo, 2s. cloth.

"The instructions given in this unpretentious little book are sufficiently clear and explicit to enable any amateur mechanic possessed of average skill and the usual tools to be found in an amateur's workshop, to build a practical dynamo machine."—*Electrician.*

Text Book of Electricity.

THE STUDENT'S TEXT-BOOK OF ELECTRICITY. By Henry M. Noad, Ph.D., F.R.S. New Edition, carefully Revised. With Introduction and Additional Chapters, by W. H. Preece, M.I.C.E. Crown 8vo, 12s. 6d. cloth.

Electricity.

A MANUAL OF ELECTRICITY: Including Galvanism, Magnetism, Dia-Magnetism, Electro-Dynamics. By Henry M. Noad, Ph.D., F.R.S. Fourth Edition (1859). 8vo, £1 4s. cloth.

ARCHITECTURE, BUILDING, etc.

Building Construction.

PRACTICAL BUILDING CONSTRUCTION: A Handbook for Students Preparing for Examinations, and a Book of Reference for Persons Engaged in Building. By JOHN PARNELL ALLEN, Surveyor, Lecturer on Building Construction at the Durham College of Science, Newcastle-on-Tyne. Medium 8vo, 450 pages, with 1,000 Illustrations. 12s. 6d. cloth.
[*Just published.*

"This volume is one of the most complete expositions of building construction we have seen. It contains all that is necessary to prepare students for the various examinations in building construction."—*Building News.*

"The author depends nearly as much on his diagrams as on his type. The pages suggest the hand of a man of experience in building operations—and the volume must be a blessing to many teachers as well as to students."—*The Architect.*

"This volume promises to be the recognised hand-book in all advanced classes where building construction is taught from a practical point of view. We strongly commend the book to the notice of all teachers of building construction."—*Technical World.*

"The work is sure to prove a formidable rival to great and small competitors alike, and it is fair to take a permanent place as a favourite students' text book. The large number of illustrations deserve particular mention for the great merit they possess for purposes of reference, in exactly corresponding to convenient scales."—*Jour. Inst. Brit. Ar'ts.*

Concrete.

CONCRETE: ITS NATURE AND USES. A Book for Architects, Builders, Contractors, and Clerks of Works. By GEORGE L. SUTCLIFFE, A.R.I.B.A. 350 pages, with numerous Illustrations. Crown 8vo, 7s. 6d. cloth.
[*Just published.*

"The author treats a difficult subject in a lucid manner. The man at first sight gap. It is careful and exhaustive, equally useful as a student's guide and a architect's book of reference."—*Journal of Royal Institution of British Architects.*

"There is room for this new book, which will probably be for some time the standard work on the subject for a builder's purpose."—*Glasgow Herald.*

"A thoroughly useful and comprehensive work."—*British Architect.*

Mechanics for Architects.

THE MECHANICS OF ARCHITECTURE: A Treatise on Applied Mechanics, especially Adapted to the Use of Architects. By E. W. TARN, M.A., Author of "The Science of Building," &c. Second Edition, Enlarged. Illust. with 125 Diagrams. Cr. 8vo, 7s. 6d. cloth. [*Just publishe'.*

"The book is a very useful and helpful manual of architectural mechanics, and really contains sufficient to enable a careful and painstaking student to grasp the principles bearing upon the majority of building problems. . . . Mr. Tarn has added, by this volume, to the debt of gratitude which is owing to him by architectural students for the many valuable works which he has produced for their use."—*The Builder.*

"The mechanics in the volume are really mechanics, and are harmoniously wrought in with the distinctive professional manner proper to the subject. The diagrams and type are commendably clear."—*The Schoolmaster.*

The New Builder's Price Book, 1894.

LOCKWOOD'S BUILDER'S PRICE BOOK FOR 1894. A Comprehensive Handbook of the Latest Prices and Data for Builders, Architects, Engineers, and Contractors. *Re-constructed, Re-written, and Greatly Enlarged.* By FRANCIS T. W. MILLER. 700 closely-printed pages. crown 8vo, 4s. cloth.

"This book is a very useful one, and should find a place in every English office connected with the building and engineering professions."—*Industries.*

"An excellent book of reference."—*Truth.*

"In its new and revised form this Price Book is what a work of this kind should be —comprehensive, reliable, well arranged, legible, and well bound. *British Architect.*

Designing Buildings.

THE DESIGN OF BUILDINGS. Being Elementary Notes on the Planning, Sanitation and Ornamentive Formation of Structures, based on Modern Practice. Illustrated with Nine Folding Plates. By W. WOODLEY, Assistant Master, Metropolitan Drawing Classes, &c. Demy 8vo, 6s. cloth.
[*Just published.*

Sir Wm. Chambers's Treatise on Civil Architecture.

THE DECORATIVE PART OF CIVIL ARCHITECTURE. By Sir WILLIAM CHAMBERS, F.R.S. With Portrait, Illustrations, Notes, and an Examination of Grecian Architecture, by JOSEPH GWILT, F.S.A. Revised and Edited by W. H. LEEDS. 66 Plates, 4to, 21s. cloth.

Villa Architecture.

A HANDY BOOK OF VILLA ARCHITECTURE: Being a Series of Designs for Villa Residences in various Styles. With Outline Specifications and Estimates. By C. Wickes, Architect, Author of "The Spires and Towers of England," &c. 61 Plates, 4to, £1 11s. 6d. half morocco.
"The whole of the designs bear evident of their being the work of an artistic architect, and they will prove very valuable and suggestive."—*Building News.*

Text-Book for Architects.

THE ARCHITECT'S GUIDE: Being a Text-Book of Useful Information for Architects, Engineers, Surveyors, Contractors, Clerks of Works, &c. &c. By FREDERICK ROGERS, Architect. Third Edition. Crown 8vo, 3s. 6d. cloth.
"As a text book of useful information for architects, engineers, surveyors, &c., it would be hard to find a handier or more complete little volume."—*Standard.*

Taylor and Cresy's Rome.

THE ARCHITECTURAL ANTIQUITIES OF ROME. By the late G. L. TAYLOR, Esq., F.R.I.B.A., and EDWARD CRESY, Esq. New Edition, thoroughly Revised by the Rev. ALEXANDER TAYLOR, M.A. (son of the late G. L. Taylor, Esq.), Fellow of Queen's College, Oxford, and Chaplain of Gray's Inn. Large folio, with 130 Plates, £3 3s. half-bound.
"Taylor and Cresy's work has from its first publication been ranked among those professional books which cannot be bettered."—*Architect.*

Linear Perspective.

ARCHITECTURAL PERSPECTIVE: The whole Course and Operations of the Draughtsman in Drawing a Large House in Linear Perspective. Illustrated by 39 Folding Plates. By F. O. FERGUSON. 8vo, 3s. 6d. boards.
"It is the most intelligible of the treatises on this subject treated . . ."—INGRESS BELL, Esq., in the *R.I.B.A. Journal.*

Architectural Drawing.

PRACTICAL RULES ON DRAWING, for the Operative Builder and Young Student in Architecture. By GEORGE PYNE. With 14 Plates, 4to, 7s. 6d. boards.

Vitruvius' Architecture.

THE ARCHITECTURE of MARCUS VITRUVIUS POLLIO. Translated by JOSEPH GWILT, F.S.A., F.R.A.S. New Edition, Revised by the Translator. With 23 Plates. Fcap. 8vo, 5s. cloth.

Designing, Measuring, and Valuing.

THE STUDENT'S GUIDE to the PRACTICE of MEASURING AND VALUING ARTIFICERS' WORK. Containing Directions for taking Dimensions, Abstracting the same, and bringing the Quantities into Bill, with Tables of Constants for Valuation of Labour, and for the Calculation of Areas and Solidities. Originally edited by EDWARD DOBSON, Architect. With Additions by E. WYNDHAM TARN, M.A. Sixth Edition. With 8 Plates and 63 Woodcuts. Crown 8vo, 7s. 6d. cloth.
"This edition will be found the most complete treatise on the principles of measuring and valuing artificers' work that has yet been published."—*Building News.*

Pocket Estimator and Technical Guide.

THE POCKET TECHNICAL GUIDE, MEASURER, AND ESTIMATOR FOR BUILDERS AND SURVEYORS. Containing Technical Directions for Measuring Work in all the Building Trades, Complete Specifications for Houses, Roads, and Drains, and an easy Method of Estimating the parts of a Building collectively. By A. C. BEATON. Sixth Edit. Waistcoat-pocket size, 1s. 6d. leather, gilt edges.
"No builder, architect, surveyor, or valuer should be without his 'Beaton.'"—*Building News.*

Donaldson on Specifications.

THE HANDBOOK OF SPECIFICATIONS; or, Practical Guide to the Architect, Engineer, Surveyor, and Builder, in drawing up Specifications and Contracts for Works and Constructions. Illustrated by Precedents of Buildings actually executed by eminent Architects and Engineers. By Professor T. L. DONALDSON, P.R.I.B.A., &c. New Edition. 8vo, with upwards of 1,000 pages of Text, and 33 Plates. £1 11s. 6d. cloth.
"Valuable as a record, and more valuable still as a book of precedents. . . . Suffice it to say that Donaldson's 'Handbook of Specifications' must be bought by all architects."—*Reader.*

Bartholomew and Rogers' Specifications.

SPECIFICATIONS FOR PRACTICAL ARCHITECTURE.
A Guide to the Architect, Engineer, Surveyor, and Builder. With an Essay on the Structure and Science of Modern Buildings. Upon the Basis of the Work by ALFRED BARTHOLOMEW, thoroughly Revised, Corrected, and greatly added to by FREDERICK ROGERS, Architect. Third Edition, Revised, with Additions. With numerous Illustrations. Medium 8vo, 15s. cloth.
"The collection of specifications prepared by Mr. Rogers on the basis of Bartholomew's work is too well known to need any recommendation from us. It is one of the books with which every young architect must be equipped."—*Architect.*

Construction.

THE SCIENCE OF BUILDING: An Elementary Treatise on the *Principles of Construction*. By E. WYNDHAM TARN, M.A., Architect. Third Edition, Revised and Enlarged. With 59 Engravings. Fcap. 8vo, 4s. cl.
"A very valuable book, which we strongly recommend to all students."—*Builder.*

House Building and Repairing.

THE HOUSE-OWNER'S ESTIMATOR: or, What will it Cost to Build, Alter, or Repair? A Price Book for Unprofessional People, as well as the Architectural Surveyor and Builder. By JAMES D. SIMON. Edited by FRANCIS T. W. MILLER, A.R.I.B.A. Fourth Edition. Crown 8vo, 3s. 6d. cloth.
"In two years it will repay its cost a hundred times over."—*Field.*

Cottages and Villas.

COUNTRY AND SUBURBAN COTTAGES AND VILLAS: How to Plan and Build Them. Containing 33 Plates, with Introduction, General Explanations, and Description of each Plate. By JAMES W. BOGLE, Architect, Author of "Domestic Architecture," &c. 4to, 10s. 6d. cloth.

Building: Civil and Ecclesiastical.

A BOOK ON BUILDING, *Civil and Ecclesiastical*, including Church Restoration; with the Theory of Domes and the Great Pyramid, &c. By Sir EDMUND BECKETT, Bart., LL.D., F.R.A.S. Second Edition. Fcap. 8vo, 5s. cloth.
"A book which is always amusing and nearly always instructive."—*Times.*

Sanitary Houses, etc.

THE SANITARY ARRANGEMENTS OF DWELLING-HOUSES. By A. J. WALLIS TAYLER, A.M. Inst. C.E. Crown 8vo, with numerous Illustrations. Price about 3s. cloth. [*Nearly ready.*

Ventilation of Buildings.

VENTILATION. *A Text Book to the Practice of the Art of Ventilating Buildings.* By W. P. BUCHAN, R.P. 12mo, 4s. cloth.
"Contains a great amount of useful practical information, as thoroughly interesting as it is technically reliable."—*British Architect.*

The Art of Plumbing.

PLUMBING. *A Text Book to the Practice of the Art or Craft of the Plumber.* By WILLIAM PATON BUCHAN, R.P. Sixth Edition, Enlarged. 12mo, 4s. cloth.
"A text-book which may be safely put in the hands of every young plumber."—*****

Geometry for the Architect, Engineer, etc.

PRACTICAL GEOMETRY, *for the Architect, Engineer, and Mechanic.* Giving Rules for the Delineation and Application of various Geometrical Lines, Figures and Curves. By E. W. TARN, M.A., Architect. 8vo, 9s. cloth.
"No book with the same object in view has ever been published in which the clearness of the rules laid down and the illustrative diagrams have been so satisfactory."—*Scotsman.*

The Science of Geometry.

THE GEOMETRY OF COMPASSES; or, *Problems Resolved by the mere Description of Circles, and the use of Coloured Diagrams and Symbols.* By OLIVER BYRNE. Coloured Plates. Crown 8vo, 3s. 6d. cloth.

CARPENTRY, TIMBER, etc.

Tredgold's Carpentry, Revised & Enlarged by Tarn.
THE ELEMENTARY PRINCIPLES OF CARPENTRY. A Treatise on the Pressure and Equilibrium of Timber Framing, the Resistance of Timber, and the Construction of Floors, Arches, Bridges, Roofs, Uniting Iron and Stone with Timber, &c. To which is added an Essay on the Nature and Properties of Timber, &c., with Descriptions of the kinds of Wood used in Building; also numerous Tables of the Scantlings of Timber for different purposes, the Specific Gravities of Materials, &c. By THOMAS TREDGOLD, C.E. With an Appendix of Specimens of Various Roofs of Iron and Stone, lately erected. Seventh Ed tion, thoroughly revised and considerably enlarged by E. WYNDHAM TARN, M A., Author of "The Science of Building," &c. With 61 Plates, Portrait of the Author, and several Woodcuts. In One large Vol., 4to, price £1 5s. cloth.

"Ought to be in every architect's and every builder's library."—*Builder.*

"A work whose merit and excellence must command it wherever skilled carpentry is concerned. The volume's merits are rather enhanced than impaired by time. The additional plates are of great intrinsic value."—*Building News.*

Woodworking Machinery.
WOODWORKING MACHINERY: Its Rise, Progress, and Construction. With Hints on the Management of Saw Mills and the Economical Conversion of Timber. Illustrated with Examples of Recent Designs by leading English, French, and American Engineers. By M. POWIS BALE, A.M.Inst.C.E., M.I.M.E. Second Ed tion, Revised, with large Additions. Large crown 8vo, 410 pp., 9s. cloth. [*Just published*

"Mr. Bale is evidently an expert on the subject and he has collected so much information that his book is all-sufficient for builders and others engaged in the conversion of timber."—*Architect.*

"The most comprehensive compendium of wood working machinery we have seen. The author is a thorough master of his subject."—*Building News.*

Saw Mills.
SAW MILLS: Their Arrangement and Management, and the Economical Conversion of Timber. (A Companion Volume to "Woodworking Machinery.") By M. POWIS BALE. Crown 8vo, 10s. 6d. cloth.

"The administration of a large sawing establishment is discussed and the subject examined from a financial standpoint. Hence the successive order as logs are converted and the course of the timber traced from its reception to its delivery in its converted state. We could not desire a more complete or practical treatise."—*Builder.*

Nicholson's Carpentry.
THE CARPENTER'S NEW GUIDE; or, Book of Lines for Carpenters; comprising all the Elementary Principles essential for acquiring a knowledge of Carpentry. Founded on the late PETER NICHOLSON'S Standard Work. New Edition. Revised by A. ASHPITEL, F.S.A. With Practical Rules on Drawing, by G. PYNE. With 74 Plates 4to, £1 1s. cloth.

Handrailing and Stairbuilding.
A PRACTICAL TREATISE ON HANDRAILING: Showing New and Simple Methods for Finding the Pitch of the Plank, Drawing the Moulds, Bevelling, Jointing-up, and Squaring the Wreath. By GEORGE COLLINGS. Second Edition, Revised and Enlarged, to which is added A TREATISE ON STAIRBUILDING. 12mo, 2s. 6d. cloth limp.

"Will be found of practical utility in the execution of the difficult branch of joinery."—*Builder.*

"Almost every difficult phase of this somewhat intricate branch of joinery is elucidated by the aid of plates and explanatory letterpress."—*Furniture Gazette.*

Circular Work.
CIRCULAR WORK IN CARPENTRY AND JOINERY: A Practical Treatise on Circular Work of Single and Double Curvature. By GEORGE COLLINGS. With Diagrams. Second Edition, 12mo, 2s 6d. cloth limp.

"An excellent example of what a book of this sort should be. Cheap in price, clear in definition and practical in the examples selected."—*Builder.*

Handrailing.
HANDRAILING COMPLETE IN EIGHT LESSONS. On the Square-Cut System. By J. S. GOLDTHORP, Teacher of Geometry and Building Construction at the Halifax Mechanic's Institute. With Eight Plates and over 150 Practical Exercises. 4to, 3s. 6d. cloth.

"Likely to be of considerable use to those artisans who wish to take a pride in good work. We heartily commend it to teachers and students."—*Timber Trades Journal.*

CARPENTRY, TIMBER, etc.

Timber Merchant's Companion.
THE TIMBER MERCHANT'S AND BUILDER'S COMPANION. Containing New and Copious Tables of the Reduced Weight and Measurement of Deals and Battens, of all sizes, from One to a Thousand Pieces, and the relative Price that each size bears per Lineal Foot to any given Price per Petersburg Standard Hundred; the Price per Cube Foot of Square Timber to any given Price per Load of 50 Feet; the proportionate Value of Deals and Battens by the Standard, to Square Timber by the Load of 50 Feet; the readiest mode of ascertaining the Price of Scantling per Lineal Foot of any size, to any given Figure per Cube Foot, &c. &c. By WILLIAM DOWSING. Fourth Edition, Revised and Corrected. Cr. 8vo, 3s cl.

"Everything is as concise and correct as it ... [illegible] ... every timber merchant ..."—*Hull Advertiser.*
"We are glad to see a fourth edition of these admirable tables, which for correctness and simplicity of arrangement leave nothing to be desired.—*Timber Trades Journal.*

Practical Timber Merchant.
THE PRACTICAL TIMBER MERCHANT. Being a Guide for the use of Building Contractors, Surveyors, Builders, &c., comprising useful Tables for all purposes connected with the Timber Trade, Marks of Wood, Essay on the Strength of Timber, Remarks on the Growth of Timber, &c. By W. RICHARDSON. Fcap 8vo, 3s 6d. cloth.

"This handy manual contains much valuable information for the use of timber merchants, builders, breeders, and all others connected with the growth, use, and manufacture of timber.—*Journal of Forestry.*

Timber Freight Book.
THE TIMBER MERCHANT'S, SAW MILLER'S, AND IMPORTER'S FREIGHT BOOK AND ASSISTANT. Comprising Rules, Tables, and Memoranda relating to the Timber Trade. By WILLIAM RICHARDSON, Timber Broker; together with a Chapter on "SPEEDS OF SAW MILL MACHINERY," by M POWIS BALE, M I M E., &c. 12mo, 3s. 6d. cl. boards.

"A very useful manual of rules, tables and memoranda relating to the timber trade. We recommend it as a compendium of calculations to all timber measurers and merchants, and as supplying a real want in the trade.—*Building News.*

Packing-Case Makers, Tables for.
PACKING-CASE TABLES; showing the number of Superficial Feet in Boxes or Packing-Cases, from six inches square and upwards. By W. RICHARDSON, Timber Broker. Third Edition. Oblong 4to, 3s. 6d. cl.
"Invaluable labour-saving tables."—*Ironmonger.*
"Will save much labour and calculation.—*Grocer.*

Superficial Measurement.
THE TRADESMAN'S GUIDE TO SUPERFICIAL MEASUREMENT. Tables calculated from 1 to 200 inches in length, by 1 to 108 inches in breadth. For the use of Architects, Surveyors, Engineers, Timber Merchants, Builders, &c. By JAMES HAWKINGS. Fourth Edition. Fcap., 3s. 6d. cloth.

"A useful collection of tables to facilitate rapid calculation of surfaces. The exact area of any surface of which the limits have been ascertained can be instantly determined. The book will be found of the greatest utility to all engaged in building operations."—*Scotsman.*
"These tables will be found of great assistance to all who require to make calculations in superficial measurement.—*English Mechanic.*

Forestry.
THE ELEMENTS OF FORESTRY. Designed to afford Information concerning the Planting and Care of Forest Trees for Ornament or Profit, with Suggestions upon the Creation and Care of Woodlands. By F. B. HOUGH. Large crown 8vo, 10s. cloth.

Timber Importer's Guide.
THE TIMBER IMPORTER'S, TIMBER MERCHANT'S, AND BUILDER'S STANDARD GUIDE. By RICHARD E. GRANDY. Comprising an Analysis of Deal Standards, Home and Foreign, with Comparative Values and Tabular Arrangements for fixing Net Landed Cost on Baltic and North American Deals, including all intermediate Expenses, Freight, Insurance, &c. &c. Together with copious Information for the Retailer and Builder. Third Edition, Revised. 12mo, 2s. cloth limp.

"Everything it pretends to be ... gradually, it leads one from a forest to a treenail, and throws in, as a makeweight, a host of material concerning ... &c.—*English Mechanic.*

DECORATIVE ARTS, etc.

Woods and Marbles (Imitation of).

SCHOOL OF PAINTING FOR THE IMITATION OF WOODS AND MARBLES, as Taught and Practised by A. R. VAN DER BURG and P. VAN DER BURG, Directors of the Rotterdam Painting Institution. Royal folio, 18¾ by 12¼ in., Illustrated with 24 large Coloured Plates; also 12 plain Plates, comprising 154 Figures. Second and Cheaper Edition. Price £1 11s. 6d.

List of Plates.

1. Various Tools required for Wood Painting—2, 3. Walnut: Preliminary Stages of Graining and Finished Specimen—4. Tools used for Marble Painting and Method of Manipulation—5, 6. St. Remi Marble: Earlier Operations and Finished Specimen. 7. Methods of Sketching different Grains, Knots, &c.—8, 9. Ash: Preliminary Stages and Finished Specimen—10. Methods of Sketching Marble Grains—11, 12. Breche Marble: Preliminary Stages of Working and Finished Specimen—13. Maple: Methods of Producing the different Grains—14, 15. Bird's-eye Maple: Preliminary Stages and Finished Specimen—16. Methods of Sketching the different Species of White Marble—17, 18. White Marble: Preliminary Stages of Process and Finished Specimen—19. Mahogany: Specimens of various Grain and Methods of Manipulation—20, 21. Mahogany: Earlier Stages and Finished Specimen—22, 23, 24. Serra Marble. Varieties of Grain, Preliminary Stages and Finished Specimen—25, 26, 27. Juniper Wood: Methods of producing Grain &c.: Preliminary Stages and Finished Specimen—28, 29, 30. Vert de Mer Marble: Varieties of Grain and Methods of Working: Unfinished and Finished Specimens—31, 32, 33. Oak: Varieties of Grain, Tools Employed and Methods of Manipulation, Preliminary Stages and Finished Specimens—34, 35, 36. Waulsort Marble: Varieties of Grain, Unfinished and Finished Specimens.

"Those who desire to attain skill in the art of painting wood and marbles will find advantage in consulting this book. . . . Some of the Working Men's Clubs should give their young men the opportunity to study it."—*Builder.*

"A comprehensive guide to the art. The explanations of the processes, the manipulation and management of the colours, and the beautifully executed plates will not be the least valuable to the student who aims at making his work a faithful transcript of nature.—*Building News.*

Wall Paper.

WALL PAPER DECORATION. By ARTHUR SEYMOUR JENNINGS, Author of "Practical Paper Hanging." With numerous Illustrations. Demy 8vo. *In preparation.*

House Decoration.

ELEMENTARY DECORATION. A Guide to the Simpler Forms of Everyday Art. Together with PRACTICAL HOUSE DECORATION. By JAMES W. FACEY. With numerous Illustrations. In One Vol., 5s. strongly half-bound.

House Painting, Graining, etc.

HOUSE PAINTING, GRAINING, MARBLING, AND SIGN WRITING, A Practical Manual of. By ELLIS A. DAVIDSON. Sixth Edition. With Coloured Plates and Wood Engravings. 12mo, 6s. cloth boards.

"A mass of information, of use to the amateur and of value to the practical man."—*English Mechanic.*

Decorators, Receipts for.

THE DECORATOR'S ASSISTANT: A Modern Guide to Decorative Artists and Amateurs, Painters, Writers, Gilders, &c. Containing upwards of 600 Receipts, Rules and Instructions; with a variety of Information for General Work connected with every Class of Interior and Exterior Decorations, &c. Fifth Edition, Revised. 152 pp., crown 8vo, 1s. in wrapper.

"Full of receipts of value to decorators, painters, gilders, &c. The book contains the gist of larger treatises on colour and technical processes. It would be difficult to meet with a work so full of varied information on the painter's art."—*Building News.*

Moyr Smith on Interior Decoration.

ORNAMENTAL INTERIORS, ANCIENT AND MODERN. By J. MOYR SMITH. Super-royal 8vo, with 32 full-page Plates and numerous smaller Illustrations, handsomely bound in cloth, gilt top, price 18s.

"The book is well illustrated and handsomely got up, and contains some true criticism and a good many good examples of decorative treatment.—*The Builder.*

British and Foreign Marbles.

MARBLE DECORATION and the Terminology of British and Foreign Marbles. A Handbook for Students. By GEORGE H. BLAGROVE, Author of "Shoring and its Application," &c. With 28 Illustrations. Crown 8vo, 3s. 6d. cloth.

"This most useful and much wanted handbook should be in the hands of every architect and builder."—*Building World.*
"A carefully and usefully written treatise; the work is essentially practical.—*Scotsman.*

Marble Working, etc.

MARBLE AND MARBLE WORKERS: A Handbook for Architects, Artists, Masons, and Students. By ARTHUR LEE, Author of "A Visit to Carrara," "The Working of Marble," &c. Small crown 8vo, 2s. cloth.

"A really valuable addition to the technical literature of architects and masons.—*Building News.*

DELAMOTTE'S WORKS ON ILLUMINATION AND ALPHABETS.

A PRIMER OF THE ART OF ILLUMINATION, for the Use of Beginners: with a Rudimentary Treatise on the Art, Practical Directions for its Exercise, and Examples taken from Illuminated MSS., printed in Gold and Colours. By F. DELAMOTTE. New and Cheaper Edition. Small 4to, 6s. ornamental boards.

"The examples of ancient MSS. recommended to the student, which, with much good sense, the author chooses from collections accessible to all, are selected with judgment and knowledge, as well as taste."—*Athenæum.*

ORNAMENTAL ALPHABETS, Ancient and Mediæval, from the Eighth Century, with Numerals; including Gothic, Church-Text, large and small, German, Italian, Arabesque, Initials for Illumination, Monograms, Crosses, &c. &c., for the use of Architectural and Engineering Draughtsmen, Missal Painters, Masons, Decorative Painters, Lithographers, Engravers, Carvers, &c. &c. Collected and Engraved by F. DELAMOTTE, and printed in Colours. New and Cheaper Edition. Royal 8vo, oblong, 2s. 6d. ornamental boards.

"For those who insert enamelled sentences round gilt leaf chalices, who blazon shop legends over shop-doors, who letter church walls with pithy sentences from the Decalogue, this book will be useful.—*Athenæum.*

EXAMPLES OF MODERN ALPHABETS, Plain and Ornamental; including German, Old English, Saxon, Italic, Perspective, Greek, Hebrew, Court Hand, Engrossing, Tuscan, Riband, Gothic, Rustic, and Arabesque; with several Original Designs, and an Analysis of the Roman and Old English Alphabets, large and small, and Numerals, for the use of Draughtsmen, Surveyors, Masons, Decorative Painters, Lithographers, Engravers, Carvers, &c. Collected and Engraved by F. DELAMOTTE, and printed in Colours. New and Cheaper Edition. Royal 8vo, oblong, 2s. 6d. ornamental boards.

"There is comprised in it every possible shape into which the letters of the alphabet and numerals can be formed, and the talent which has been expended in the conception of the various plain and ornamental letters is wonderful."—*Standard.*

MEDIÆVAL ALPHABETS AND INITIALS FOR ILLUMINATORS. By F. G. DELAMOTTE. Containing 21 Plates and Illuminated Title, printed in Gold and Colours. With an Introduction by J. WILLIS BROOKS. Fourth and Cheaper Edition. Small 4to, 4s. ornamental boards.

"A volume in which the letters of the alphabet come forth glorified in gilding and all the colours of the prism interwoven and intertwined and intermingled.—*Sun.*

THE EMBROIDERER'S BOOK OF DESIGN. Containing Initials, Emblems, Cyphers, Monograms, Ornamental Borders, Ecclesiastical Devices, Mediæval and Modern Alphabets, and National Emblems. Collected by F. DELAMOTTE, and printed in Colours. Oblong royal 8vo, 1s. 6d. ornamental wrapper.

"The book will be of great assistance to ladies and young children who are endowed with the art of plying the needle in this most ornamental and useful pretty work.'—*East Anglian Times.*

Wood Carving.

INSTRUCTIONS IN WOOD-CARVING, for Amateurs; with Hints on Design. By A LADY. With Ten Plates. New and Cheaper Edition. Crown 8vo, 2s. in emblematic wrapper.

"The handicraft of the wood-carver, so well as a book can impart it, may be learnt from 'A Lady's publication.'—*Athenæum.*

NATURAL SCIENCE, etc.

The Heavens and their Origin.
THE VISIBLE UNIVERSE: Chapters on the Origin and Construction of the Heavens. By J. E. GORE, F.R.A.S., Author of "Star Groups," &c. Illustrated by 6 Stellar Photographs and 12 Plates. Demy 8vo, 16s. cloth, gilt top.

"A valuable and lucid summary of recent astronomical theory, rendered more valuable and attractive by a series of stellar photographs and other illustrations."—*The Times.*

"In presenting a clear and concise account of the present state of our knowledge, Mr Gore has made a valuable addition to the literature of the subject."—*Nature.*

"One of the finest works on astronomical science that has recently appeared in our language. In spirit and in method it is scientific from cover to cover, but the style is so clear and attractive that it will be as acceptable and as readable to those who make no scientific pretensions as to those who devote themselves specially to matters astronomical."—*Leeds Mercury.*

"As interesting as a novel, and instructive withal; the text being made still more luminous by stellar photographs and other illustrations. . . . A most valuable book."—*Manchester Examiner.*

The Constellations.
STAR GROUPS: A Student's Guide to the Constellations. By J. ELLARD GORE, F.R.A.S., M.R.I.A., &c., Author of "The Visible Universe," "The Scenery of the Heavens." With 30 Maps. Small 4to, 5s. cloth, silvered.

"A knowledge of the principal constellations visible in our latitudes may be easily acquired from the thirty maps and accompanying text contained in this work."—*Nature.*

"The volume contains thirty maps showing stars of the sixth magnitude—the usual naked eye limit—and each is accompanied by a brief commentary, adapted to facilitate recognition and bring to notice objects of special interest. For the purpose of a preliminary survey of the midnight pomp of the heavens, nothing could be better than a set of delineations averaging scarcely twenty square inches in area, and including nothing that cannot at once be identified."—*Saturday Review.*

"A very compact and handy guide to the constellations."—*Athenæum.*

Astronomical Terms.
AN ASTRONOMICAL GLOSSARY: or, Dictionary of Terms used in Astronomy. With Tables of Data and Lists of Remarkable and Interesting Celestial Objects. By J. ELLARD GORE, F.R.A.S., Author of "The Visible Universe," &c., Small crown 8vo, 2s 6d. cloth.

"A very useful little work for beginners in astronomy, and not to be despised by more advanced students."—*The Time.*

"A very handy book. . . . the utility of which is much increased by its valuable tables of astronomical data."—*The Athenæum.*

"Astronomers of all kinds will be glad to have it for reference."—*Guardian.*

The Microscope.
THE MICROSCOPE: Its Construction and Management, including Technique, Photo-micrography, and the Past and Future of the Microscope. By Dr. HENRI VAN HEURCK, Director of the Antwerp Botanical Gardens. English Edition, Re-Edited and Augmented by the Author from the Fourth French Edition, and Translated by WYNNE E. BAXTER, F.R.M.S., F.G.S., &c. About 400 pages, with Three Plates and upwards of 250 Woodcuts. Imp. 8vo, 18s. cloth gilt.

"A translation of a well-known work, at once popular and comprehensive."—*Times.*

"The translation is as felicitous as it is accurate."—*Nature.*

Astronomy.
ASTRONOMY. By the late Rev. ROBERT MAIN, M.A., F R S. Third Edition, Revised, by WM. THYNNE LYNN, B.A., F.R.A.S., formerly of the Royal Observatory, Greenwich. 12mo, 2s. cloth limp.

"A sound and simple treatise, and a capital book for beginners."—*Knowledge.*

"Accurately brought down to the requirements of the present time."—*Educational Times.*

Recent and Fossil Shells.
A MANUAL OF THE MOLLUSCA: Being a Treatise on Recent and Fossil Shells. By S. P. WOODWARD, A.L.S., F.G.S., late Assistant Palæontologist in the British Museum. With an Appendix on Recent and Fossil Conchological Discoveries, by RALPH TATE, A.L.S., F.G.S. Illustrated by A. N. WATERHOUSE and JOSEPH WILSON LOWRY. With 23 Plates and upwards of 300 Woodcuts. Reprint of Fourth Ed., 1880. Cr. 8vo, 7s. 6d. cl.

"A most valuable storehouse of conchological and geological information."—*Science Gossip.*

Geology and Genesis.
THE TWIN RECORDS OF CREATION; or, Geology and Genesis: their Perfect Harmony and Wonderful Concord. By GEORGE W. VICTOR LE VAUX. Fcap. 8vo, 5s. cloth.

"A valuable contribution to the evidences of Revelation, and disposes very conclusively of the arguments of those who would set God's Works against God's Word. No real difficulty is shirked and no sophistry is left unexposed."—*The Rock.*

DR. LARDNER'S COURSE OF NATURAL PHILOSOPHY.

THE HANDBOOK OF MECHANICS. Enlarged and almost Rewritten by BENJAMIN LOEWY, F.R.A.S. With 378 Illustrations. Post 8vo, 6s. cloth.

"The perspicuity of the original has been retained, and chapters which had become obsolete have been replaced by others of more modern character. The explanations throughout are studiously popular, and care has been taken to show the application of the various branches of physics to the industrial arts, and to the practical business of life."—*Mining Journal.*

"Mr. Loewy has carefully revised the book, and brought it up to modern requirements."—*Nature.*

"Natural philosophy has had few exponents more able or better skilled in the art of popularising the subject than Dr. Lardner; and Mr. Loewy is doing good service in fitting this treatise, and the others of the series, for use at the present time."—*Scotsman.*

THE HANDBOOK OF HYDROSTATICS AND PNEUMATICS. New Edition, Revised and Enlarged, by BENJAMIN LOEWY, F.R.A.S. With 236 Illustrations. Post 8vo, 5s. cloth.

"For those 'who desire to attain an accurate knowledge of physical science without the profound methods of mathematical investigation,' this work is not merely intended, but well adapted."—*Chemical News.*

"The volume before us has been carefully edited, augmented to nearly twice the bulk of the former edition, and all the most recent matter has been added. . . . It is a valuable text-book."—*Nature.*

"Candidates for pass examinations will find it, we think, specially suited to their requirements.—*English Mechanic.*

THE HANDBOOK OF HEAT. Edited and almost entirely Rewritten by BENJAMIN LOEWY, F.R.A.S., &c. 117 Illusts. Post 8vo, 6s. cloth.

"The style is always clear and precise, and conveys instruction without leaving any cloudiness or lurking doubts behind."—*Engineering.*

"A most exhaustive book on the subject on which it treats, and is so arranged that it can be understood by all who desire to attain an accurate knowledge of physical science. . . . Mr. Loewy has included all the latest discoveries in the varied laws and effects of heat."—*Standard.*

"A complete and handy text-book for the use of students and general readers."—*English Mechanic.*

THE HANDBOOK OF OPTICS. By DIONYSIUS LARDNER, D.C.L., formerly Professor of Natural Philosophy and Astronomy in University College, London. New Edition. Edited by T. OLVER HARDING, B.A. Lond., of University College, London. With 298 Illustrations. Small 8vo, 448 pages, 5s. cloth.

"Written by one of the ablest English scientific writers, beautifully and elaborately illustrated."—*Mechanic's Magazine.*

THE HANDBOOK OF ELECTRICITY, MAGNETISM, AND ACOUSTICS. By Dr. LARDNER. Ninth Thousand. Edit. by GEORGE CAREY FOSTER, B.A., F.C.S. With 400 Illustrations. Small 8vo, 5s. cloth.

"The book could not have been entrusted to anyone better calculated to preserve the terse and lucid style of Lardner, while correcting his errors and bringing up his work to the present state of scientific knowledge."—*Popular Science Review.*

THE HANDBOOK OF ASTRONOMY. Forming a Companion to the "Handbook of Natural Philosophy." By DIONYSIUS LARDNER, D.C.L., formerly Professor of Natural Philosophy and Astronomy in University College, London. Fourth Edition, Revised and Edited by EDWIN DUNKIN, F.R.A.S., Royal Observatory, Greenwich. With 38 Plates and upwards of 100 Woodcuts. In One Vol., small 8vo, 550 pages, 9s. 6d. cloth.

"Probably no other book contains the same amount of information in so compendious and well-arranged a form—certainly none at the price at which this is offered to the public."—*Athenæum.*

"We can do no other than pronounce this work a most valuable manual of astronomy, and we strongly recommend it to all who wish to acquire a general—but at the same time correct—acquaintance with this sublime science."—*Quarterly Journal of Science.*

"One of the most deservedly popular books on the subject . . . We would recommend not only the student of the elementary principles of the science, but he who aims at mastering the higher and mathematical branches of astronomy, not to be without this work beside him."—*Practical Magazine.*

Geology.

RUDIMENTARY TREATISE ON GEOLOGY, PHYSICAL AND HISTORICAL. Consisting of "Physical Geology," which sets forth the leading Principles of the Science; and "Historical Geology," which treats of the Mineral and Organic Conditions of the Earth at each successive epoch, especial reference being made to the British Series of Rocks. By RALPH TATE, A.L.S., F.G.S., &c. With 250 Illustrations. 12mo, 5s cl. bds.

"The fulness of the matter has elevated the book into a manual. Its information is exhaustive and well arranged."—*School Board Chronicle.*

D

DR. LARDNER'S MUSEUM OF SCIENCE AND ART.

THE MUSEUM OF SCIENCE AND ART. Edited by Dionysius Lardner, D.C.L., formerly Professor of Natural Philosophy and Astronomy in University College, London. With upwards of 1,200 Engravings on Wood. In 6 Double Volumes, £1 1s. in a new and elegant cloth binding; or handsomely bound in half morocco, 31s. 6d.

*** OPINIONS OF THE PRESS.

"This series, besides affording popular but sound information on scientific subjects, with which the humblest man in the country ought to be acquainted, also undertakes that thorough of 'Common Things' which every well-wisher of his kind is anxious to promote. Many thousand copies of this serviceable publication have been printed, in the belief and hope that the desire for instruction and improvement widely prevails; and we have no fear that such enlightened faith will meet with disappointment."—*Times*.

"A cheap and interesting publication, alike informing and attractive. The papers combine subjects of importance and great scientific knowledge, considerable inductive powers, and a popular style of treatment."—*Spectator*.

"The 'Museum of Science and Art' is the most valuable contribution that has ever been made to the Scientific Instruction of every class of society."—Sir DAVID BREWSTER, in the *North British Review*.

"Whether we consider the liberality and beauty of the illustrations, the charm of the writing, or the durable interest of the matter, we must express our belief that there is hardly to be found among the new books one that would be welcomed by people of so many ages and classes as a valuable present."—*Examiner*.

*** *Separate books formed from the above, suitable for Workmen's Libraries, Science Classes, etc.*

Common Things Explained. Containing Air, Earth, Fire, Water, Time, Man, the Eye, Locomotion, Colour, Clocks and Watches, &c. 233 Illustrations, cloth gilt, 5s.

The Microscope. Containing Optical Images, Magnifying Glasses, Origin and Description of the Microscope, Microscopic Objects, the Solar Microscope, Microscopic Drawing and Engraving, &c. 147 Illustrations, cloth gilt, 2s.

Popular Geology. Containing Earthquakes and Volcanoes, the Crust of the Earth, &c. 201 Illustrations, cloth gilt, 2s. 6d.

Popular Physics. Containing Magnitude and Minuteness, the Atmosphere, Meteoric Stones, Popular Fallacies, Weather Prognostics, the Thermometer, the Barometer, Sound, &c. 85 Illustrations, cloth gilt, 2s. 6d.

Steam and its Uses. Including the Steam Engine, the Locomotive, and Steam Navigation. 89 Illustrations, cloth gilt, 2s.

Popular Astronomy. Containing How to observe the Heavens—The Earth, Sun, Moon, Planets, Light, Comets, Eclipses, Astronomical Influences, &c. 182 Illustrations, cloth gilt, 4s. 6d.

The Bee and White Ants: Their Manners and Habits. With Illustrations of Animal Instinct and Intelligence. 135 Illustrations, cloth gilt, 2s.

The Electric Telegraph Popularized. To render intelligible to all who can Read, irrespective of any previous Scientific Acquirements, the various forms of Telegraphy in Actual Operation. 100 Illustrations, cloth gilt, 1s. 6d.

Dr. Lardner's School Handbooks.

NATURAL PHILOSOPHY FOR SCHOOLS. By Dr. LARDNER. 328 Illustrations. Sixth Edition. One Vol., 3s. 6d. cloth.

"A very convenient class-book for junior students in private schools. It is intended to convey in clear and precise terms, general notions of all the principal divisions of Physical Science."—*British Quarterly Review*.

ANIMAL PHYSIOLOGY FOR SCHOOLS. By Dr. LARDNER. With 190 Illustrations. Second Edition. One Vol., 3s. 6d. cloth.

"Clearly written, well arranged, and excellently illustrated."—*Gardener's Chronicle*.

Lardner and Bright on the Electric Telegraph.

THE ELECTRIC TELEGRAPH. By Dr. LARDNER. Revised and Re-written by E. B. BRIGHT, F.R.A.S. 140 Illustrations. Small 8vo, 2s. 6d. cloth.

"One of the most readable books extant on the Electric Telegraph."—*English Mechanic*.

CHEMICAL MANUFACTURES, CHEMISTRY.

Chemistry for Engineers, etc.

ENGINEERING CHEMISTRY: A Practical Treatise for the Use of Analytical Chemists, Engineers, Iron Masters, Iron Founders, Students, and others. Comprising Methods of Analysis and Valuation of the Principal Materials used in Engineering Work, with numerous Analyses, Examples, and Suggestions. By H. JOSHUA PHILLIPS, F.I.C., F.C.S. formerly Analytical and Consulting Chemist to the Great Eastern Railway. Second Edition, Revised and Enlarged. Crown 8vo, 400 pp., with Illustrations, 10s. 6d. cloth. [*Just published.*

"In this work the author has rendered no small service to a numerous body of practical men. . . . The analytical methods may be pronounced most satisfactory, being as accurate as the despatch required of engineering chemists permits."—*Chemical News.*

"Those in search of a handy treatise on the subject of analytical chemistry as applied to the every-day requirements of workshop practice will find this volume of great assistance."—*Iron.*

"The first attempt to bring forward a Chemistry specially written for the use of engineers, and we have no hesitation whatever in saying that it should at once be in the possession of every railway engineer."—*The Railway Engineer.*

"The book will be very useful to those who require a handy and concise *resume* of approved methods of analysing and valuing metals, oils, fuels, &c. It is, in fact, a work for chemists, a guide to the routine of the engineering laboratory. . . . The book is full of good things. As a handbook of technical analysis, it is very welcome."—*Builder.*

"Considering the extensive ground which such a subject as Engineering Chemistry covers, the work is complete, and recommends itself to both the practising analyst and the analytical student."—*Chemical Trade Journal.*

"The analytical methods given are, as a whole, such as are likely to give rapid and trustworthy results in experienced hands. There is much excellent descriptive matter in the work, the chapter on 'Oils and Lubrication' being specially noticeable in this respect."—*Engineer.*

Alkali Trade, Manufacture of Sulphuric Acid, etc.

A MANUAL OF THE ALKALI TRADE, including the Manufacture of Sulphuric Acid, Sulphate of Soda, and Bleaching Powder. By JOHN LOMAS, Alkali Manufacturer, Newcastle-upon-Tyne and London. With 232 Illustrations and Working Drawings, and containing 390 pages of Text. Second Edition, with Additions. Super-royal 8vo, £1 10s. cloth.

"This book is written by a manufacturer for manufacturers. The working details of the most approved forms of apparatus are given, and these are accompanied by no less than 232 wood engravings, all of which may be used for the purposes of construction. Every step in the manufacture is very fully described in this manual, and each improvement explained."—*Athenæum.*

"We find not merely a sound and luminous explanation of the chemical principles of the trade, but a notice of numerous matters which have a most important bearing on the successful conduct of alkali works, but which are generally overlooked by even experienced technological authors."—*Chemical Review.*

The Blowpipe.

THE BLOWPIPE IN CHEMISTRY, MINERALOGY, AND GEOLOGY. Containing all known Methods of Anhydrous Analysis, many Working Examples, and Instructions for Making Apparatus. By Lieut.-Colonel W. A. ROSS, R.A., F.G.S. With 120 Illustrations. Second Edition. Revised and Enlarged. Crown 8vo, 5s. cloth.

"The student who goes through the course of experimentation here laid down will gain a better insight into inorganic chemistry and mineralogy than if he had 'got up' any of the best text-books, and passed any number of examinations in their contents."—*Chemical News.*

Commercial Chemical Analysis.

THE COMMERCIAL HANDBOOK OF CHEMICAL ANALYSIS; or, Practical Instructions for the determination of the Intrinsic or Commercial Value of Substances used in Manufactures, in Trades, and in the Arts. By A. NORMANDY, Editor of Rose's "Treatise on Chemical Analysis." New Edition, to a great extent Re-written by HENRY M. NOAD, Ph.D., F.R.S. With numerous Illustrations. Crown 8vo, 12s. 6d. cloth.

"We strongly recommend this book to our readers as a guide, alike indispensable to the housewife as to the pharmaceutical practitioner."—*Medical Times.*

"Essential to the analysts appointed under the new Act. The most recent results are given and the work is well edited and carefully written."—*Nature.*

Dye-Wares and Colours.

THE MANUAL OF COLOURS AND DYE-WARES: Their Properties, Applications, Valuations, Impurities, and Sophistications. For the use of Dyers, Printers, Drysalters, Brokers, &c. By J. W. SLATER. Second Edition, Revised and greatly Enlarged. Crown 8vo, 7s. 6d. cloth.

"A complete encyclopædia of the *materia tinctoria*. The information given respecting each article is full and precise, and the methods of determining the value of articles such as these, so liable to sophistication, are given with clearness, and are practical as well as valuable."—*Chemist and Druggist.*

"There is no other work which covers precisely the same ground. To students preparing for examinations in dyeing and printing it will prove exceedingly useful."—*Chemical News.*

Modern Brewing and Malting.

A HANDYBOOK FOR BREWERS: Being a Practical Guide to the Art of Brewing and Malting. Embracing the Conclusions of Modern Research which bear upon the Practice of Brewing. By HERBERT EDWARDS WRIGHT, M.A., Author of "A Handbook for Young Brewers." Crown 8vo, 550 pp., 12s. 6d. cloth.

"May be consulted with advantage by the student who is preparing himself for examinational tests, while the scientific brewer will find in it a résumé of all the most important discoveries of modern times. The work is written throughout in a clear and intelligible style, and the author shews great care to discriminate between vague theories, and well-ascertained facts."—*Brewers' Journal.*

"We have great pleasure in recommending this handybook, as I have no hesitation in saying that it is one of the best, if not the best, which has yet been written on the subject of beer-brewing in this country, and it should have a place on the shelves of every brewer's library."—*The Brewers' Guardian.*

"Although the requirements of the student are primarily considered, a practical tane [*sic*] an hour's duty the cannot fail to impress the practical brewer with the sense of its value. It is a trustworthy guide and practical counsellor in brewery matters."—*Chemical Trades Journal.*

Analysis and Valuation of Fuels.

FUELS: SOLID, LIQUID, AND GASEOUS, Their Analysis and Valuation. For the Use of Chemists and Engineers. By H. J. PHILLIPS, F.C.S., formerly Analytical and Consulting Chemist to the Great Eastern Railway. Second Edition, Revised and Enlarged. Crown 8vo, 5s. cloth.

"Ought to have its place in the laboratory of every metallurgical establishment, and wherever fuel is used on a large scale."—*Chemical News.*

"Cannot fail to be of wide interest, especially at the present time."—*Railway News.*

Pigments.

THE ARTIST'S MANUAL OF PIGMENTS. Showing their Composition, Conditions of Permanency, Non-Permanency, and Adulterations; Effects in Combination with Each Other and with Vehicles, and the most Reliable Tests of Purity. Together with the Science and Art Department's Examination Questions on Painting. By H. C. STANDAGE. Second Edition. Crown 8vo, 2s. 6d. cloth.

"This work is indeed *multum-in-parvo*, and we can, with good conscience, recommend it to all who come in contact with pigments, whether as makers, dealers or users."—*Chemical Review.*

Gauging. Tables and Rules for Revenue Officers, Brewers, etc.

A POCKET BOOK OF MENSURATION AND GAUGING: Containing Tables, Rules and Memoranda for Revenue Officers, Brewers, Spirit Merchants, &c. By J. B. MANT (Inland Revenue). Second Edition, Revised. 18mo, 4s. leather.

"This handy and useful book is adapted to the requirements of the Inland Revenue Department, and will be a favourite book of reference. The range of subjects is comprehensive, and the arrangement simple and clear."—*Civilian.*

"Should be in the hands of every practical brewer."—*Brewers' Journal.*

INDUSTRIAL ARTS, TRADES, AND MANUFACTURES.

Cotton Spinning.

COTTON MANUFACTURE: A Practical Manual. Embracing the various operations of Cotton Manufacture, Dyeing, &c. For the Use of Operatives, Overlookers, and Manufacturers. By JOHN LISTER, Technical Instructor, Pendleton. With numerous Illustrations. Demy 8vo, 7s. 6d. cloth. [*Just published.*

Flour Manufacture, Milling, etc.

FLOUR MANUFACTURE: A Treatise on Milling Science and Practice. By FRIEDRICH KICK, Imperial Regierungsrath, Professor of Mechanical Technology in the Imperial German Polytechnic Institute, Prague. Translated from the Second Enlarged and Revised Edition with Supplement. By H. H. P. POWLES, Assoc. Memb. Institution of Civil Engineers. Nearly 400 pp. Illustrated with 28 Folding Plates, and 167 Woodcuts. Royal 8vo, 25s. cloth.

"This valuable work is, and will remain, the standard authority on the science of milling.... The miller who has read and digested this work will have laid the foundation, so to speak, of a successful career; he will have acquired a number of general principles which he can proceed to apply. In this handsome volume we at last have the accepted text-book of modern milling in good, sound English, which has little, if any, trace of the German idiom."—*The Miller.*

"The appearance of this celebrated work in English is very opportune, and British millers will, we are sure, not be slow in availing themselves of its pages."—*Millers' Gazette.*

Agglutinants.

CEMENTS, PASTES, GLUES AND GUMS: A Practical Guide to the Manufacture and Application of the various Agglutinants required in the Building, Metal-Working, Wood-Working and Leather-Working Trades, and for Workshop, Laboratory or Office Use. With upwards of 900 Recipes and Formulæ. By H. C. STANDAGE, Chemist. Crown 8vo, 2s. 6d. cloth. [*Just published.*

"We have pleasure in speaking favourably of this volume. So far as we have had experience, which is not inconsiderable, this manual is trustworthy."—*Athenæum.*

"As a revelation of what are considered trade secrets, this book will arouse an amount of curiosity among the large number of industries it touches."—*Daily Chronicle.*

"In this goodly collection of receipts it would be strange if a cement for any purpose cannot be found."—*Oil and Colourman's Journal.*

Soap-making.

THE ART OF SOAP-MAKING: A Practical Handbook of the Manufacture of Hard and Soft Soaps, Toilet Soaps, etc. Including many New Processes, and a Chapter on the Recovery of Glycerine from Waste Leys. By ALEXANDER WATT. Fourth Edition, Enlarged. Crown 8vo, 7s. 6d. cloth

"The work will prove very useful, not merely to the technological student, but to the practical soap-boiler who wishes to understand the theory of his art."—*Chemical News.*

"A thoroughly practical treatise on an art which has almost no literature in our language. We congratulate the author on the success of his endeavour to fill a void in English technical literature."—*Nature.*

Paper Making.

PRACTICAL PAPER-MAKING: A Manual for Paper-makers and Owners and Managers of Paper-Mills. With Tables, Calculations, &c. By G. CLAPPERTON, Paper-maker. With Illustrations of Fibres from Micro-Photographs. Crown 8vo, 5s. cloth. [*Just published.*

"The author caters for the requirements of responsible mill hands, apprentices, &c., whilst his manual will be found of great service to students of technology, as well as to veteran paper makers and mill owners. The illustrations form an excellent feature."—*Paper Trade Review.*

"We recommend everybody interested in the trade to get a copy of this thoroughly practical book."—*Paper Making.*

Paper Making.

THE ART OF PAPER MAKING: A Practical Handbook of the Manufacture of Paper from Rags, Esparto, Straw, and other Fibrous Materials, Including the Manufacture of Pulp from Wood Fibre, with a Description of the Machinery and Appliances used. To which are added Details of Processes for Recovering Soda from Waste Liquors. By ALEXANDER WATT, Author of "The Art of Soap-Making" With Illusts. Crown 8vo, 7s. 6d. cloth.

"It may be regarded as the standard work on the subject. The book is full of valuable information. The 'Art of Paper-making,' is in every respect a model of a text-book, either for a technical class or for the private student."—*Paper and Printing Trades Journal.*

Leather Manufacture.

THE ART OF LEATHER MANUFACTURE. Being a Practical Handbook, in which the Operations of Tanning, Currying, and Leather Dressing are fully Described, and the Principles of Tanning Explained, and many Recent Processes Introduced; as also the Methods for the Estimation of Tannin, and a Description of the Arts of Glue Boiling, Gut Dressing, &c. By ALEXANDER WATT, Author of "Soap-Making," &c. Second Edition. Crown 8vo, 9s. cloth.

"A sound, comprehensive treatise on tanning and its accessories. It is an eminently valuable production, which redounds to the credit of both author and publishers."—*Chemical Review.*

Boot and Shoe Making.

THE ART OF BOOT AND SHOE-MAKING. A Practical Handbook, including Measurement, Last-Fitting, Cutting-Out, Closing, and Making, with a Description of the most approved Machinery employed. By JOHN B. LENO, late Editor of *St. Crispin,* and *The Boot and Shoe-Maker* 12mo, 2s. cloth limp.

"This excellent treatise is by far the best work ever written. The chapter on clicking, which shows how waste may be prevented, will save fifty times the price of the book."
Scottish Leather Trader.

Dentistry Construction.

MECHANICAL DENTISTRY: A Practical Treatise on the Construction of the various kinds of Artificial Dentures. Comprising also Useful Formulæ, Tables, and Receipts for Gold Plate, Clasps, Solders, &c. &c. By CHARLES HUNTER. Third Edition. Crown 8vo, 3s. 6d. cloth.

"We can strongly recommend Mr. Hunter's treatise to all students preparing for the profession of dentistry, as well as to every mechanical dentist."—*Dublin Journal of Medical Science.*

Wood Engraving.

WOOD ENGRAVING: A Practical and Easy Introduction to the Study of the Art. By WILLIAM NORMAN BROWN. Second Edition. With numerous Illustrations. 12mo, 1s. 6d. cloth limp.

"The book is clear and complete, and will be useful to anyone wanting to understand the first elements of the beautiful art of wood engraving."—*Graphic*

Horology.

A TREATISE ON MODERN HOROLOGY, in Theory and Practice. Translated from the French of CLAUDIUS SAUNIER, ex-Director of the School of Horology at Maçon, by JULIEN TRIPPLIN, F.R.A.S., Besançon Watch Manufacturer, and EDWARD RIGG, M.A., Assayer in the Royal Mint. With 78 Woodcuts and 22 Coloured Copper Plates. Second Edition. Super-royal 8vo, £2 2s. cloth; £2 10s. half-calf.

"There is no horological work in the English language at all to be compared to this production of M. Saunier's ... It is a sheer language for the student and as a reference for the experienced horologist at his own workbench."—*Horological Journal*.

"The latest, the most complete, and the most readable of those hitherto produced ... continental watchmakers require to be tested for the rest ... at superiority on either length both rows ... in fact, the Book Clock of M. Saunier's Treatise."—*Watchmaker, Jeweller and Silversmith*.

Watchmaking.

THE WATCHMAKER'S HANDBOOK. Intended as a Workshop Companion for those engaged in Watchmaking and the Allied Mechanical Arts. Translated from the French of CLAUDIUS SAUNIER, and considerably enlarged by JULIEN TRIPPLIN, F.R.A.S., Vice-President of the Horological Institute, and EDWARD RIGG, M.A., Assayer in the Royal Mint. With numerous Woodcuts and 14 Copper Plates. Third Edition. Crown 8vo, 9s. cloth.

"Each part is truly a treatise in itself. The arrangement is good and the language is clear and concise. It is an admirable guide for the young watchmaker."—*Engineering*.

"It is impossible to speak too highly of its excellence. It fulfils every requirement in a handbook intended for the use of a workman. Should be found in every workshop."—*Watch and Clockmaker*.

"This book contains an immense number of practical details bearing on the daily occupation of a watchmaker."—*Watchmaker and Metalworker* (Chicago).

Watches and Timekeepers.

A HISTORY OF WATCHES AND OTHER TIMEKEEPERS. By JAMES F. KENDAL, M.B.H.Inst. 1s. 6d. boards; or 2s. 6d. cloth, gilt.

"Mr. Kendal's book, for its size, is the best which has yet appeared on the subject in the English language."—*Industries*.

"Open the book where you may, there is interesting matter in it concerning the ingenious devices of the ancient or modern horologer. The subject is treated in a learned and entertaining spirit, as might be expected of a historian who is a master of the craft."—*Saturday Review*.

Electrolysis of Gold, Silver, Copper, etc.

ELECTRO-DEPOSITION: A Practical Treatise on the Electrolysis of Gold, Silver, Copper, Nickel, and other Metals and Alloys. With descriptions of Voltaic Batteries, Magneto and Dynamo-Electric Machines, Thermopiles, and of the Materials and Processes used in every Department of the Art, and several Chapters on Electro-Metallurgy. By ALEXANDER WATT, Author of "Electro-Metallurgy," &c. Third Edition, Revised. Crown 8vo, 9s. cloth.

"Eminently a book for the practical worker in electro-deposition. It contains practical descriptions of methods, processes and materials as actually pursued and used in the workshop."—*Engineer*.

Electro-Metallurgy.

ELECTRO-METALLURGY; Practically Treated. By ALEXANDER WATT, Author of "Electro-Deposition," &c. Ninth Edition, including the most recent Processes. 12mo, 4s. cloth boards.

"From this book both amateur and artisan may learn everything necessary for the successful prosecution of electroplating."—*Iron*.

Working in Gold.

THE JEWELLER'S ASSISTANT IN THE ART OF WORKING IN GOLD: A Practical Treatise for Masters and Workmen, Compiled from the Experience of Thirty Years' Workshop Practice. By GEORGE E. GEE, Author of "The Goldsmith's Handbook," &c. Cr. 8vo, 7s. 6d. cloth.

"This manual of technical education is apparently destined to be a valuable auxiliary to a handicraft which is certainly capable of great improvement."—*The Times*.

"Very useful in the workshop, as the knowledge is practical, having been acquired by long experience, and all the recipes and directions are guaranteed to be successful."—*Jeweller and Metalworker*.

Electroplating.

ELECTROPLATING: A Practical Handbook on the Deposition of Copper, Silver, Nickel, Gold, Aluminium, Brass, Platinum, &c. &c. With Descriptions of the Chemicals, Materials, Batteries, and Dynamo Machines used in the Art. By J. W. URQUHART, C.E., Author of "Electric Light," &c. Third Edition, Revised, with Additions. Numerous Illustrations. Crown 8vo, 5s. cloth.

"An excellent practical manual."—*Engineering.*
"An excellent work, giving the newest information."—*Horological Journal.*

Electrotyping.

ELECTROTYPING: The Reproduction and Multiplication of Printing Surfaces and Works of Art by the Electro-deposition of Metals. By J. W. URQUHART, C.E. Crown 8vo, 5s. cloth.

"The book is thoroughly practical. The reader is, therefore, conducted through the leading laws of electricity, then through the metals used by electrotypers, the apparatus, and the depositing processes, up to the final preparation of the work."—*Art Journal.*

Goldsmiths' Work.

THE GOLDSMITH'S HANDBOOK. By GEORGE E. GEE, Jeweller, &c. Third Edition, considerably Enlarged. 12mo, 3s. 6d. cl. bds.

"A good, sound educator, and will be generally accepted as an authority."—*Horological Journal.*

Silversmiths' Work.

THE SILVERSMITH'S HANDBOOK. By GEORGE E. GEE, Jeweller, &c. Second Edition, Revised, with numerous Illustrations. 12mo, 3s. 6d. cloth boards.

"The chief merit of the work is its practical character. . . The workers in the trade will speedily discover its merits when they sit down to study it."—*English Mechanic.*

** The above two works together, strongly half-bound, price 7s.

Bread and Biscuit Baking.

THE BREAD AND BISCUIT BAKER'S AND SUGAR-BOILER'S ASSISTANT. Including a large variety of Modern Recipes. With Remarks on the Art of Bread-making. By ROBERT WELLS, Practical Baker. Second Edition, with Additional Recipes. Crown 8vo, 2s. cloth.

"A large number of wrinkles for the ordinary cook, as well as the baker."—*Saturday Review.*

Confectionery for Hotels and Restaurants.

THE PASTRYCOOK AND CONFECTIONER'S GUIDE. For Hotels, Restaurants and the Trade in general, adapted also for Family Use. By ROBERT WELLS, Author of "The Bread and Biscuit Baker's and Sugar-Boiler's Assistant." Crown 8vo, 2s. cloth.

"We cannot speak too highly of this really excellent work. In these days of keen competition our readers cannot do better than purchase this book."—*Bakers' Times.*

Ornamental Confectionery.

ORNAMENTAL CONFECTIONERY: A Guide for Bakers. Confectioners and Pastrycooks; including a variety of Modern Recipes, and Remarks on Decorative and Coloured Work. With 129 Original Designs. By ROBERT WELLS, Practical Baker, Author of "The Bread and Biscuit Baker's and Sugar-Boiler's Assistant," &c. Crown 8vo, cloth gilt, 5s.

"A valuable work, practical, and should be in the hands of every baker and confectioner. The illustrative designs are alone worth treble the amount charged for the whole work."—*Bakers' Times.*

Flour Confectionery.

THE MODERN FLOUR CONFECTIONER. Wholesale and Retail. Containing a large Collection of Recipes for Cheap Cakes, Biscuits, &c. With Remarks on the Ingredients used in their Manufacture. To which are added Recipes for Dainties for the Working Man's Table. By R. WELLS, Author of "The Bread and Biscuit Baker," &c. Crown 8vo, 2s. cl.

"The work is of a decidedly practical character, and in every recipe regard is had to economical working."—*North British Daily Mail.*

Laundry Work.

LAUNDRY MANAGEMENT. A Handbook for Use in Private and Public Laundries, Including Descriptive Accounts of Modern Machinery and Appliances for Laundry Work. By the EDITOR of "The Laundry Journal." With numerous Illustrations. Second Edition. Crown 8vo, 2s. 6d. cloth.

"This book should certainly occupy an honoured place on the shelves of all housekeepers who wish to keep themselves au courant of the newest appliances and methods."—*The Queen.*

HANDYBOOKS FOR HANDICRAFTS.

By PAUL N. HASLUCK,

EDITOR OF "WORK" (NEW SERIES); AUTHOR OF "LATHE-WORK," "MILLING MACHINES,' &c.

Crown 8vo, 144 pages, cloth, price 1s. each.

☞ *These* HANDYBOOKS *have been written to supply information for* WORKMEN, STUDENTS, *and* AMATEURS *in the several Handicraft, on the actual* PRACTICE *of the* WORKSHOP, *and are intended to convey in plain language* TECHNICAL KNOWLEDGE *of the several* CRAFTS. *In describing the processes employed, and the manipulation of material, workshop terms are used, workshop practice is fully explained; and the text is freely illustrated with drawings of modern tools, appliances, and processes.*

THE METAL TURNER'S HANDYBOOK. A Practical Manual for Workers at the Foot-Lathe. With over 100 Illustrations. Price 1s.
"The book will be of service alike to the amateur at Lathe and turner. It displays thorough knowledge of the subject."—*Scotsman.*

THE WOOD TURNER'S HANDYBOOK. A Practical Manual for Workers at the Lathe. With over 100 Illustrations. Price 1s.
"We recommend the book to young turners and amateurs. A multitude of workmen have hitherto sought in vain for a manual of this special industry."—*Mechanical World.*

THE WATCH JOBBER'S HANDYBOOK. A Practical Manual on Cleaning, Repairing, and Adjusting. With upwards of 100 Illustrations. Price 1s.
"We strongly advise all young persons connected with the watch trade to acquire and study this inexpensive work."—*Clerkenwell Chronicle.*

THE PATTERN MAKER'S HANDYBOOK. A Practical Manual on the Construction of Patterns for Founders. With upwards of 100 Illustrations. Price 1s.
"A most valuable, if not indispensable, manual for the pattern maker."—*Knowledge.*

THE MECHANIC'S WORKSHOP HANDYBOOK. A Practical Manual on Mechanical Manipulation. Embracing Information on various Handicraft Processes, with Useful Notes and Miscellaneous Memoranda. Comprising about 200 Subjects. Price 1s.
"A very clever and useful book, which should be found in every workshop; and it should certainly find a place in all technical schools."—*Saturday Review.*

THE MODEL ENGINEER'S HANDYBOOK. A Practical Manual on the Construction of Model Steam Engines. With upwards of 100 Illustrations. Price 1s.
"Mr. Hasluck has produced a very good little book."—*Builder.*

THE CLOCK JOBBER'S HANDYBOOK. A Practical Manual on Cleaning, Repairing, and Adjusting. With upwards of 100 Illustrations. Price 1s.
"It is of inestimable service to those commencing the trade."—*Coventry Standard.*

THE CABINET WORKER'S HANDYBOOK: A Practical Manual on the Tools, Materials, Appliances, and Processes employed in Cabinet Work. With upwards of 100 Illustrations. Price 1s.
"Mr. Hasluck's thoroughgoing little Handybook is amongst the most practical guides we have seen for beginners in cabinet-work."—*Saturday Review.*

THE WOODWORKER'S HANDYBOOK OF MANUAL INSTRUCTION. Embracing Information on the Tools, Materials, Appliances and Processes employed in Woodworking. With 104 Illustrations. Price 1s.
[*Just published.*

THE METALWORKER'S HANDYBOOK. With upwards of 100 Illustrations. [*In preparation.*

. OPINIONS OF THE PRESS.

"Written by a man who knows, not only how work ought to be done, but how to do it, and how to convey his knowledge to others."—*Engineering.*
"Mr. Hasluck writes admirably, and gives complete instructions."—*Engineer.*
"Mr. Hasluck combines the experience of a practical teacher with the manipulative skill and scientific knowledge of processes of the trained mechanician, and the manuals are marvels of what can be produced at a popular price."—*Schoolmaster.*
"Helpful to workmen of all ages and degrees of experience."—*Daily Chronicle.*
"Practical, sensible, and remarkably cheap."—*Journal of Education.*
"Concise, clear and practical."—*Saturday Review.*

COMMERCE, COUNTING-HOUSE WORK, TABLES, etc.

Commercial Education.
LESSONS IN COMMERCE. By Professor R. GAMBARO, of the Royal High Commercial School at Genoa. Edited and Revised by JAMES GAULT, Professor of Commerce and Commercial Law in King's College, London. Crown 8vo, 3s. 6d. cloth.

"The publishers of this work have rendered considerable service to the cause of commercial education by the opportune production of this volume. . . . The work is peculiarly acceptable to English readers and an admirable addition to existing class-books. In a phrase, we think the work attains its object in furnishing a brief account of those laws and customs of British trade with which the commercial man interested therein should be familiar."—*Chamber of Commerce Journal.*

"An invaluable guide in the hands of those who are preparing for a commercial career."—*Counting House.*

Foreign Commercial Correspondence.
THE FOREIGN COMMERCIAL CORRESPONDENT: Being Aids to Commercial Correspondence in Five Languages—English, French, German, Italian, and Spanish. By CONRAD E. BAKER. Second Edition. Crown 8vo, 3s. 6d. cloth.

"Whoever wishes to correspond in all the languages mentioned by Mr. Baker cannot do better than study this work, the materials of which are excellent and conveniently arranged. They consist not of entire specimen letters but—what are far more useful—short passages, sentences, or phrases expressing the same general idea in various forms."—*Athenæum.*

"A careful examination has convinced us that it is unusually complete, well arranged, and reliable. The book is a thoroughly good one."—*Schoolmaster.*

Accounts for Manufacturers.
FACTORY ACCOUNTS: Their Principles and Practice. A Handbook for Accountants and Manufacturers, with Appendices on the Nomenclature of Machine Details; the Income Tax Acts; the Rating of Factories; Fire and Boiler Insurance; the Factory and Workshop Acts, &c., including also a Glossary of Terms and a large number of Specimen Rulings. By EMILE GARCKE and J. M. FELLS. Fourth Edition, Revised and Enlarged. Demy 8vo, 250 pages. 6s. strongly bound.

"A very interesting description of the requirements of Factory Accounts. . . . the principle of assimilating the Factory Accounts to the general commercial books is one which we thoroughly agree with."—*Accountants' Journal.*

"Characterised by extreme thoroughness. There are few owners of factories who would not derive great benefit from the perusal of this most admirable work."—*Local Government Chronicle.*

Intuitive Calculations.
THE COMPENDIOUS CALCULATOR; or, Easy and Concise Methods of Performing the various Arithmetical Operations required in Commercial and Business Transactions, together with Useful Tables. By DANIEL O'GORMAN. Corrected and Extended by Professor J. R. YOUNG. Twenty-seventh Edition, Revised by C. NORRIS. Fcap. 8vo, 2s. 6d. cloth limp; or, 3s. 6d. strongly half-bound in leather.

"It would be difficult to exaggerate the usefulness of a book like this to everyone engaged in commerce or manufacturing industry. It is crammed full of rules and formulæ for shortening and employing calculations."—*Knowledge.*

Modern Metrical Units and Systems.
MODERN METROLOGY: A Manual of the Metrical Units and Systems of the Present Century. With an Appendix containing a proposed English System. By LOWIS D'A. JACKSON, A.M.Inst.C.E., Author of "Aid to Survey Practice," &c. Large crown 8vo, 12s. 6d. cloth.

"We recommend the work to all interested in the practical reform of our weights and measures."—*Nature.*

The Metric System and the British Standards.
A SERIES OF METRIC TABLES, in which the British Standard Measures and Weights are compared with those of the Metric System at present in Use on the Continent. By C. H. DOWLING, C.E. 8vo, 10s. 6d. strongly bound.

"Mr. Dowling's Tables are well put together as a ready-reckoner for the conversion of one system into the other."—*Athenæum.*

Iron and Metal Trades' Calculator.
THE IRON AND METAL TRADES' COMPANION. For expeditiously ascertaining the Value of any Goods bought or sold by Weight, from 1s. per cwt. to 112s. per cwt., and from one farthing per pound to one shilling per pound. By THOMAS DOWNIE. 396 pp., 9s. leather.

"A most useful set of tables; nothing like them before existed."—*Building News.*

"Although specially adapted to the iron and metal trades, the tables will be found useful in every other business in which merchandise is bought and sold by weight."—*Railway News.*

Chadwick's Calculator for Numbers and Weights Combined.

THE NUMBER, WEIGHT, AND FRACTIONAL CALCULATOR. Containing upwards of 250,000 Separate Calculations, showing at a glance the value at 422 different rates, ranging from 1/32th of a Penny to 20s. each, or per cwt., and £20 per ton, of any number of articles consecutively, from 1 to 470.—Any number of cwts., qrs., and lbs., from 1 cwt to 470 cwts.—Any number of tons, cwts., qrs., and lbs., from 1 to 1,000 tons. By WILLIAM CHADWICK, Public Accountant. Third Edition, Revised and Improved. 8vo, 18s., strongly bound for Office wear and tear.

☞ *Is adapted for the use of Accountants and Auditors, Railway Companies, Canal Companies, Shippers, Shipping Agents, General Carriers, etc. Ironfounders, Brassfounders, Metal Merchants, Iron Manufacturers, Ironmongers, Engineers, Machinists, Boiler Makers, Millwrights, Roofing, Bridge and Girder Makers, Colliery Proprietors, etc. Timber Merchants, Builders, Contractors, Architects, Surveyors, Auctioneers, Valuers, Brokers, Mill Owners and Manufacturers, Mill Furnishers, Merchants, and General Wholesale Tradesmen. Also for the Apportionment of Mileage Charges for Railway Traffic.*

** OPINIONS OF THE PRESS.

"It is easy of reference if any answer any number of answers as a discovery and the references are even more quickly made. For making up accounts or estimates too quick and prove invaluable to all who have any materia to quantity of calculating to revising (the and measure in any combination to do."—*Engineer.*

"The most complete and practical already reckoner which it has been our fortune yet to see. It is difficult to imagine a treasure of more importance in the life of the great merchant, or nearer in saving human labour than the King work. The publishers have placed within the reach of every commercial man an invaluable and unfailing assistant."—*The Miller.*

"The most perfect work of the kind yet prepared."—*City and Hall.*

Harben's Comprehensive Weight Calculator.

THE WEIGHT CALCULATOR. Being a Series of Tables upon a New and Comprehensive Plan, exhibiting at One Reference the exact Value of any Weight from 1 lb. to 15 tons, at 300 Progressive Rates, from 1d. to 168s. per cwt., and containing 186,000 Direct Answers, which, with their Combinations, consisting of a single addition (mostly to be performed at sight), will afford an aggregate of 10,266,000 Answers; the whole being calculated and designed to ensure correctness and promote despatch. By HENRY HARBEN, Accountant. Fourth Edition, carefully Corrected. Royal 8vo, £1 5s. strongly half-bound.

"A practical and useful work of reference for men of business generally; it is the best of the kind we have seen."—*Ironmonger.*

"Of priceless value to business men, it is a necessary book in all mercantile offices."—*Sheffield Independent.*

Harben's Comprehensive Discount Guide.

THE DISCOUNT GUIDE. Comprising several Series of Tables for the use of Merchants, Manufacturers, Ironmongers, and others, by which may be ascertained the exact Profit arising from any mode of using Discounts, either in the Purchase or Sale of Goods, and the method of either Altering a Rate of Discount or Advancing a Price, so as to produce, by one operation, a sum that will realise any required profit after allowing one or more Discounts: to which are added Tables of Profit or Advance from 1¼ to 90 per cent., Tables of Discount from 1¼ to 98⅜ per cent., and Tables of Commission, &c., from ⅛ to 10 per cent. By HENRY HARBEN, Accountant, Author of "The Weight Calculator." New Edition, carefully Revised and Corrected. Demy 8vo, 544 pp., £1 5s. half-bound.

"A book such as this can only be appreciated by business men, to whom the saving of time means saving of money. We have the high authority of Professor J. R. Young that the tables throughout the work are constructed upon strictly accurate principles. The work is a model of typographical clearness, and must prove of great value to merchants, manufacturers, and general traders."—*British Trade Journal.*

Iron Shipbuilders' and Merchants' Weight Tables.

IRON-PLATE WEIGHT TABLES: For Iron Shipbuilders, Engineers, and Iron Merchants. Containing the Calculated Weights of upwards of 150,000 different sizes of Iron Plates, from 1 foot by 6 in. by ¼ in. to 10 feet by 5 feet by 1 in. Worked out on the basis of 40 lbs. to the square foot of Iron of 1 inch in thickness. Carefully compiled and thoroughly Revised by H. BURLINSON and W. H. SIMPSON. Oblong 4to, 25s. half-bound

"This work will be found of great utility. The authors have had much practical experience of what is wanting in making estimates; and the use of the book will save much time in making elaborate calculations."—*English Mechanic.*

AGRICULTURE, FARMING, GARDENING, etc.

Dr. Fream's New Edition of "The Standard Treatise on Agriculture."

THE COMPLETE GRAZIER, and FARMER'S and CATTLE-BREEDER'S ASSISTANT: A Compendium of Husbandry. Originally Written by WILLIAM YOUATT. Thirteenth Edition, entirely Re-written, considerably Enlarged, and brought up to the Present Requirements of Agricultural Practice, by WILLIAM FREAM, LL.D., Steven Lecturer in the University of Edinburgh, Author of "The Elements of Agriculture," &c. Royal 8vo, 1,100 pp., with over 450 Illustrations. £1 11s. 6d. strongly and handsomely bound.

EXTRACT FROM PUBLISHERS' ADVERTISEMENT.

"A treatise that made its original appearance in the first decade of the century, and that enters upon its Thirteenth Edition before the century has run its course, has undoubtedly established its position as a work of permanent value... The phenomenal progress of the last dozen years in the Practice and Science of Farming has rendered it necessary, however, that the volume should be re-written, . . . and for this undertaking the publishers were fortunate enough to secure the services of Dr. FREAM, whose high attainments in all matters pertaining to agriculture have been so emphatically recognised by the highest professional and official authorities. In carrying out his editorial duties, Dr. FREAM has been favoured with valuable contributions by Prof. J. WORTLEY AXE, Mr. E. BROWN, Dr. BERNARD DYER, Mr. W. J. MALDEN, Mr. R. H. REW, Prof. SHELDON, Mr. J. SINCLAIR, Mr. SANDERS SPENCER, and others.

"As regards the illustrations of the work, no pains have been spared to make them as representative and characteristic as possible, so as to be practically useful to the Farmer and Grazier."

SUMMARY OF CONTENTS.

BOOK I. ON THE VARIETIES, BREEDING, REARING, FATTENING, AND MANAGEMENT OF CATTLE.
BOOK II. ON THE ECONOMY AND MANAGEMENT OF THE DAIRY.
BOOK III. ON THE BREEDING, REARING, AND MANAGEMENT OF HORSES.
BOOK IV. ON THE BREEDING, REARING, AND FATTENING OF SHEEP.
BOOK V. ON THE BREEDING, REARING, AND FATTENING OF SWINE.
BOOK VI. ON THE DISEASES OF LIVE STOCK.
BOOK VII. ON THE BREEDING, REARING, AND MANAGEMENT OF POULTRY.
BOOK VIII. ON FARM OFFICES AND IMPLEMENTS OF HUSBANDRY.
BOOK IX. ON THE CULTURE AND MANAGEMENT OF GRASS LANDS.
BOOK X. ON THE CULTIVATION AND APPLICATION OF GRASSES, PULSE, AND ROOTS.
BOOK XI. ON MANURES AND THEIR APPLICATION TO GRASS LAND & CROPS
BOOK XII. MONTHLY CALENDARS OF FARMWORK.

*** OPINIONS OF THE PRESS ON THE NEW EDITION.

"Dr. Fream is to be congratulated on the successful attempt he has made to give us a work which will at once become the standard classic of the farm practice of the country. We believe that it will be found that it has no compeer among the many works at present in existence. . . . The illustrations are admirable, while the frontispiece, which represents the well-known bull, New Year's Gift, bred by the Queen, is a work of art."—*The Times*.

"The book must he recognised as occupying the proud position of the most exhaustive work of reference in the English language on the subject with which it deals."—*Athenæum*.

"The most comprehensive guide to modern farm practice that exists in the English language to-day. . . . The book is one that ought to be on every farm and in the library of every landowner."—*Mark Lane Express*.

"In point of exhaustiveness and accuracy the work will certainly hold a pre-eminent and unique position among books dealing with scientific agricultural practice. It is, in fact, an agricultural library of itself."—*North British Agriculturist*.

"A compendium of authoratative and well-ordered knowledge on every conceivable branch of the work of the live stock farmer; probably without an equal in this or any other country."—*Yorkshire Post*.

"The best and brightest guide to the practice of husbandry, one that has no superior—no equal we might truly say—among the agricultural literature now before the public. . . . In every section in which we have tested it, the work has been found thoroughly up to date."—*Bell's Weekly Messenger*.

British Farm Live Stock.

FARM LIVE STOCK OF GREAT BRITAIN. By ROBERT WALLACE, F.L.S., F.R.S.E., &c., Professor of Agriculture and Rural Economy in the University of Edinburgh. Third Edition, thoroughly Revised and considerably Enlarged. With over 120 Phototypes of Prize Stock. Demy 8vo, 384 pp., with 79 Plates and Maps, 12s. 6d. cloth.

"A really complete work on the history, breeds, and management of the farm stock of Great Britain, and one which is likely to find its way to the shelves of every country gentleman's library."—*The Times*.

"The latest edition of 'Farm Live Stock of Great Britain' is a production to be proud of, and its issue not the least of the services which its author has rendered to agricultural science."—*Scottish Farmer*.

"The book is very attractive . . . and we can scarcely imagine the existence of a farmer who would not like to have a copy of this beautiful work."—*Mark Lane Express*.

"A work which will long be regarded as a standard authority whenever a concise history and description of the breeds of live stock in the British Isles is required."—*Bell's Weekly Messenger*.

Dairy Farming.

BRITISH DAIRYING. A Handy Volume on the Work of the Dairy-Farm. For the Use of Technical Instruction Classes, Students in Agricultural Colleges, and the Working Dairy Farmer. By Prof. J. P. SHELDON, late Special Commissioner of the Canadian Government, Author of "Dairy Farming," &c. With numerous Illustrations. Crown 8vo, 2s. 6d. cloth.

"May be confidently recommended as a useful text-book.—*Dairy*" *Agricultural Gazette.*

"Probably the best half-crown manual of dairy work that has yet appeared."—*North British Agriculturist.*

"It is the soundest little work we have yet seen on the subject."—*Times.*

Dairy Manual.

MILK, CHEESE AND BUTTER: Their Composition, Character and the Processes of their Production. A Practical Manual for Students and Dairy Farmers. By JOHN OLIVER, late Principal of the Western Dairy Institute, Berkeley. Crown 8vo, 350 pages, with Coloured Test Sheets and numerous Illustrations, 7s. 6d. cloth. *Just published.*

Agricultural Facts and Figures.

NOTE-BOOK OF AGRICULTURAL FACTS AND FIGURES FOR FARMERS AND FARM STUDENTS. By PRIMROSE MCCONNELL, B.Sc. Fifth Edition. Royal 32mo, roan, gilt edges, with band, 4s.

"Literally teems with information, and we can cordially recommend it to all connected with agriculture."—*North British Agriculturist.*

Small Farming.

SYSTEMATIC SMALL FARMING; or, *The Lessons of my Farm.* Being an Introduction to Modern Farm Practice for Small Farmers. By ROBERT SCOTT BURN, Author of "Outlines of Modern Farming," &c. With numerous Illustrations, crown 8vo, 6s. cloth.

"This is the completest book of its class we have seen, and one which every amateur farmer will read with pleasure and accept as a guide."—*Field.*

Modern Farming.

OUTLINES OF MODERN FARMING. By R. SCOTT BURN. Soils, Manures, and Crops—Farming and Farming Economy—Cattle, Sheep, and Horses — Management of Dairy, Pigs, and Poultry — Utilisation of Town-Sewage, Irrigation, &c. Sixth Edition. In One Vol., 1,250 pp., half-bound, profusely Illustrated, 12s.

"The aim of the author has been to make his work at once comprehensive and trustworthy, and he has succeeded to a degree which entitles him to much credit."—*Morning Advertiser.*

Agricultural Engineering.

FARM ENGINEERING, THE COMPLETE TEXT-BOOK OF. Comprising Draining and Embanking; Irrigation and Water Supply; Farm Roads, Fences, and Gates; Farm Buildings; Barn Implements and Machines; Field Implements and Machines; Agricultural Surveying, &c. By Prof. JOHN SCOTT. In One Vol., 1,150 pages, half-bound, with over 600 Illustrations, 12s.

"Written with great care, as well as with knowledge and ability. The author has done his work well; we have found him a very trustworthy guide wherever we have tested his statements. The volume will be of great value to agricultural students."—*Mark Lane Express.*

Agricultural Text-Book.

THE FIELDS OF GREAT BRITAIN: A Text-Book of Agriculture, adapted to the Syllabus of the Science and Art Department. For Elementary and Advanced Students. By HUGH CLEMENTS (Board of Trade). Second Edition, Revised, with Additions. 18mo, 2s. 6d. cloth.

"A most comprehensive volume, giving a mass of information."—*Agricultural Economist.*

"It is a long time since we have seen a book which has pleased us more, or which contains such a vast and useful fund of knowledge."—*Educational Times.*

Tables for Farmers, etc.

TABLES, MEMORANDA, AND CALCULATED RESULTS for Farmers, Graziers, Agricultural Students, Surveyors, Land Agents, Auctioneers, etc. With a New System of Farm Book-keeping. Selected and Arranged by SIDNEY FRANCIS. Third Edition, Revised. 272 pp., waistcoat-pocket size, 1s. 6d. limp leather.

"Weighing less than 1 oz., and occupying no more space than a match box, it contains a mass of facts and calculations which has never before, in such handy form, been obtainable. Every operation on the farm is dealt with. The work may be taken as thoroughly accurate, the whole of the tables having been revised by Dr. Fream. We cordially recommend it."—*Bell's Weekly Messenger.*

AGRICULTURE, FARMING, GARDENING, etc.

The Management of Bees.
BEES FOR PLEASURE AND PROFIT: A Guide to the Manipulation of Bees, the Production of Honey, and the General Management of the Apiary. By G. GORDON SAMSON. With numerous Illustrations. Crown 8vo, 1s. cloth.
"The intending bee-keeper will find exactly the kind of information required to enable him to make a successful start with his hives. The author is a thoroughly competent teacher, and his book may be commended."—*Morning Post.*

Farm and Estate Book-keeping.
BOOK-KEEPING FOR FARMERS & ESTATE OWNERS. A Practical Treatise, presenting, in Three Plans, a System adapted for all Classes of Farms. By JOHNSON M. WOODMAN, Chartered Accountant. Second Edition, Revised. Crown 8vo, 3s. 6d. cloth boards; or 2s. 6d. cloth limp.
"The volume is a capital study of a most important subject."—*Agricultural Gazette.*
"The young farmer, land agent, and surveyor will find Mr. Woodman's treatise more than repay its cost and study."—*Building News.*

Farm Account Book.
WOODMAN'S YEARLY FARM ACCOUNT BOOK. Giving a Weekly Labour Account and Diary, and showing the Income and Expenditure under each Department of Crops, Live Stock, Dairy, &c. &c. With Valuation, Profit and Loss Account, and Balance Sheet at the end of the Year. By JOHNSON M. WOODMAN, Chartered Accountant, Author of "Book-keeping for Farmers." Folio, 7s. 6d. half bound. [*culture.*
"Contains every requisite form for keeping farm accounts readily and accurately."—*Agri-*

Early Fruits, Flowers, and Vegetables.
THE FORCING GARDEN; or, How to Grow Early Fruits, Flowers, and Vegetables. With Plans and Estimates for Building Glass-houses, Pits, and Frames. With Illustrations. By SAMUEL WOOD. Crown 8vo, 3s. 6d. cloth.
"A good book, and fairly fills a place that was in some degree vacant. The book is written with great care, and contains a great deal of valuable teaching."—*Gardeners' Magazine.*

Good Gardening.
A PLAIN GUIDE TO GOOD GARDENING; or, How to Grow Vegetables, Fruits, and Flowers. By S. WOOD. Fourth Edition, with considerable Additions, &c., and numerous Illustrations. Crown 8vo, 3s. 6d. cl.
"A very good book, and one to be highly recommended as a practical guide. The practical directions are excellent."—*Athenæum.*
"May be recommended to young gardeners, cottagers, and specially to amateurs, for the plain, simple, and trustworthy information it gives on common matters too often neglected."—*Gardeners' Chronicle.*

Gainful Gardening.
MULTUM-IN-PARVO GARDENING; or, How to make One Acre of Land produce £620 a-year by the Cultivation of Fruits and Vegetables; also, How to Grow Flowers in Three Glass Houses, so as to realise £176 per annum clear Profit. By SAMUEL WOOD, Author of "Good Gardening," &c. Fifth and Cheaper Edition, Revised, with Additions. Crown 8vo, 1s. sewed.
"We are bound to recommend it as not only suited to the case of the amateur and gentleman's gardener, but to the market grower."—*Gardeners' Magazine.*

Gardening for Ladies.
THE LADIES' MULTUM-IN-PARVO FLOWER GARDEN, and Amateurs' Complete Guide. With Illusts. By S. WOOD. Cr. 8vo, 3s. 6d. cl.
"This volume contains a good deal of sound common sense instruction."—*Florist.*
"Full of shrewd hints and useful instructions, based on a lifetime of experience."—*Scotsman.*

Receipts for Gardeners.
GARDEN RECEIPTS. Edited by CHARLES W. QUIN. 12mo, 1s. 6d. cloth limp.
"A useful and handy book, containing a good deal of valuable information."—*Athenæum.*

Market Gardening.
MARKET AND KITCHEN GARDENING. By Contributors to "The Garden." Compiled by C. W. SHAW, late Editor of "Gardening Illustrated." 12mo, 3s. 6d. cloth boards.
"The most valuable compendium of kitchen and market-garden work published."—*Farmer.*

Cottage Gardening.
COTTAGE GARDENING; or, Flowers, Fruits, and Vegetables for Small Gardens. By E. HOBDAY. 12mo, 1s. 6d. cloth limp.
"Contains much useful information at a small charge."—*Glasgow Herald.*

AUCTIONEERING, VALUING, LAND SURVEYING ESTATE AGENCY, etc.

Auctioneer's Assistant.

THE APPRAISER, AUCTIONEER, BROKER, HOUSE AND ESTATE AGENT AND VALUER'S POCKET ASSISTANT, for the Valuation for Purchase, Sale, or Renewal of Leases, Annuities and Reversions, and of property generally; with Prices for Inventories, &c. By JOHN WHEELER, Valuer, &c. Sixth Edition, Re-written and greatly extended by C. NORRIS, Surveyor, Valuer, &c. Royal 32mo, 5s. cloth.

"A neat and conte book of reference, containing an admirable and clearly arranged set of prices for inventories, and a very practical guide to determine the value of furniture, &c."—*Standard.*
"Contains a large quantity of varied and useful information as to the valuation for purchase, sale, or renewal of leases, annuities and reversions, and of property generally, with prices for Inventories, and is a guide to determine the value of interior fittings and other effects."—*Builder.*

Auctioneering.

AUCTIONEERS: THEIR DUTIES AND LIABILITIES. A Manual of Instruction and Counsel for the Young Auctioneer. By ROBERT SQUIBBS, Auctioneer. Second Edition, Revised and partly Re-written. Demy 8vo, 12s. 6d. cloth.

*** OPINIONS OF THE PRESS.

"The standard text-book on the topics of which it treats."—*Athenæum.*
"The work is one of general excellent character, and gives much information in a compendious and scholarly form."—*Builder.*
"May be recommended as giving a great deal of information on the law relating to auctioneers, in a very readable form."—*Law Journal.*
"Auctioneers may be congratulated on having so pleasing a writer to minister to their special needs."—*Solicitors' Journal.*
"Every auctioneer ought to possess a copy of this excellent work."—*Ironmonger.*
"Of great value to the profession. . . . We readily welcome this book from the fact that it treats the subject in a manner somewhat new to the profession."—*Estates Gazette.*

Inwood's Estate Tables.

TABLES FOR THE PURCHASING OF ESTATES, Freehold, Copyhold, or Leasehold; Annuities, Advowsons, etc., and for the Renewing of Leases held under Cathedral Churches, Colleges, or other Corporate bodies for Terms of Years certain, and for Lives; also for Valuing Reversionary Estates, Deferred Annuities, Next Presentations, &c.; together with SMART'S Five Tables of Compound Interest, and an Extension of the same to Lower and Intermediate Rates. By W. INWOOD. 24th Edition, with considerable Additions, and new and valuable Tables of Logarithms for the more Difficult Computations of the Interest of Money, Discount, Annuities, &c., by M. FEDOR THOMAN, of the Société Crédit Mobilier of Paris. Crown 8vo, 8s. cloth.

"Those interested in the purchase and sale of estates, and in the adjustment of compensation cases, as well as in transactions in annuities, life insurances, &c., will find the present edition of eminent service."—*Engineering.*
"'Inwood's Tables' still maintain a most enviable reputation. The new issue has been enriched by large additional contributions by M. Fedor Thoman, whose carefully arranged Tables cannot fail to be of the utmost utility."—*Mining Journal.*

Agricultural Valuer's Assistant.

THE AGRICULTURAL VALUER'S ASSISTANT. A Practical Handbook on the Valuation of Landed Estates; including Rules and Data for Measuring and Estimating the Contents, Weights, and Values of Agricultural Produce and Timber, and the Values of Feeding Stuffs, Manures, and Labour; with Forms of Tenant-Right-Valuations, Lists of Local Agricultural Customs, Scales of Compensation under the Agricultural Holdings Act, &c. &c. By TOM BRIGHT, Agricultural Surveyor. Second Edition, much Enlarged. Crown 8vo, 5s. cloth.

"Full of tables and examples in connection with the valuation of tenant-right, estates, labour, contents, and weights of timber, and farm produce of all kinds."—*Agricultural Gazette.*
"An eminently practical handbook, full of practical tables and data of undoubted interest and value to surveyors and auctioneers in preparing valuations of all kinds."—*Farmer.*

Plantations and Underwoods.

POLE PLANTATIONS AND UNDERWOODS: A Practical Handbook on Estimating the Cost of Forming, Renovating, Improving, and Grubbing Plantations and Underwoods, their Valuation for Purposes of Transfer, Rental, Sale, or Assessment. By TOM BRIGHT, Author of "The Agricultural Valuer's Assistant," &c. Crown 8vo, 3s. 6d. cloth.

"To valuers, foresters and agents it will be a welcome aid."—*North British Agriculturist.*
"Well calculated to assist the valuer in the discharge of his duties, and of undoubted interest and use both to surveyors and auctioneers in preparing valuations of all kinds."—*Kent Herald.*

Hudson's Land Valuer's Pocket-Book.
THE LAND VALUER'S BEST ASSISTANT: Being Tables on a very much Improved Plan, for Calculating the Value of Estates. With Tables for reducing Scotch, Irish, and Provincial Customary Acres to Statute Measure, &c. By R. HUDSON, C.E. New Edition. Royal 32mo, leather, elastic band, 4s.
"Of incalculable value to the country gentleman and professional man."—*Farmers' Journal*

Ewart's Land Improver's Pocket-Book.
THE LAND IMPROVER'S POCKET-BOOK OF FORMULÆ, TABLES, *and MEMORANDA required in any Computation relating to the Permanent Improvement of Landed Property.* By JOHN EWART, Land Surveyor and Agricultural Engineer. Second Edition, Revised. Royal 32mo, oblong, leather, gilt edges, with elastic band, 4s.
"A compendious and handy little volume."—*Spectator.*

Complete Agricultural Surveyor's Pocket-Book.
THE LAND VALUER'S AND LAND IMPROVER'S COMPLETE POCKET-BOOK. Being of the above Two Works bound together. Leather, with strap, 7s. 6d.

House Property.
HANDBOOK OF HOUSE PROPERTY. A Popular and Practical Guide to the Purchase, Mortgage, Tenancy, and Compulsory Sale of Houses and Land, including the Law of Dilapidations and Fixtures; with Examples of all kinds of Valuations, Useful Information on Building, and Suggestive Elucidations of Fine Art. By E. L. TARBUCK, Architect and Surveyor. Fifth Edition, Enlarged. 12mo, 5s. cloth.
"The advice is thoroughly practical."—*Law Journal.*
"For all who have dealings with house property, this is an indispensable guide."—*Decoration.*
"Carefully brought up to date, and much improved by the addition of a division on fine art. . . . A well written and thoughtful work."—*Land Agent's Record.*

LAW AND MISCELLANEOUS.

Private Bill Legislation and Provisional Orders.
HANDBOOK FOR THE USE OF SOLICITORS AND ENGINEERS Engaged in Promoting Private Acts of Parliament and Provisional Orders, for the Authorization of Railways, Tramways, Works for the Supply of Gas and Water, and other undertakings of a like character. By L. LIVINGSTON MACASSEY, of the Middle Temple, Barrister-at-Law, M.Inst.C.E.; Author of "Hints on Water Supply." Demy 8vo, 950 pp., 25s. cl.
"The author's double experience as an engineer and barrister has enabled him to approach the subject alike from an engineering and legal point of view."—*Local Government Chronicle.*

Law of Patents.
PATENTS FOR INVENTIONS, AND HOW TO PROCURE THEM. Compiled for the Use of Inventors, Patentees and others. By G. G. M. HARDINGHAM, Assoc.Mem.Inst.C.E., &c. Demy 8vo, 1s. 6d. cloth.

Labour Disputes.
INDUSTRIAL CONCILIATION AND ARBITRATION: An Historical Sketch, with Practical Suggestions for the Settlement of Labour Disputes. By J. S. JEANS, Author of "Railway Problems," "England's Supremacy," &c. Crown 8vo, 200 pp., 2s. 6d. cloth. [*Just published.*

Pocket-Book for Sanitary Officials.
THE HEALTH OFFICER'S POCKET-BOOK: A Guide to Sanitary Practice and Law. For Medical Officers of Health, Sanitary Inspectors, Members of Sanitary Authorities, &c. By EDWARD F. WILLOUGHBY, M.D. (Lond.), &c., Author of "Hygiene and Public Health." Fcap. 8vo, 7s. 6d. cloth, red edges, rounded corners. [*Just published.*
"A mine of condensed information of a pertinent and useful kind on the various subjects of which it treats. The matter seems to have been carefully compiled and arranged for facility of reference, and it is well illustrated by diagrams and woodcuts. The different subjects are succinctly but fully and scientifically dealt with."—*The Lancet.*
"Ought to be welcome to those for whose use it is designed, since it practically boils down a reference library into a pocket volume. . . . It combines, with an uncommon degree of efficiency, the qualities of accuracy, conciseness and comprehensiveness."—*Scotsman.*
"An excellent publication, dealing with the scientific, technical and legal matters connected with the duties of medical officers of health and sanitary inspectors. The work is replete with information."—*Local Government Journal.*

A Complete Epitome of the Laws of this Country.

EVERY MAN'S OWN LAWYER: A Handy-Book of the Principles of Law and Equity. By A BARRISTER. Thirty-first Edition, carefully Revised, and Including the Legislation of 1893. Comprising (amongst other Acts) the *Voluntary Conveyances Act*, 1893; the *Married Women's Property Act*, 1893; the *Trustee Act*, 1893; the *Savings Bank Act*, 1893; the *Barbed Wire Act*, 1893; the *Industrial and Provident Societies Act*, 1893; the *Hours of Labour of Railway Servants Act*, 1893; the *Fertiliser and Feeding Stuffs Act*, 1893, &c., as well as the *Betting and Loans (Infants) Act*, 1892; the *Gaming Act*, 1892, the *Shop Hours Act*, 1892; the *Conveyancing and Real Property Act*, 1892; the *Small Holdings Act*, 1892, and many other new Acts. Crown 8vo, 700 pp., price 6s. 8d. (saved at every consultation!), strongly bound in cloth. *[Just published.*

. *The Book will be found to comprise (amongst other matter)—*

THE RIGHTS AND WRONGS OF INDIVIDUALS - LANDLORD AND TENANT - VENDORS AND PURCHASERS - PARTNERS AND AGENTS—COMPANIES AND ASSOCIATIONS—MASTERS, SERVANTS, AND WORKMEN—LEASES AND MORTGAGES—LIBEL AND SLANDER - CONTRACTS AND AGREEMENTS - BONDS AND BILLS OF SALE—CHEQUES, BILLS, AND NOTES—RAILWAY AND SHIPPING LAW - BANKRUPTCY AND INSURANCE - BORROWERS, LENDERS, AND SURETIES—CRIMINAL LAW - PARLIAMENTARY ELECTIONS—COUNTY COUNCILS—MUNICIPAL CORPORATIONS - PARISH LAW, CHURCHWARDENS, ETC. - PUBLIC HEALTH AND NUISANCES—COPYRIGHT AND PATENTS—TRADE MARKS AND DESIGNS - HUSBAND AND WIFE, DIVORCE, ETC.—TRUSTEES AND EXECUTORS - GUARDIAN AND WARD, INFANTS, ETC.—GAME LAWS AND SPORTING - HORSES, HORSE DEALING, AND DOGS—INN-KEEPERS, LICENSING, ETC.—FORMS OF WILLS, AGREEMENTS ETC. ETC.

☞ *The object of this work is to enable those who consult it to help themselves to the law; and thereby to dispense, as far as possible, with professional assistance and advice. There are many wrongs and grievances which persons submit to from time to time through not knowing how or where to apply for redress; and many persons have as great a dread of a lawyer's office as of a lion's den. With this book at hand it is believed that many a* SIX-AND-EIGHTPENCE *may be saved; many a wrong redressed; many a right reclaimed; many a law suit avoided; and many an evil abated. The work has established itself as the standard legal adviser of all classes, and has also made a reputation for itself as a useful book of reference for lawyers residing at a distance from law libraries, who are glad to have at hand a work embodying recent decisions and enactments.*

. OPINIONS OF THE PRESS.

" It is a complete code of English Law, written in plain language, which all can understand. Should be in the hands of every business man, and all who wish to abolish lawyers' bills. — *Weekly Times.*

" A useful and concise epitome of the law, compiled with considerable care."—*Law Magazine.*

" A complete digest of the most useful facts which constitute English law. —*Globe.*

" This excellent handbook. . . . Admirably done, admirably arranged, and admirably cheap."—*Leeds Mercury.*

" A concise, cheap and complete epitome of the English law. So plainly written that he who runs may read, and he who reads may understand. —*Figaro.*

" A dictionary of legal facts well put together. The book is a very useful one."—*Spectator.*

" A work which has long been wanted, which is thoroughly well done, and which we most cordially recommend. —*Sunday Times.*

" The latest edition of this popular book ought to be in every business establishment, and on every library table."—*Sheffield Post.*

" A complete epitome of the law; thoroughly intelligible to non-professional readers."—*Bee's Life.*

Legal Guide for Pawnbrokers.

THE PAWNBROKERS', FACTORS' AND MERCHANTS' GUIDE TO THE LAW OF LOANS AND PLEDGES. With the Statutes and a Digest of Cases. By H. C. FOLKARD, Esq., Barrister-at-Law. Fcap. 8vo, 3s. 6d. cloth.

The Law of Contracts.

LABOUR CONTRACTS: A Popular Handbook on the Law of Contracts for Works and Services. By DAVID GIBBONS. Fourth Edition, Appendix of Statutes by T. F. UTTLEY, Solicitor. Fcap. 8vo, 3s. 6d. cloth.

The Factory Acts.

SUMMARY OF THE FACTORY AND WORKSHOP ACTS (1878-1891). For the Use of Manufacturers and Managers. By EMILE GARCKE and J. M. FELLS. (Reprinted from "FACTORY ACCOUNTS." Crown 8vo, 6d. sewed.

Weale's Rudimentary Series.

LONDON, 1862.
THE PRIZE MEDAL
Was awarded to the Publishers of
"WEALE'S SERIES."

A NEW LIST OF
WEALE'S SERIES
RUDIMENTARY SCIENTIFIC, EDUCATIONAL, AND CLASSICAL.

Comprising nearly Three Hundred and Fifty distinct works in almost every department of Science, Art, and Education, recommended to the notice of Engineers, Architects, Builders, Artisans, and Students generally, as well as to those interested in Workmen's Libraries, Literary and Scientific Institutions, Colleges, Schools, Science Classes, &c., &c.

☞ "WEALE'S SERIES includes Text-Books on almost every branch of Science and Industry, comprising such subjects as Agriculture, Architecture and Building, Civil Engineering, Fine Arts, Mechanics and Mechanical Engineering, Physical and Chemical Science, and many miscellaneous Treatises. The whole are constantly undergoing revision, and new editions, brought up to the latest discoveries in scientific research, are constantly issued. The prices at which they are sold are as low as their excellence is assured."—*American Literary Gazette*.

"Amongst the literature of technical education, WEALE'S SERIES has ever enjoyed a high reputation, and the additions being made by Messrs. CROSBY LOCKWOOD & SON render the series more complete, and bring the information upon the several subjects down to the present time."—*Mining Journal*.

"It is not too much to say that no books have ever proved more popular with, or more useful to, young engineers and others than the excellent treatises comprised in WEALE'S SERIES."—*Engineer*.

"The excellence of WEALE'S SERIES is now so well appreciated, that it would be wasting our space to enlarge upon their general usefulness and value."—*Builder*.

"The volumes of WEALE'S SERIES form one of the best collections of elementary technical books in any language."—*Architect*.

"WEALE'S SERIES has become a standard as well as an unrivalled collection of treatises in all branches of art and science."—*Public Opinion*.

PHILADELPHIA, 1876.
THE PRIZE MEDAL
Was awarded to the Publishers for
Books: Rudimentary, Scientific,
"WEALE'S SERIES," ETC.

CROSBY LOCKWOOD & SON,
7, STATIONERS' HALL COURT, LUDGATE HILL, LONDON, E.C.

WEALE'S RUDIMENTARY SCIENTIFIC SERIES.

*** The volumes of this series are freely Illustrated with Woodcuts, or otherwise, where required. They are put up in the following List it must be understood that the books are issued in limp cloth, unless otherwise stated; but the volumes marked with a † may also be had strongly bound in cloth boards 1s. 6d. extra.

N.B.—In ordering from this List it is recommended, as a means of facilitating business and obviating error, to quote the numbers affixed to the volumes, as well as the titles and prices.

CIVIL ENGINEERING, SURVEYING, ETC.

No.
31. *WELLS AND WELL-SINKING.* By JOHN GEO. SWINDELL, A.R.I.B.A., and G. R. BURNELL, C.E. Revised Edition. With a New Appendix on the Qualities of Water. Illustrated. 2s.
35. *THE BLASTING AND QUARRYING OF STONE,* for Building and other Purposes. By Gen. Sir J. BURGOYNE, Bart. 1s. 6d.
43. *TUBULAR, AND OTHER IRON GIRDER BRIDGES,* particularly describing the Britannia and Conway Tubular Bridges. By G. DRYSDALE DEMPSEY, C.E. Fourth Edition. 2s.
44. *FOUNDATIONS AND CONCRETE WORKS,* with Practical Remarks on Footings, Sand, Concrete, Béton, Pile-driving, Caissons, and Cofferdams, &c. By E. DOBSON. Seventh Edition. 1s. 6d.
60. *LAND AND ENGINEERING SURVEYING.* By T. BAKER, C.E. Fifteenth Edition, revised by Professor J. R. YOUNG. 2s.‡
80*. *EMBANKING LANDS FROM THE SEA.* With examples and Particulars of actual Embankments, &c. By J. WIGGIN, F.G.S. 2s.
81. *WATER WORKS,* for the Supply of Cities and Towns. With a Description of the Principal Geological Formations of England as influencing Supplies of Water, &c. By S. HUGHES, C.E. New Edition. 4s.‡
118. *CIVIL ENGINEERING IN NORTH AMERICA,* a Sketch of. By DAVID STEVENSON, F.R.S.E., &c. Plates and Diagrams. 3s.
167. *IRON BRIDGES, GIRDERS, ROOFS, AND OTHER WORKS.* By FRANCIS CAMPIN, C.E. 2s. 6d.‡
197. *ROADS AND STREETS.* By H. LAW, C.E., revised and enlarged by D. K. CLARK, C.E., including pavements of Stone, Wood, Asphalte, &c. 4s. 6d.‡
203. *SANITARY WORK IN THE SMALLER TOWNS AND IN VILLAGES.* By C. SLAGG, A.M.I.C.E. Revised Edition. 3s.‡
212. *GAS-WORKS, THEIR CONSTRUCTION AND ARRANGEMENT;* and the Manufacture and Distribution of Coal Gas. Originally written by SAMUEL HUGHES, C.E. Re-written and enlarged by WILLIAM RICHARDS, C.E. Eighth Edition, with important additions. 5s. 6d.‡
213. *PIONEER ENGINEERING.* A Treatise on the Engineering Operations connected with the Settlement of Waste Lands in New Countries. By EDWARD DOBSON, Assoc. Inst. C.E. 4s. 6d.‡
216. *MATERIALS AND CONSTRUCTION;* A Theoretical and Practical Treatise on the Strains, Designing, and Erection of Works of Construction. By FRANCIS CAMPIN, C.E. Second Edition, revised. 3s.‡
219. *CIVIL ENGINEERING.* By HENRY LAW, M.Inst. C.E. Including HYDRAULIC ENGINEERING by GEO. R. BURNELL, M.Inst. C.E. Seventh Edition, revised, with large additions by D. KINNEAR CLARK, M.Inst. C.E. 6s. 6d., Cloth boards, 7s 6d.
268. *THE DRAINAGE OF LANDS, TOWNS, & BUILDINGS.* By G. D. DEMPSEY, C.E. Revised, with large Additions on Recent Practice in Drainage Engineering, by D. KINNEAR CLARK, M I C.E. Second Edition, Corrected. 4s. 6d.‡

☞ *The ‡ indicates that these vols. may be had strongly bound at 6d. extra.*

LONDON : CROSBY LOCKWOOD AND SON,

MECHANICAL ENGINEERING, ETC.

33. *CRANES*, the Construction of, and other Machinery for Raising Heavy Bodies. By Joseph Glynn, F.R.S. Illustrated. 1s. 6d.
34. *THE STEAM ENGINE*. By Dr. Lardner. Illustrated. 1s. 6d.
59. *STEAM BOILERS*: their Construction and Management. By R. Armstrong, C.E. Illustrated. 1s. 6d.
82. *THE POWER OF WATER*, as applied to drive Flour Mills, and to give motion to Turbines, &c. By Joseph Glynn, F.R.S. 2s.‡
98. *PRACTICAL MECHANISM*, the Elements of; and Machine Tools. By T. Baker, C.E. With Additions by J. Nasmyth, C.E. 2s. 6d.‡
139. *THE STEAM ENGINE*, a Treatise on the Mathematical Theory of, with Rules and Examples for Practical Men. By T. Baker, C.E. 1s. 6d.
164. *MODERN WORKSHOP PRACTICE*, as applied to Steam Engines, Bridges, Ship-building, &c. By J. G. Winton. New Edition. 3s. 6d.‡
165. *IRON AND HEAT*, exhibiting the Principles concerned in the Construction of Iron Beams, Pillars, and Girders. By J. Armour. 2s. 6d.‡
166. *POWER IN MOTION*: Horse-Power, Toothed-Wheel Gearing, Long and Short Driving Bands, and Angular Forces. By J. Armour. 2s.‡
171. *THE WORKMAN'S MANUAL OF ENGINEERING DRAWING*. By J. Maxton. 7th Edn. With 7 Plates and 350 Cuts. 3s. 6d.‡
190. *STEAM AND THE STEAM ENGINE*, Stationary and Portable. By J. Sewell and D. K. Clark, C.E. 3s. 6d.‡
200. *FUEL*, its Combustion and Economy. By C. W. Williams. With Recent Practice in the Combustion and Economy of Fuel—Coal, Coke, Wood, Peat, Petroleum, &c.—by D. K. Clark, M.I.C.E. 3s. 6d.‡
202. *LOCOMOTIVE ENGINES*. By G. D. Dempsey, C.E.; with large additions by D. Kinnear Clark, M.I.C.E. 3s.‡
211. *THE BOILERMAKER'S ASSISTANT* in Drawing, Templating, and Calculating Boiler and Tank Work. By John Courtney, Practical Boiler Maker. Edited by D. K. Clark, C.E. 100 Illustrations. 2s.
217. *SEWING MACHINERY*: Its Construction, History, &c., with full Technical Directions for Adjusting, &c. By J. W. Urquhart, C.E. 2s.‡
223. *MECHANICAL ENGINEERING*. Comprising Metallurgy, Moulding, Casting, Forging, Tools, Workshop Machinery, Manufacture of the Steam Engine, &c. By Francis Campin, C.E. Second Edition. 2s. 6d.‡
236. *DETAILS OF MACHINERY*. Comprising Instructions for the Execution of various Works in Iron. By Francis Campin, C.E. 3s.‡
237. *THE SMITHY AND FORGE*; including the Farrier's Art and Coach Smithing. By W. J. E. Crane. Illustrated. 2s. 6d.‡
238. *THE SHEET-METAL WORKER'S GUIDE*; a Practical Handbook for Tinsmiths, Coppersmiths, Zincworkers, &c. With 94 Diagrams and Working Patterns. By W. J. E. Crane. Second Edition, revised. 1s. 6d.
251. *STEAM AND MACHINERY MANAGEMENT*: with Hints on Construction and Selection. By M. Powis Bale, M.I.M.E. 2s. 6d.‡
254. *THE BOILERMAKER'S READY-RECKONER*. By J. Courtney. Edited by D. K. Clark, C.E. 4s.

*** Nos. 211 and 254 in One Vol., half-bound, entitled "The Boilermaker's Ready-Reckoner and Assistant." By J. Courtney and D. K. Clark. 7s.

255. *LOCOMOTIVE ENGINE-DRIVING*. A Practical Manual for Engineers in charge of Locomotive Engines. By Michael Reynolds, M.S.E. Eighth Edition. 3s. 6d., limp; 4s. 6d. cloth boards.
256. *STATIONARY ENGINE-DRIVING*. A Practical Manual for Engineers in charge of Stationary Engines. By Michael Reynolds, M.S.E. Fourth Edition. 3s. 6d. limp; 4s. 6d. cloth boards.
260. *IRON BRIDGES OF MODERATE SPAN*: their Construction and Erection. By Hamilton W. Pendred, C.E. 2s.

☞ *The ‡ indicates that these vols. may be had strongly bound at 6d. extra.*

7, STATIONERS' HALL COURT, LUDGATE HILL, E.C.

MINING, METALLURGY, ETC.

4. *MINERALOGY*, Rudiments of, a concise View of the General Properties of Minerals. By A. Ramsay, F.G.S., F.R.G.S., &c. Third Edition, revised and enlarged. Illustrated. 3s. 6d.‡

117. *SUBTERRANEOUS SURVEYING*, with and without the Magnetic Needle. By T. Fenwick and T. Baker, C.E. Illustrated. 2s. 6d.

135. *ELECTRO-METALLURGY*, Practically Treated. By Alexander Watt. Ninth Edition, enlarged and revised, with additional Illustrations, and including the most recent Processes. 3s. 6d.‡

172. *MINING TOOLS*, Manual of. For the Use of Mine Managers, Agents, Students, &c. By William Morgans. 2s. 6d.

172*. *MINING TOOLS, ATLAS* of Engravings to Illustrate the above, containing 235 Illustrations, drawn to Scale. 4to. 4s. 6d.

176. *METALLURGY OF IRON*. Containing History of Iron Manufacture, Methods of Assay, and Analyses of Iron Ores, Processes of Manufacture of Iron and Steel, &c. By H. Bauerman, F.G.S. Sixth Edition, revised and enlarged. 5s.‡

180. *COAL AND COAL MINING*. By the late Sir Warington W. Smyth, M.A., F.R.S. Seventh Edition, revised. 3s. 6d.‡

195. *THE MINERAL SURVEYOR AND VALUER'S COMPLETE GUIDE*. By W. Lintern, M.E. Third Edition, including Magnetic and Angular Surveying. With Four Plates. 3s. 6d.‡

214. *SLATE AND SLATE QUARRYING*, Scientific, Practical, and Commercial. By D. C. Davies, F.G.S., Mining Engineer, &c. 3s.‡

264. *A FIRST BOOK OF MINING AND QUARRYING*, with the Sciences connected therewith, for Primary Schools and Self Instruction. By J. H. Collins, F.G.S. Second Edition, with additions. 1s. 6d.

ARCHITECTURE, BUILDING, ETC.

16. *ARCHITECTURE—ORDERS*—The Orders and their Æsthetic Principles. By W. H. Leeds. Illustrated. 1s. 6d.

17. *ARCHITECTURE—STYLES*—The History and Description of the Styles of Architecture of Various Countries, from the Earliest to the Present Period. By T. Talbot Bury, F.R.I.B.A., &c. Illustrated. 2s.
⁎ Orders and Styles of Architecture, in One Vol., 3s. 6d

18. *ARCHITECTURE—DESIGN*—The Principles of Design in Architecture, as deducible from Nature and exemplified in the Works of the Greek and Gothic Architects. By E. L. Garbett, Architect. Illustrated. 2s. 6d.
⁎ The three preceding Works, in One handsome Vol., half bound, entitled "Modern Architecture," price 6s.

22. *THE ART OF BUILDING*, Rudiments of. General Principles of Construction, Materials used in Building, Strength and Use of Materials, Working Drawings, Specifications, and Estimates. By E. Dobson. 2s.‡

25. *MASONRY AND STONECUTTING:* Rudimentary Treatise on the Principles of Masonic Projection and their application to Construction. By Edward Dobson, M.R.I.B.A., &c. 2s. 6d.‡

42. *COTTAGE BUILDING*. By C. Bruce Allen, Architect. Eleventh Edition, revised and enlarged. With a Chapter on Economic Cottages for Allotments, by Edward E. Allen, C.E. 2s.

45. *LIMES, CEMENTS, MORTARS, CONCRETES, MASTICS, PLASTERING*, &c. By G. R. Burnell, C.E. Fourteenth Edition. 1s. 6d.

57. *WARMING AND VENTILATION*. An Exposition of the General Principles as applied to Domestic and Public Buildings, Mines, Lighthouses, Ships, &c. By C. Tomlinson, F.R.S., &c. Illustrated. 3s.

111. *ARCHES, PIERS, BUTTRESSES &c.:* Experimental Essays on Principles of Construction. By W. Bland. Illustrated. 1s. 6d

Architecture, Building, etc., *continued.*

116. *THE ACOUSTICS OF PUBLIC BUILDINGS;* or, The Principles of the Science of Sound applied to the purposes of the Architect and Builder. By T. ROGER SMITH, M.R.I.B.A., Architect. Illustrated. 1s. 6d.
127. *ARCHITECTURAL MODELLING IN PAPER*, the Art of. By T. A. RICHARDSON, Architect. Illustrated. 1s. 6d.
128. *VITRUVIUS—THE ARCHITECTURE OF MARCUS VITRUVIUS POLLO.* In Ten Books. Translated from the Latin by JOSEPH GWILT, F.S.A., F.R.A.S. With 23 Plates. 5s.
130. *GRECIAN ARCHITECTURE*, An Inquiry into the Principles of Beauty in; with an Historical View of the Rise and Progress of the Art in Greece. By the EARL OF ABERDEEN. 1s.

*** The two preceding Works in One handsome Vol., half bound, entitled "*ANCIENT ARCHITECTURE,*" price 6s.*

132. *THE ERECTION OF DWELLING-HOUSES.* Illustrated by a Perspective View, Plans, Elevations, and Sections of a pair of Semi-detached Villas, with the Specification, Quantities, and Estimates, &c. By S. H. BROOKS. New Edition, with Plates. 2s. 6d.‡
156. *QUANTITIES & MEASUREMENTS* in Bricklayers', Masons', Plasterers', Plumbers', Painters', Paperhangers', Gilders', Smiths', Carpenters' and Joiners' Work. By A. C. BEATON, Surveyor. Ninth Edition. 1s. 6d.
175. *LOCKWOOD'S BUILDER'S PRICE BOOK FOR* 1893. A Comprehensive Handbook of the Latest Prices and Data for Builders, Architects, Engineers, and Contractors. Re-constructed, Re-written, and further Enlarged. By FRANCIS T. W. MILLER, A.R.I.B.A. 700 pages. 3s. 6d.; cloth boards, 4s. [*Just Published.*
182. *CARPENTRY AND JOINERY*—THE ELEMENTARY PRINCIPLES OF CARPENTRY. Chiefly composed from the Standard Work of THOMAS TREDGOLD, C.E. With a TREATISE ON JOINERY by E. WYNDHAM TARN. M.A. Fifth Edition, Revised. 3s. 6d.‡
182*. *CARPENTRY AND JOINERY.* ·ATLAS of 35 Plates to accompany the above. With Descriptive Letterpress. 4to. 6s.
185. *THE COMPLETE MEASURER;* the Measurement of Boards, Glass, &c.; Unequal-sided, Square-sided, Octagonal-sided, Round Timber and Stone, and Standing Timber, &c. By RICHARD HORTON. Fifth Edition. 4s.; strongly bound in leather, 5s.
187. *HINTS TO YOUNG ARCHITECTS.* By G. WIGHTWICK. New Edition. By G. H. GUILLAUME. Illustrated. 3s. 6d.‡
188. *HOUSE PAINTING. GRAINING, MARBLING, AND SIGN WRITING:* with a Course of Elementary Drawing for House-Painters, Sign-Writers, &c., and a Collection of Useful Receipts. By ELLIS A. DAVIDSON. Sixth Edition. With Coloured Plates. 5s. cloth limp; 6s. cloth boards.
189. *THE RUDIMENTS OF PRACTICAL BRICKLAYING.* In Six Sections: General Principles; Arch Drawing, Cutting, and Setting; Pointing; Paving. Tiling, Materials; Slating and Plastering; Practical Geometry, Mensuration, &c. By ADAM HAMMOND. Seventh Edition. 1s. 6d.
191. *PLUMBING.* A Text-Book to the Practice of the Art or Craft of the Plumber. With Chapters upon House Drainage and Ventilation. Sixth Edition. With 380 Illustrations. By W. P. BUCHAN. 3s. 6d.‡
192. *THE TIMBER IMPORTER'S, TIMBER MERCHANT'S*, and BUILDER'S STANDARD GUIDE. By R. E. GRANDY. 2s.
206. *A BOOK ON BUILDING, Civil and Ecclesiastical,* including CHURCH RESTORATION. With the Theory of Domes and the Great Pyramid, &c. By Sir EDMUND BECKETT, Bart., LL.D., Q.C., F.R.A.S. 4s. 6d.‡
226. *THE JOINTS MADE AND USED BY BUILDERS* in the Construction of various kinds of Engineering and Architectural Works. By WYVILL J. CHRISTY, Architect. With upwards of 160 Engravings on Wood. 3s.‡
228. *THE CONSTRUCTION OF ROOFS OF WOOD AND IRON.* By E. WYNDHAM TARN, M.A., Architect. Second Edition, revised. 1s. 6d.

☞ *The ‡ indicates that these vols. may be had strongly bound at 6d. extra.*

7, STATIONERS' HALL COURT, LUDGATE HILL, E.C.

Architecture, Building, etc., *continued.*

229. *ELEMENTARY DECORATION:* as applied to the Interior and Exterior Decoration of Dwelling Houses, &c. By J. W. FACEY. 2s.

257. *PRACTICAL HOUSE DECORATION.* A Guide to the Art of Ornamental Painting. By JAMES W. FACEY. 2s. 6d.

*** *The two preceding Works, in One handsome Vol., half-bound, entitled "House Decoration, Elementary and Practical," price 5s.*

230. *A PRACTICAL TREATISE ON HANDRAILING.* Showing New and Simple Methods. By G. COLLINGS. Second Edition, Revised, including A TREATISE ON STAIRBUILDING. Plates. 2s. 6d.

247. *BUILDING ESTATES:* a Rudimentary Treatise on the Development, Sale, Purchase, and General Management of Building Land. By FOWLER MAITLAND, Surveyor. Second Edition, revised. 2s.

248. *PORTLAND CEMENT FOR USERS.* By HENRY FAIJA, Assoc. M. Inst. C.I. Third Edition, corrected. Illustrated. 2s.

252. *BRICKWORK:* a Practical Treatise, embodying the General and Higher Principles of Bricklaying, Cutting and Setting, &c. By F. WALKER. Third Edition, Revised and Enlarged. 1s. 6d.

23. *THE PRACTICAL BRICK AND TILE BOOK.* Comprising:
189. BRICK AND TILE MAKING, by E. DOBSON, A.I.C.E.; PRACTICAL BRICKLAY-
265. ING, by A. HAMMOND; BRICKCUTTING AND SETTING, by A. HAMMOND. 534 pp. with 270 Illustrations. 6s. Strongly half-bound.

253. *THE TIMBER MERCHANT'S, SAW-MILLER'S, AND IMPORTER'S FREIGHT-BOOK AND ASSISTANT.* By Wm. RICHARDSON. With Additions by M. POWIS BALE, A.M.Inst.C.E. 3s.

258. *CIRCULAR WORK IN CARPENTRY AND JOINERY.* A Practical Treatise on Circular Work of Single and Double Curvature. By GEORGE COLLINGS. Second Edition. 2s. 6d.

259. *GAS FITTING:* A Practical Handbook treating of every Description of Gas Laying and Fitting. By JOHN BLACK. 2s. 6d.‡

261. *SHORING AND ITS APPLICATION:* A Handbook for the Use of Students. By GEORGE H. BLAGROVE. 1s. 6d.

265. *THE ART OF PRACTICAL BRICK CUTTING & SETTING.* By ADAM HAMMOND. With 90 Engravings. 1s. 6d.

267. *THE SCIENCE OF BUILDING:* An Elementary Treatise on the Principles of Construction. By E. WYNDHAM TARN, M.A. Lond. Third Edition, Revised and Enlarged. 3s. 6d.‡

271. *VENTILATION:* a Text-book to the Practice of the Art of Ventilating Buildings. By W. P. BUCHAN, R.P., Sanitary Engineer, Author of "Plumbing," &c. 3s. 6d.‡

272. *ROOF CARPENTRY;* Practical Lessons in the Framing of Wood Roofs. For the Use of Working Carpenters. By GEO. COLLINGS, Author of "Handrailing and Stairbuilding," &c. 2s. [*Just published.*

273. *THE PRACTICAL PLASTERER:* A Compendium of Plain and Ornamental Plaster Work. By WILFRED KEMP. 2s. [*Just published.*

SHIPBUILDING, NAVIGATION, ETC.

51. *NAVAL ARCHITECTURE.* An Exposition of the Elementary Principles. By J. PEAKE. Fifth Edition, with Plates. 3s. 6d.‡

53*. *SHIPS FOR OCEAN & RIVER SERVICE,* Elementary and Practical Principles of the Construction of. By H. A. SOMMERFELDT. 1s. 6d.

53**. *AN ATLAS OF ENGRAVINGS* to Illustrate the above. Twelve large folding plates. Royal 4to, cloth. 7s. 6d.

54. *MASTING, MAST-MAKING, AND RIGGING OF SHIPS,* Also Tables of Spars, Rigging, Blocks; Chain, Wire, and Hemp Ropes, &c., relative to every class of vessels. By ROBERT KIPPING, N.A. 2s.

☞ *The* ‡ *indicates that these vols. may be had strongly bound at 6d. extra.*

LONDON : CROSBY LOCKWOOD AND SON,

Shipbuilding, Navigation, Marine Engineering, etc., *cont.*

54*. *IRON SHIP-BUILDING.* With Practical Examples and Details. By JOHN GRANTHAM, C.E. Fifth Edition. 4s.

55. *THE SAILOR'S SEA BOOK:* a Rudimentary Treatise on Navigation. By JAMES GREENWOOD, B.A. With numerous Woodcuts and Coloured Plates. New and enlarged edition. By W. H. ROSSER. 2s. 6d.‡

80. *MARINE ENGINES AND STEAM VESSELS.* By ROBERT MURRAY, C.E. Eighth Edition, thoroughly Revised, with Additions by the Author and by GEORGE CARLISLE, C.E. 4s. 6d. limp; 5s. cloth boards.

83*bis*. *THE FORMS OF SHIPS AND BOATS.* By W. BLAND. Eighth Edition, Revised, with numerous Illustrations and Models. 1s. 6d.

99. *NAVIGATION AND NAUTICAL ASTRONOMY*, in Theory and Practice. By Prof. J. R. YOUNG. New Edition. 2s. 6d.

106. *SHIPS' ANCHORS*, a Treatise on. By G. COTSELL, N.A. 1s. 6d.

149. *SAILS AND SAIL-MAKING.* With Draughting, and the Centre of Effort of the Sails; Weights and Sizes of Ropes; Masting, Rigging, and Sails of Steam Vessels, &c. 12th Edition. By R. KIPPING. N.A. 2s. 6d.‡

155. *ENGINEER'S GUIDE TO THE ROYAL & MERCANTILE NAVIES.* By a PRACTICAL ENGINEER. Revised by D. F. M'CARTHY. 3s.

55 & 204. *PRACTICAL NAVIGATION.* Consisting of The Sailor's Sea-Book. By JAMES GREENWOOD and W. H. ROSSER. Together with the requisite Mathematical and Nautical Tables for the Working of the Problems. By H. LAW, C.E., and Prof. J. R. YOUNG. 7s. Half-bound.

AGRICULTURE, GARDENING, ETC.

61*. *A COMPLETE READY RECKONER FOR THE ADMEA-SUREMENT OF LAND*, &c. By A. ARMAN. Third Edition, revised and extended by C. NORRIS, Surveyor, Valuer, &c. 2s.

131. *MILLER'S, CORN MERCHANT'S, AND FARMER'S READY RECKONER.* Second Edition, with a Price List of Modern Flour-Mill Machinery, by W. S. HUTTON, C.E. 2s.

140. *SOILS, MANURES, AND CROPS.* (Vol. 1. OUTLINES OF MODERN FARMING.) By R. SCOTT BURN. Woodcuts. 2s.

141. *FARMING & FARMING ECONOMY*, Notes, Historical and Practical, on. (Vol. 2. OUTLINES OF MODERN FARMING.) By R. SCOTT BURN. 3s.

142. *STOCK; CATTLE, SHEEP, AND HORSES.* (Vol. 3. OUTLINES OF MODERN FARMING.) By R. SCOTT BURN. Woodcuts. 2s. 6d.

145. *DAIRY, PIGS, AND POULTRY*, Management of the. By R. SCOTT BURN. (Vol. 4. OUTLINES OF MODERN FARMING.) 2s.

146. *UTILIZATION OF SEWAGE, IRRIGATION, AND RECLAMATION OF WASTE LAND.* (Vol. 5. OUTLINES OF MODERN FARMING.) By R. SCOTT BURN. Woodcuts. 2s. 6d.

⁎ Nos. 140-1-2-5-6, *in One Vol., handsomely half-bound, entitled* "OUTLINES OF MODERN FARMING." *By* ROBERT SCOTT BURN. *Price* 12s.

177. *FRUIT TREES*, The Scientific and Profitable Culture of. From the French of DU BREUIL. Revised by GEO. GLENNY. 187 Woodcuts. 3s. 6d.‡

198. *SHEEP; THE HISTORY, STRUCTURE, ECONOMY, AND DISEASES OF.* By W. C. SPOONER, M.R.V.C., &c. Fifth Edition, enlarged, including Specimens of New and Improved Breeds. 3s. 6d.‡

201. *KITCHEN GARDENING MADE EASY.* By GEORGE M. F. GLENNY. Illustrated. 1s. 6d.‡

207. *OUTLINES OF FARM MANAGEMENT*, and the Organization *of Farm Labour.* By R. SCOTT BURN. 2s. 6d.‡

208. *OUTLINES OF LANDED ESTATES MANAGEMENT.* By R. SCOTT BURN. 2s. 6d.

⁎ Nos. 207 & 208 *in One Vol., handsomely half-bound, entitled* "OUTLINES OF LANDED ESTATES AND FARM MANAGEMENT." *By* R. SCOTT BURN. *Price* 6s.

☞ The ‡ *indicates that these vols. may be had strongly bound at 6d. extra.*

7, STATIONERS' HALL COURT, LUDGATE HILL, E.C.

Agriculture, Gardening, etc., *continued.*

209. *THE TREE PLANTER AND PLANT PROPAGATOR.* A Practical Manual on the Propagation of Forest Trees, Fruit Trees, Flowering Shrubs, Flowering Plants, &c. By SAMUEL WOOD. **2s.**
210. *THE TREE PRUNER.* A Practical Manual on the Pruning of Fruit Trees, including also their Training and Renovation; also the Pruning of Shrubs, Climbers, and Flowering Plants. By SAMUEL WOOD. **1s. 6d.**

*** *Nos. 209 & 210 in One Vol., handsomely half bound entitled* "THE TREE PLANTER, PROPAGATOR, AND PRUNER." *By* SAMUEL WOOD. *Price* **3s. 6d.**

218. *THE HAY AND STRAW MEASURER:* Being New Tables for the Use of Auctioneers, Valuers, Farmers, Hay and Straw Dealers, &c. By JOHN STEELE. Fifth Edition. **2s.**
222. *SUBURBAN FARMING.* The Laying-out and Cultivation of Farms, adapted to the Produce of Milk, Butter, and Cheese, Eggs, Poultry, and Pigs. By Prof. JOHN DONALDSON and R. SCOTT BURN. **3s. 6d.‡**
231. *THE ART OF GRAFTING AND BUDDING.* By CHARLES BALTET. With Illustrations. **2s. 6d.‡**
232. *COTTAGE GARDENING;* or, Flowers, Fruits, and Vegetables for Small Gardens. By E. HOBDAY. **1s. 6d.**
233. *GARDEN RECEIPTS.* Edited by CHARLES W. QUIN. **1s. 6d.**
234. *MARKET AND KITCHEN GARDENING.* By C. W. SHAW, late Editor of "Gardening Illustrated." **3s.‡**
239. *DRAINING AND EMBANKING.* A Practical Treatise, embodying the most recent experience in the Application of Improved Methods. By JOHN SCOTT, late Professor of Agriculture and Rural Economy at the Royal Agricultural College, Cirencester. With 68 Illustrations. **1s. 6d.**
240. *IRRIGATION AND WATER SUPPLY.* A Treatise on Water Meadows, Sewage Irrigation, and Warping; the Construction of Wells, Ponds, and Reservoirs, &c. By Prof. JOHN SCOTT. With 34 Illus. **1s. 6d.**
241. *FARM ROADS, FENCES, AND GATES.* A Practical Treatise on the Roads, Tramways, and Waterways of the Farm; the Principles of Enclosures; and the different kinds of Fences, Gates, and Stiles. By Professor JOHN SCOTT. With 75 Illustrations. **1s. 6d.**
242. *FARM BUILDINGS.* A Practical Treatise on the Buildings necessary for various kinds of Farms, their Arrangement and Construction, with Plans and Estimates. By Prof. JOHN SCOTT. With 105 Illus. **2s.**
243. *BARN IMPLEMENTS AND MACHINES.* A Practical Treatise on the Application of Power to the Operations of Agriculture; and on various Machines used in the Threshing-barn, in the Stock-yard, and in the Dairy, &c. By Prof. J. SCOTT. With 123 Illustrations. **2s.**
244. *FIELD IMPLEMENTS AND MACHINES.* A Practical Treatise on the Varieties now in use, with Principles and Details of Construction, their Points of Excellence, and Management. By Professor JOHN SCOTT. With 138 Illustrations. **2s.**
245. *AGRICULTURAL SURVEYING.* A Practical Treatise on Land Surveying, Levelling, and Setting-out; and on Measuring and Estimating Quantities, Weights, and Values of Materials, Produce, Stock, &c. By Prof. JOHN SCOTT. With 62 Illustrations. **1s. 6d.**

*** *Nos. 239 to 245 in One Vol., handsomely half-bound, entitled* "THE COMPLETE TEXT BOOK OF FARM ENGINEERING." *By Professor* JOHN SCOTT. *Price* **12s.**

250. *MEAT PRODUCTION.* A Manual for Producers, Distributors, &c. By JOHN EWART. **2s. 6d.‡**
266. *BOOK-KEEPING FOR FARMERS & ESTATE OWNERS.* By J. M. WOODMAN, Chartered Accountant. **2s. 6d.** cloth limp; **3s. 6d.** cloth boards.

☞ *The ‡ indicates that these vols. may be had strongly bound at 6d. extra.*

LONDON: CROSBY LOCKWOOD AND SON,

MATHEMATICS, ARITHMETIC, ETC.

32. *MATHEMATICAL INSTRUMENTS*, a Treatise on; Their Construction, Adjustment, Testing, and Use concisely Explained. By J. F. HEATHER, M.A. Fourteenth Edition, revised, with additions, by A. T. WALMISLEY, M.I.C.E., Fellow of the Surveyors' Institution. Original Edition, in 1 vol., Illustrated. 2s.‡

∗ *In ordering the above, be careful to say, "Original Edition" (No. 32), to distinguish it from the Enlarged Edition in 3 vols. (Nos. 168-9-70.)*

76. *DESCRIPTIVE GEOMETRY*, an Elementary Treatise on; with a Theory of Shadows and of Perspective, extracted from the French of G. MONGE To which is added, a description of the Principles and Practice of Isometrical Projection. By J. F. HEATHER, M.A. With 14 Plates. 2s.

178. *PRACTICAL PLANE GEOMETRY:* giving the Simplest Modes of Constructing Figures contained in one Plane and Geometrical Construction of the Ground. By J. F. HEATHER, M.A. With 215 Woodcuts. 2s.

83. *COMMERCIAL BOOK-KEEPING*. With Commercial Phrases and Forms in English, French, Italian, and German. By JAMES HADDON, M.A., Arithmetical Master of King's College School, London. 1s. 6d.

84. *ARITHMETIC*, a Rudimentary Treatise on: with full Explanations of its Theoretical Principles, and numerous Examples for Practice. By Professor J. R. YOUNG. Eleventh Edition. 1s. 6d.

84*. A KEY to the above, containing Solutions in full to the Exercises, together with Comments, Explanations, and Improved Processes, for the Use of Teachers and Unassisted Learners. By J. R. YOUNG. 1s. 6d.

85. *EQUATIONAL ARITHMETIC*, applied to Questions of Interest, Annuities, Life Assurance, and General Commerce; with various Tables by which all Calculations may be greatly facilitated. By W. HIPSLEY. 2s.

86. *ALGEBRA*, the Elements of. By JAMES HADDON, M.A. With Appendix, containing miscellaneous Investigations, and a Collection of Problems in various parts of Algebra. 2s.

86*. A KEY AND COMPANION to the above Book, forming an extensive repository of Solved Examples and Problems in Illustration of the various Expedients necessary in Algebraical Operations. By J. R. YOUNG. 1s. 6d.

88. *EUCLID*, THE ELEMENTS OF: with many additional Propositions
89. and Explanatory Notes: to which is prefixed, an Introductory Essay on Logic. By HENRY LAW, C.E. 2s. 6d.‡

∗ *Sold also separately, viz.:—*

88. EUCLID, The First Three Books. By HENRY LAW, C.E. 1s. 6d.
89. EUCLID, Books 4, 5, 6, 11, 12. By HENRY LAW, C.E. 1s. 6d.

90. *ANALYTICAL GEOMETRY AND CONIC SECTIONS*, By JAMES HANN. A New Edition, by Professor J. R. YOUNG. 2s.‡

91. *PLANE TRIGONOMETRY*, the Elements of. By JAMES HANN, formerly Mathematical Master of King's College, London. 1s. 6d.

92. *SPHERICAL TRIGONOMETRY*, the Elements of. By JAMES HANN. Revised by CHARLES H. DOWLING, C.E. 1s.

∗ *Or with "The Elements of Plane Trigonometry," in One Volume, 2s. 6d.*

93. *MENSURATION AND MEASURING*. With the Mensuration and Levelling of Land for the Purposes of Modern Engineering. By T. BAKER, C.E. New Edition by E. NUGENT, C.E. Illustrated. 1s. 6d.

101. *DIFFERENTIAL CALCULUS*, Elements of the. By W. S. B. WOOLHOUSE, F.R.A.S., &c. 1s. 6d.

102. *INTEGRAL CALCULUS*, Rudimentary Treatise on the. By HOMERSHAM COX, B.A. Illustrated. 1s.

136. *ARITHMETIC*, Rudimentary, for the Use of Schools and Self-Instruction. By JAMES HADDON, M.A. Revised by A. ARMAN. 1s. 6d.

137. A KEY TO HADDON'S RUDIMENTARY ARITHMETIC. By A. ARMAN. 1s. 6d.

☞ *The ‡ indicates that these vols. may be had strongly bound at 6d. extra.*

7, STATIONERS' HALL COURT, LUDGATE HILL, E.C.

Mathematics, Arithmetic, etc., *continued.*

168. *DRAWING AND MEASURING INSTRUMENTS.* Including I. Instruments employed in Geometrical and Mechanical Drawing, and in the Construction, Copying, and Measurement of Maps and Plans. II. Instruments used for the purposes of Accurate Measurement, and for Arithmetical Computations. By J. F. HEATHER, M.A. Illustrated. 1s. 6d

169. *OPTICAL INSTRUMENTS.* Including (more especially) Telescopes, Microscopes, and Apparatus for producing copies of Maps and Plans by Photography. By J. F. HEATHER, M.A. Illustrated. 1s. 6d

170. *SURVEYING AND ASTRONOMICAL INSTRUMENTS.* Including—I. Instruments Used for Determining the Geometrical Features of a portion of Ground. II. Instruments Employed in Astronomical Observations. By J. F. HEATHER, M.A. Illustrated. 1s. 6d.

⁂ *The above three volumes form an enlargement of the Author's original work "Mathematical Instruments." (See No. 32 in the Series.)*

168.⎱
169.⎰ *MATHEMATICAL INSTRUMENTS.* By J. F. HEATHER, M.A. Enlarged Edition, for the most part entirely re-written. The 3 Parts as
170.⎰ above, in One thick Volume. With numerous Illustrations. 4s. 6d.‡

158. *THE SLIDE RULE, AND HOW TO USE IT;* containing full, easy, and simple Instructions to perform all Business Calculations with unexampled rapidity and accuracy. By CHARLES HOARE, C.E. Sixth Edition. With a Slide Rule in tuck of cover. 2s. 6d.‡

196. *THEORY OF COMPOUND INTEREST AND ANNUITIES;* with Tables of Logarithms for the more Difficult Computations of Interest, Discount, Annuities, &c. By FEDOR THOMAN. Fourth Edition. 4s.‡

199. *THE COMPENDIOUS CALCULATOR;* or, Easy and Concise Methods of Performing the various Arithmetical Operations required in Commercial and Business Transactions; together with Useful Tables. By D. O'GORMAN. Twenty-seventh Edition, carefully revised by C. NORRIS. 2s. 6d., cloth limp; 3s. 6d., strongly half-bound in leather.

204. *MATHEMATICAL TABLES,* for Trigonometrical, Astronomical, and Nautical Calculations; to which is prefixed a Treatise on Logarithms. By HENRY LAW, C.E. Together with a Series of Tables for Navigation and Nautical Astronomy. By Prof. J. R. YOUNG. New Edition. 4s.

204*. *LOGARITHMS.* With Mathematical Tables for Trigonometrical, Astronomical, and Nautical Calculations. By HENRY LAW, M.Inst.C.E. New and Revised Edition. (Forming part of the above Work). 3s.

221. *MEASURES, WEIGHTS, AND MONEYS OF ALL NATIONS,* and an Analysis of the Christian, Hebrew, and Mahometan Calendars. By W. S. B. WOOLHOUSE, F.R.A.S., F.S.S. Seventh Edition. 2s. 6d.‡

227. *MATHEMATICS AS APPLIED TO THE CONSTRUCTIVE ARTS.* Illustrating the various processes of Mathematical Investigation, by means of Arithmetical and Simple Algebraical Equations and Practical Examples. By FRANCIS CAMPIN, C.E. Second Edition. 3s.‡

PHYSICAL SCIENCE, NATURAL PHILOSOPHY, ETC.

1. *CHEMISTRY.* By Professor GEORGE FOWNES, F.R.S. With an Appendix on the Application of Chemistry to Agriculture. 1s.

2. *NATURAL PHILOSOPHY,* Introduction to the Study of. By C. TOMLINSON. Woodcuts. 1s. 6d.

6. *MECHANICS,* Rudimentary Treatise on. By CHARLES TOMLINSON. Illustrated. 1s. 6d.

7. *ELECTRICITY;* showing the General Principles of Electrical Science, and the purposes to which it has been applied. By Sir W. SNOW HARRIS, F.R.S., &c. With Additions by R. SABINE, C.E., F.S.A. 1s. 6d.

7*. *GALVANISM.* By Sir W. SNOW HARRIS. New Edition by ROBERT SABINE, C.E., F.S.A. 1s. 6d.

8. *MAGNETISM;* being a concise Exposition of the General Principles of Magnetical Science. By Sir W. SNOW HARRIS. New Edition, revised by H. M. NOAD, Ph.D. With 165 Woodcuts. 3s. 6d.‡

☞ *The ‡ indicates that these vols. may be had strongly bound at 6d. extra.*

LONDON : CROSBY LOCKWOOD AND SON,

WEALE'S RUDIMENTARY SERIES.

Physical Science, Natural Philosophy, etc., *continued.*

11. *THE ELECTRIC TELEGRAPH;* its History and Progress; with Descriptions of some of the Apparatus. By R. Sabine, C.E., F.S.A. 3s.
12. *PNEUMATICS,* including Acoustics and the Phenomena of Wind Currents, for the Use of Beginners. By Charles Tomlinson, F.R.S. Fourth Edition, enlarged. Illustrated. 1s. 6d.
72. *MANUAL OF THE MOLLUSCA;* a Treatise on Recent and Fossil Shells. By Dr. S. P. Woodward, A.L.S. Fourth Edition. With Plates and 300 Woodcuts. 7s. 6d., cloth.
96. *ASTRONOMY.* By the late Rev. Robert Main, M.A. Third Edition, by William Thynne Lynn, B.A., F.R.A.S. 2s.
97. *STATICS AND DYNAMICS,* the Principles and Practice of; embracing also a clear development of Hydrostatics, Hydrodynamics, and Central Forces. By T. Baker, C.E. Fourth Edition. 1s. 6d.
173. *PHYSICAL GEOLOGY,* partly based on Major-General Portlock's "Rudiments of Geology." By Ralph Tate, A.L.S., &c. Woodcuts. 2s.
174. *HISTORICAL GEOLOGY,* partly based on Major-General Portlock's "Rudiments." By Ralph Tate, A.L.S., &c. Woodcuts. 2s. 6d.
173 & 174. *RUDIMENTARY TREATISE ON GEOLOGY,* Physical and Historical. Partly based on Major-General Portlock's "Rudiments of Geology." By Ralph Tate, A.L.S., F.G.S., &c. In One Volume. 4s. 6d.‡
183 & 184. *ANIMAL PHYSICS,* Handbook of. By Dr. Lardner, D.C.L., formerly Professor of Natural Philosophy and Astronomy in University College, Lond. With 520 Illustrations. In One Vol. 7s. 6d., cloth boards.
*** *Sold also in Two Parts, as follows:*—
183. Animal Physics. By Dr. Lardner. Part I., Chapters I.—VII. 4s.
184. Animal Physics. By Dr. Lardner. Part II., Chapters VIII.—XVIII. 3s.
269. *LIGHT:* an Introduction to the Science of Optics, for the Use of Students of Architecture, Engineering, and other Applied Sciences. By E. Wyndham Tarn, M.A. 1s. 6d. [*Just published.*

FINE ARTS.

20. *PERSPECTIVE FOR BEGINNERS.* Adapted to Young Students and Amateurs in Architecture, Painting, &c. By George Pyne. 2s.
40. *GLASS STAINING, AND THE ART OF PAINTING ON GLASS.* From the German of Dr. Gessert and Emanuel Otto Fromberg. With an Appendix on The Art of Enamelling. 2s. 6d.
69. *MUSIC,* A Rudimentary and Practical Treatise on. With numerous Examples. By Charles Child Spencer. 2s. 6d.
71. *PIANOFORTE,* The Art of Playing the. With numerous Exercises & Lessons from the Best Masters. By Charles Child Spencer. 1s. 6d.
69-71. *MUSIC & THE PIANOFORTE.* In one vol. Half bound, 5s.
181. *PAINTING POPULARLY EXPLAINED,* including Fresco, Oil, Mosaic, Water Colour, Water-Glass, Tempera, Encaustic, Miniature, Painting on Ivory, Vellum, Pottery, Enamel, Glass, &c. With Historical Sketches of the Progress of the Art by Thomas John Gullick, assisted by John Timbs, F.S.A. Sixth Edition, revised and enlarged. 5s.‡
186. *A GRAMMAR OF COLOURING,* applied to Decorative Painting and the Arts. By George Field. New Edition, enlarged and adapted to the Use of the Ornamental Painter and Designer. By Ellis A. Davidson. With two new Coloured Diagrams, &c. 3s.‡
246. *A DICTIONARY OF PAINTERS, AND HANDBOOK FOR PICTURE AMATEURS;* including Methods of Painting, Cleaning, Relining and Restoring, Schools of Painting, &c. With Notes on the Copyists and Imitators of each Master. By Philippe Daryl. 2s. 6d.‡

☞ *The ‡ indicates that these vols. may be had strongly bound at 6d. extra.*

7, STATIONERS' HALL COURT, LUDGATE HILL, E.C.

INDUSTRIAL AND USEFUL ARTS.

23. *BRICKS AND TILES*, Rudimentary Treatise on the Manufacture of. By E. Dobson, M.R.I.B.A. Illustrated, 3s.‡
67. *CLOCKS, WATCHES, AND BELLS*, a Rudimentary Treatise on. By Sir Edmund Beckett, LL.D., Q.C. Seventh Edition, revised and enlarged. 4s. 6d. limp; 5s. 6d. cloth boards.
83**. *CONSTRUCTION OF DOOR LOCKS*. Compiled from the Papers of A. C. Hobbs, and Edited by Charles Tomlinson, F.R.S. 2s. 6d.
162. *THE BRASS FOUNDER'S MANUAL*; Instructions for Modelling, Pattern-Making, Moulding, Turning, Filing, Burnishing, Bronzing, &c. With copious Receipts, &c. By Walter Graham. 2s.‡
205. *THE ART OF LETTER PAINTING MADE EASY*. By J. G. Badenoch. Illustrated with 12 full-page Engravings of Examples. 1s. 6d.
215. *THE GOLDSMITH'S HANDBOOK*, containing full Instructions for the Alloying and Working of Gold. By George E. Gee. 3s.‡
225. *THE SILVERSMITH'S HANDBOOK*, containing full Instructions for the Alloying and Working of Silver. By George E. Gee. 3s.‡
₊ *The two preceding Works, in One handsome Vol., half-bound, entitled "The Goldsmith's & Silversmith's Complete Handbook," 7s.*
249. *THE HALL-MARKING OF JEWELLERY PRACTICALLY CONSIDERED*. By George E. Gee. 3s.‡
224. *COACH BUILDING*. A Practical Treatise, Historical and Descriptive. By J. W. Burgess. 2s. 6d.‡
235. *PRACTICAL ORGAN BUILDING*. By W. E. Dickson, M.A., Precentor of Ely Cathedral. Illustrated. 2s. 6d.‡
262. *THE ART OF BOOT AND SHOEMAKING*. By John Bedford Leno. Numerous Illustrations. Third Edition. 2s.
263. *MECHANICAL DENTISTRY*: A Practical Treatise on the Construction of the Various Kinds of Artificial Dentures, with Formulæ, Tables, Receipts, &c. By Charles Hunter. Third Edition. 3s.‡
270. *WOOD ENGRAVING*: A Practical and Easy Introduction to the Study of the Art. By W. N. Brown. 1s. 6d.

MISCELLANEOUS VOLUMES.

36. *A DICTIONARY OF TERMS used in ARCHITECTURE, BUILDING, ENGINEERING, MINING, METALLURGY, ARCHÆOLOGY, the FINE ARTS, &c*. By John Weale. Sixth Edition. Revised by Robert Hunt, F.R.S. Illustrated. 5s. limp; 6s. cloth boards.
50. *LABOUR CONTRACTS*. A Popular Handbook on the Law of Contracts for Works and Services. By David Gibbons. Fourth Edition. Revised, with Appendix of Statutes by T. F. Uttley, Solicitor, 3s. 6d. cloth.
112. *MANUAL OF DOMESTIC MEDICINE*. By R. Gooding, B.A., M.D. A Family Guide in all Cases of Accident and Emergency. 2s.
112*. *MANAGEMENT OF HEALTH*. A Manual of Home and Personal Hygiene. By the Rev. James Baird, B.A. 1s.
150. *LOGIC*, Pure and Applied. By S. H. Emmens. 1s. 6d.
153. *SELECTIONS FROM LOCKE'S ESSAYS ON THE HUMAN UNDERSTANDING*. With Notes by S. H. Emmens. 2s.
154. *GENERAL HINTS TO EMIGRANTS*. 2s.
157. *THE EMIGRANT'S GUIDE TO NATAL*. By R. Mann. 2s.
193. *HANDBOOK OF FIELD FORTIFICATION*. By Major W. W. Knollys, F.R.G.S. With 163 Woodcuts. 3s.‡
194. *THE HOUSE MANAGER*: Being a Guide to Housekeeping. Practical Cookery, Pickling and Preserving, Household Work, Dairy Management, &c. By An Old Housekeeper. 3s. 6d.‡
194, 112 & 112*. *HOUSE BOOK (The)*. Comprising:—I. The House Manager. By an Old Housekeeper. II. Domestic Medicine. By R. Gooding, M.D. III. Management of Health. By J. Baird. In One Vol., half-bound, 6s.

☞ *The ‡ indicates that these vols. may be had strongly bound at 6d. extra.*

LONDON : CROSBY LOCKWOOD AND SON,

EDUCATIONAL AND CLASSICAL SERIES.

HISTORY.

1. **England, Outlines of the History of;** more especially with reference to the Origin and Progress of the English Constitution. By WILLIAM DOUGLAS HAMILTON, F.S.A., of Her Majesty's Public Record Office. 4th Edition, revised. 5s.; cloth boards. 6s.
5. **Greece, Outlines of the History of;** in connection with the Rise of the Arts and Civilization in Europe. By W. DOUGLAS HAMILTON, of University College, London, and EDWARD LEVIEN, M.A., of Balliol College, Oxford. 2s. 6d.; cloth boards, 3s. 6d.
7. **Rome, Outlines of the History of:** from the Earliest Period to the Christian Era and the Commencement of the Decline of the Empire. By EDWARD LEVIEN, of Balliol College, Oxford. Map, 2s. 6d.; cl. bds. 3s. 6d.
9. **Chronology of History, Art, Literature, and Progress,** from the Creation of the World to the Present Time. The Continuation by W. D. HAMILTON, F.S.A. 3s.; cloth boards, 3s. 6d.
50. **Dates and Events in English History,** for the use of Candidates in Public and Private Examinations. By the Rev. E. RAND. 1s.

ENGLISH LANGUAGE AND MISCELLANEOUS.

11. **Grammar of the English Tongue,** Spoken and Written. With an Introduction to the Study of Comparative Philology. By HYDE CLARKE, D.C.L. Fifth Edition. 1s. 6d.
12. **Dictionary of the English Language,** as Spoken and Written. Containing above 100,000 Words. By HYDE CLARKE, D.C.L. 3s. 6d.; cloth boards, 4s. 6d.; complete with the GRAMMAR, cloth bds., 5s. 6d.
48. **Composition and Punctuation,** familiarly Explained for those who have neglected the Study of Grammar. By JUSTIN BRENAN. 18th Edition. 1s. 6d.
49. **Derivative Spelling-Book:** Giving the Origin of Every Word from the Greek, Latin, Saxon, German, Teutonic, Dutch, French, Spanish, and other Languages; with their present Acceptation and Pronunciation. By J. ROWBOTHAM, F.R.A.S. Improved Edition. 1s. 6d.
51. **The Art of Extempore Speaking:** Hints for the Pulpit, the Senate, and the Bar. By M. BAUTAIN, Vicar-General and Professor at the Sorbonne. Translated from the French. 8th Edition, carefully corrected. 2s. 6d.
54. **Analytical Chemistry,** Qualitative and Quantitative, a Course of. To which is prefixed, a Brief Treatise upon Modern Chemical Nomenclature and Notation. By WM. W. PINK and GEORGE E. WEBSTER. 2s.

THE SCHOOL MANAGERS' SERIES OF READING BOOKS,

Edited by the Rev. A. R. GRANT, Rector of Hitcham, and Honorary Canon of Ely; formerly H.M. Inspector of Schools.

INTRODUCTORY PRIMER, 3d.

	s.	d.		s.	d.
FIRST STANDARD	0	6	FOURTH STANDARD	1	2
SECOND "	0	10	FIFTH "	1	6
THIRD "	1	0	SIXTH "	1	6

LESSONS FROM THE BIBLE. Part I. Old Testament. 1s.
LESSONS FROM THE BIBLE. Part II. New Testament, to which is added THE GEOGRAPHY OF THE BIBLE, for very young Children. By Rev. C. THORNTON FORSTER. 1s. 2d. *** Or the Two Parts in One Volume. 2s.

7, STATIONERS' HALL COURT, LUDGATE HILL, E.C.

FRENCH.

24. French Grammar. W... ...
25. French-English Dictionary. ...
  English-French Dictionary. By ...
25,26. French Dictionary ... ... Vol., 3s.;
   ...
47. French and English Phrase Book: ...

GERMAN.

39. German Grammar. Adapted for English Students from ... Practical Grammar, by Dr. G. L. ... 1s. 6d.
40. German Reader: A Series of Extracts, carefully ... from the ... authors of Germany; with Notes, Philological and Explanatory. G. L. ...
41-43. German Triglot Dictionary. By N. E. S. A. HAMILTON. In Three Parts. Part I. German-French-English. Part II. English-German-French. Part III. French-German-English. 3s. ...
41-43. German Triglot Dictionary as above, together with German
& 39. Grammar. ... In One Vol., cloth boards. 5s.

ITALIAN.

27. Italian Grammar, arranged in Twenty Lessons, with a Course of Exercises. By ALFRED ELWES. 1s. 6d.
28. Italian Triglot Dictionary, wherein the Genders of all the Italian and French Nouns are carefully noted down. By ALFRED ELWES. Vol. 1. Italian-English-French. 1s. 6d.
30. Italian Triglot Dictionary. By A. ELWES. Vol. 2. English-French-Italian. 1s. 6d.
32. Italian Triglot Dictionary. By ALFRED ELWES. Vol. 3. French-Italian-English. 1s. 6d.
28,30. Italian Triglot Dictionary (as above). In One Vol., 7s. 6d.
32. Cloth boards.

SPANISH AND PORTUGUESE.

34. Spanish Grammar, in a Simple and Practical Form. With a Course of Exercises. By ALFRED ELWES. 1s. 6d.
35. Spanish-English and English-Spanish Dictionary. Including a large number of Technical Terms used in Mining, Engineering, &c. with the proper Accents and the Gender of every Noun. By ALFRED ELWES. 4s.; cloth boards. 5s. *** Or with the GRAMMAR, cloth boards. 6s.
55. Portuguese Grammar, in a Simple and Practical Form. With a Course of Exercises. By ALFRED ELWES. 1s. 6d.
56. Portuguese-English and English-Portuguese Dictionary. Including a large number of Technical Terms used in Mining, Engineering, &c., with the proper Accents and the Gender of every Noun. By ALFRED ELWES. Second Edition, Revised. 5s.; cloth boards. 6s. *** Or with the GRAMMAR, cloth boards. 7s.

HEBREW.

46*. Hebrew Grammar. By Dr. BRESSLAU. 1s. 6d.
44. Hebrew and English Dictionary, Biblical and Rabbinical; containing the Hebrew and Chaldee Roots of the Old Testament; Post-Rabbinical Writers. By Dr. BRESSLAU. 6s.
46. English and Hebrew Dictionary. By Dr. BRESSLAU. 3s.
44-46. Hebrew Dictionary as above, in Two Vols., complete, with
46*. the GRAMMAR, cloth boards. 12s.

LONDON: CROSBY LOCKWOOD AND SON,

LATIN.

19. **Latin Grammar.** Containing the Inflections and Elementary Principles of Translation and Construction. By the Rev. THOMAS GOODWIN, M.A., Head Master of the Greenwich Proprietary School. 1s. 6d.
20. **Latin-English Dictionary.** By the Rev. THOMAS GOODWIN, M.A. 2s.
22. **English-Latin Dictionary**; together with an Appendix of French and Italian Words which have their origin from the Latin. By the Rev. THOMAS GOODWIN, M.A. 1s. 6d.
20,22. **Latin Dictionary** as above. Complete in One Vol. 3s. 6d. cloth boards, 4s. 6d. ∴ Or with the GRAMMAR, cloth boards, 5s. 6d.

LATIN CLASSICS. With Explanatory Notes in English.

1. **Latin Delectus.** Containing Extracts from Classical Authors with Genealogical Vocabularies and Explanatory Notes, by H. YOUNG. 1s. 6d.
2. **Cæsaris Commentarii de Bello Gallico.** Notes, and a Geographical Register for the Use of Schools, by H. YOUNG. 2s.
3. **Cornelius Nepos.** With Notes. By H. YOUNG. 1s.
4. **Virgilii Maronis Bucolica et Georgica.** With Notes on the Bucolics by W. RUSHTON, M.A., and on the Georgics by H. YOUNG. 1s. 6d.
5. **Virgilii Maronis Æneis.** With Notes. Critical and Explanatory, by H. YOUNG. New Edition, revised and improved. With copious Additional Notes by Rev. T. H. L. LEARY, D.C.L., formerly Scholar of Brasenose College, Oxford. 3s.
5*. ——— Part 1. Books i.—vi. 1s. 6d.
5** ——— Part 2. Books vii.—xii. 2s.
6. **Horace**; Odes, Epode, and Carmen Sæculare. Notes by H. YOUNG. 1s. 6d.
7. **Horace**; Satires, Epistles, and Ars Poetica. Notes by W. BROWNRIGG SMITH, M.A., F.R.G.S. 1s. 6d.
8. **Sallustii Crispi Catalina et Bellum Jugurthinum.** Notes, Critical and Explanatory, by W. M. DONNE, B.A., Trin. Coll., Cam. 1s. 6d.
9. **Terentii Andria et Heautontimorumenos.** With Notes, Critical and Explanatory, by the Rev. JAMES DAVIES. M.A. 1s. 6d.
10. **Terentii Adelphi, Hecyra, Phormio.** Edited, with Notes, Critical and Explanatory, by the Rev. JAMES DAVIES. M.A. 2s.
11. **Terentii Eunuchus, Comœdia.** Notes, by Rev. J. DAVIES, M.A. 1s. 6d.
12. **Ciceronis Oratio pro Sexto Roscio Amerino.** Edited, with an Introduction, Analysis, and Notes, Explanatory and Critical, by the Rev. JAMES DAVIES, M.A. 1s. 6d.
13. **Ciceronis Orationes in Catilinam, Verrem, et pro Archia.** With Introduction, Analysis, and Notes, Explanatory and Critical, by Rev. T. H. L. LEARY, D.C.L. formerly Scholar of Brasenose College, Oxford. 1s. 6d.
14. **Ciceronis Cato Major, Lælius, Brutus, sive de Senectute, de Amicitia, de Claris Oratoribus Dialogi.** With Notes by W. BROWNRIGG SMITH, M.A., F.R.G.S. 2s.
16. **Livy**: History of Rome. Notes by H. YOUNG and W. B. SMITH, M.A. Part 1. Books i., ii., 1s. 6d.
16*. ——— Part 2. Books iii., iv., v., 1s. 6d.
17. ——— Part 3. Books xxi., xxii., 1s. 6d.
19. **Latin Verse Selections**, from Catullus, Tibullus, Propertius, and Ovid. Notes by W. B. DONNE, M.A., Trinity College, Cambridge. 2s.
20. **Latin Prose Selections**, from Varro, Columella, Vitruvius, Seneca, Quintilian, Florus, Velleius Paterculus, Valerius Maximus, Suetonius, Apuleius, &c. Notes by W. B. DONNE, M.A. 2s.
21. **Juvenalis Satiræ.** With Prolegomena and Notes by T. H. S. ESCOTT, B.A., Lecturer on Logic at King's College, London. 2s.

GREEK.

14. **Greek Grammar**, in accordance with the Principles and Philological Researches of the most eminent Scholars of our own day. By Hans Claude Hamilton. 1s. 6d.
15, 17. **Greek Lexicon**. Containing all the Words in General Use, with their Significations, Inflections, and Doubtful Quantities. By Henry R. Hamilton. Vol. 1, Greek-English, 2s. 6d.; Vol. 2, English-Greek, 2s. Or the Two Vols. in One, 4s. 6d.; cloth boards, 5s.
14, 15. **Greek Lexicon** (as above). Complete, with the GRAMMAR, in One Vol., cloth boards, 6s.

GREEK CLASSICS. With Explanatory Notes in English.

1. **Greek Delectus.** Containing Extracts from Classical Authors, with Genealogical Vocabularies and Explanatory Notes, by H. Young. New Edition, with an improved and enlarged Supplementary Vocabulary, by John Hutchison, M.A., of the High School, Glasgow. 1s. 6d.
2, 3. **Xenophon's Anabasis;** or, The Retreat of the Ten Thousand. Notes and a Geographical Register, by H. Young. Part 1. Books i. to iii., 1s. Part 2. Books iv. to vii., 1s.
4. **Lucian's Select Dialogues.** The Text carefully revised, with Grammatical and Explanatory Notes, by H. Young. 1s. 6d.
5-12. **Homer, The Works of.** According to the Text of BAEUMLEIN. With Notes, Critical and Explanatory, drawn from the best and latest Authorities, with Preliminary Observations and Appendices, by T. H. L. Leary, M.A., D.C.L.

THE ILIAD:	Part 1. Books i. to vi., 1s. 6d.	Part 3. Books xiii. to xviii., 1s. 6d.
	Part 2. Books vii. to xii., 1s. 6d.	Part 4. Books xix. to xxiv., 1s. 6d.
THE ODYSSEY:	Part 1. Books i. to vi., 1s. 6d.	Part 3. Books xiii. to xviii., 1s. 6d.
	Part 2. Books vii. to xii., 1s. 6d.	Part 4. Books xix. to xxiv., and Hymns, 2s.

13. **Plato's Dialogues:** The Apology of Socrates, the Crito, and the Phædo. From the Text of C. F. HERMANN. Edited with Notes, Critical and Explanatory, by the Rev. JAMES DAVIES, M.A. 2s.
14-17. **Herodotus, The History of,** chiefly after the Text of GAISFORD. With Preliminary Observations and Appendices, and Notes, Critical and Explanatory, by T. H. L. LEARY, M.A., D.C.L.
    Part 1. Books i., ii. (The Clio and Euterpe), 2s.
    Part 2. Books iii., iv. (The Thalia and Melpomene), 2s.
    Part 3. Books v.-vii. (The Terpsichore, Erato, and Polymnia), 2s.
    Part 4. Books viii., ix. (The Urania and Calliope) and Index, 1s. 6d.
18. **Sophocles:** Œdipus Tyrannus. Notes by H. YOUNG. 1s.
20. **Sophocles:** Antigone. From the Text of DINDORF. Notes, Critical and Explanatory, by the Rev. JOHN MILNER, B.A. 2s.
23. **Euripides:** Hecuba and Medea. Chiefly from the Text of DINDORF. With Notes, Critical and Explanatory, by W. BROWNRIGG SMITH, M.A., F.R.G.S. 1s. 6d.
26. **Euripides:** Alcestis. Chiefly from the Text of DINDORF. With Notes, Critical and Explanatory, by JOHN MILNER, B.A. 1s. 6d.
30. **Æschylus:** Prometheus Vinctus: The Prometheus Bound. From the Text of DINDORF. Edited, with English Notes, Critical and Explanatory, by the Rev. JAMES DAVIES, M.A. 1s.
32. **Æschylus:** Septem Contra Thebes: The Seven against Thebes. From the Text of DINDORF. Edited, with English Notes, Critical and Explanatory, by the Rev. JAMES DAVIES, M.A. 1s.
40. **Aristophanes:** Acharnians. Chiefly from the Text of C. H. WEISE. With Notes, by C. S. T. TOWNSHEND, M.A. 1s. 6d.
41. **Thucydides:** History of the Peloponnesian War. Notes by H. YOUNG. Book 1. 1s. 6d.
42. **Xenophon's Panegyric on Agesilaus.** Notes and Introduction by Ll. F. W. JEWITT. 1s. 6d.
43. **Demosthenes.** The Oration on the Crown and the Philippics. With English Notes. By Rev. T. H. L. LEARY, D.C.L., formerly Scholar of Brasenose College, Oxford. 1s. 6d.

CROSBY LOCKWOOD AND SON, 7, STATIONERS' HALL COURT, E.C.

www.ingramcontent.com/pod-product-compliance
Lightning Source LLC
Chambersburg PA
CBHW031949230426
43672CB00010B/2106